ISLAM AND THE MAKING OF THE NATION

VERHANDELINGEN
VAN HET KONINKLIJK INSTITUUT
VOOR TAAL-, LAND- EN VOLKENKUNDE

282

CHIARA FORMICHI

ISLAM AND THE MAKING OF THE NATION

Kartosuwiryo and political Islam in twentieth-century Indonesia

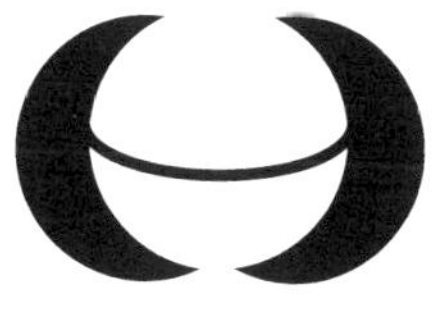

KITLV Press
Leiden
2012

Published by:
KITLV Press
Koninklijk Instituut voor Taal-, Land- en Volkenkunde
(Royal Netherlands Institute of Southeast Asian and Caribbean Studies)
P.O. Box 9515
2300 RA Leiden
The Netherlands
website: www.kitlv.nl
e-mail: kitlvpress@kitlv.nl

KITLV is an institute of the Royal Netherlands Academy of Arts and Sciences (KNAW)

KONINKLIJKE NEDERLANDSE
AKADEMIE VAN WETENSCHAPPEN

Cover: samgobin.nl

ISBN 978 90 6718 386 4

Printed editions manufactured in the Netherlands

To my mother,
and the loving memory of my father

Contents

Acknowledgements

This book would never have materialized without the support of many individuals and institutions. Above all are my PhD supervisor William Gervase Clarence-Smith at the School of Oriental and African Studies (SOAS) at the University of London, my post-doctoral mentor Michael Feener at the Asia Research Institute (ARI), and the colleagues, family and friends who supported my decision to embark on a doctoral programme and have encouraged me to further expand the thesis into a monograph.

I began this research in 2006 as the foundation for the PhD dissertation I defended in the History Department of SOAS, in September 2009. The research was conducted with the invariably resourceful administrative help of the Faculty of Arts and Humanities at SOAS. It had the financial support of this Faculty, the University of London Central Research Fund, the Royal Historical Society and the Sir Richard Stapley Educational Trust. During the period of archival research in The Hague and Leiden, I was affiliated with the Koninklijk Instituut voor Taal-, Land- en Volkenkunde (KITLV), which proved to be a most valuable source of inspiration, informal mentoring and long-lasting friendships. That KITLV Press published the final product of this research is an honour to me. I am indebted to the ever helpful staff at the library, and to Rosemarijn Hofte who has been a committed editor.

Fieldwork in Indonesia would have been impossible without Universitas Islam Negeri (UIN) Syarif Hidayatullah in Jakarta, the Fakultas Ilmu Budaya of the Gadjah Mada University in Yogyakarta and the staff members of the National Archives in Ampera and the National Library in Salemba. The Priangan would still be a mysterious place had it not been for my assistant Dede Syarif, lecturer at the IAIN Bandung, and my friend Dede Rohati.

Many have untiringly listened to my conference presentations, giving valuable feedback and insights. Some have gone through the burden of reading early drafts of the dissertation and chapters of this book. Amongst them, I wish to thank William Gervase Clarence-Smith, Michael Feener, Bob Elson, Martin van Bruinessen, Michael Laffan, Henk Schulte-Nordholt, Gerry van Klinken,

Annelieke Dirks and Juliana Finucane. Regardless, all mistakes remain mine.

My utmost gratitude rests with my *keluarga angkat* in Yogyakarta, who took me in as a daughter and a sister and took care of me throughout the drafting of the dissertation. The Pujos' affection and guidance is what ultimately made it possible for the results of this research to see the light, whilst keeping me sound in body, mind and heart. To Claudia, Andi and little Anna goes my affection for the many Sundays and evenings spent trying to get Kartosuwiryo out of my mind. With them I was able to experience a glimpse of normal life at an otherwise very difficult time.

The lengthy, and at times painful, process of rewriting the dissertation into this book was undertaken during a post-doctoral fellowship at the 'Religion and Globalization' research cluster of the Asia Research Institute, National University of Singapore. I can't express enough how important the administrative, intellectual and human support received at ARI has been to me, and a special dedication goes to my colleague and dear friend Juliana Finucane.

Note on spelling and transliteration

Addressing the political manifestation of Islam in modern Indonesia carries the problems of transliteration from Arabic and pre-reform spelling. First, Arabic Islamic terminology has been, throughout the centuries, adapted to the local languages of the archipelago; secondly, *bahasa Indonesia* radically changed its spelling rules in the 1940s. In this book I have followed the convention of modern Indonesian spelling as it appears in the *Kamus Besar Bahasa Indonesia* (2001 edition) for all terms still in use today, unless quoting directly from a source, in which case the original spelling has been retained. The 'old' Dutch-influenced spelling (where *u* is rendered by *oe*, *j* by *dj*, and *y* by *j*) has been retained in names of organizations, institutions, newspapers and periodicals, as well as in personal names when these are commonly written in the pre-conversion spelling (Hizboellah, but Masyumi and Nahdatul Ulama)

List of abbreviations

AABRI	Arsip Angkatan Bersenjata Republik Indonesia
AAS	Archief van de Algemene Secretarie, 1944-1950
ABRI	Angkatan Bersenjata Republik Indonesia
AIntel	Archief van de Marine en Leger Inlichtingendienst, Netherlands Forces Intelligence Service en Centrale Militaire Inlichtingendienst in Nederlands-Indië
AMK	Archief van het Ministerie van Koloniën, 1900-1963
AMK RI	Archief van het Ministerie van Koloniën, Rapportage Indonesië, 1945-1950
Amusa	Angkatan Muslim Sedar
ANRI	Arsip Nasional Republik Indonesia
APG	Archief van de Procureur-Generaal
APRA	Angkatan Perang Ratu Adil
AS	Archieven Strijdkrachten in Nederlands-Indië
BAKIN	Badan Koordinasi Intelijen Negara
BPRI	Barisan Pemberontak Rakyat Indonesia
CMI	Centrale Militaire Inlichtingendienst
DI-TII	Darul Islam/Tentara Islam Indonesia
DPOI	Dewan Pertahanan Oemmat Islam
EI2	Encyclopaedia of Islam, 2nd Edition, Brill Online, 2008
FO	Foreign Office
GAPI	Gaboengan Politik Indonesia
Gerindo	Gerakan Rakjat Indonesia
GMr	Geheime Mailrapporten
Golkar	Partai Golongan Karya
GPII	Gerakan Pemoeda Islam Indonesia
ICMI	Ikatan Cendekiawan Muslim Indonesia
JI	Jemaah Islamiyah
JIB	Jong Islamieten Bond
JogjaDoc	Jogjakarta Documenten, 1946-1948 (Archive)

K.H.	Kiyai Haji
KabPerd	Kabinet Perdana Menteri Republik Indonesia Yogyakarta, 1949-1950 (Archive)
KabPres	Kabinet Presiden Republik Indonesia, 1950-1959 (Archive)
KemPert	Kementrian Pertahanan Republik Indonesia (Archive)
KepNeg	Kepolisian Negara Republik Indonesia, 1947-1949 (Archive)
KITLV	Koninklijk Instituut voor Taal-, Land- en Volkenkunde
KNIL	Koninklijk Nederlands Indisch Leger
KNIP	Komite Nasional Indonesia Pusat
KPK-PSII	Komite Pertahanan Kebenaran-PSII
KR	Kedaulatan Rakyat
KVG	Kabinet Verbaal Geheim
Masyumi	Majelis Syuro Muslimin Indonesia
MD	Ministerie van Defensie
MDPP	Markas Dewan Pimpinan Perdjoeangan
MIAI	Majelis Islam A'la Indonesia
MMI	Majelis Mujahidin Indonesia
MO	Majelis Oelama
MOI	Majelis Oemmat Islam
MPOI	Majelis Pertahanan Oemmat Islam
MPPP	Majelis Persatoean Perdjoeangan Priangan or Markas Pimpinan Perjoeangan Priangan
NA	Nationaal Archief
NAUK	National Archives of the United Kingdom
NEFIS	Netherlands Forces Intelligence Service
NIAS	Nederlandsch Indische Artsen School
NICA	Netherlands Indies Civil Administration
NII	Negara Islam Indonesia
NU	Nahdatul Ulama
OSVIA	Opleidingsschool voor Inlandsche Ambtenaren
Parindra	Partai Indonesia Raja
Partii	Partij Politiek Islam Indonesia
Partindo	Partai Indonesia
PAS	Parti Islam Se-Malaysia
PDI	Partai Demokrat Indonesia
PDRI	Pemerintah Darurat RI, 1949 (Archive)

Permesta	Perdjuangan Semesta
Persis	Persatuan Islam
Perti	Persatuan Tarbiah Islamiyah
Pesindo	Pemoeda Sosialis Indonesia
Peta	Pembela Tanah Air
PII	Partai Islam Indonesia
PKI	Partai Komunis Indonesia
PMI	Pemoeda Moeslimin Indonesia
PNI	Partai Nasional Indonesia
PNI	Perserikatan Nasional Indonesia
PNI Baru	Pendidikan Nasional Indonesia
PNRI	Perpustakaan Nasional Republik Indonesia
PPO	Politiek-politioneele overzichten van Nederlandsch-Indië
PPP	Partai Persatuan dan Pembangunan
PPPKI	Permoefakatan Perhimpoenan-Perhimpoenan Politiek Kebangsaan Indonesia
PRRI	Pemerintah Revolusioner Republik Indonesia
PSI	Partai Sarekat Islam (Indonesia)
PUSA	Persatuan Ulama Seluruh Aceh
Putera	Pusat Tenaga Rakjat
RI	Republik Indonesia
RIS	Republik Indonesia Serikat
RIS ANRI	Kabinet Presiden Republik Indonesia Serikat, 1949-1950 (Archive)
RTP	Resimen Tentara Perdjoeangan
SEAC	South East Asia Command
SI	Sarekat Islam
SIAP	Sarekat Islam Angkatan/Afdeeling Pemuda
SMIAI	Soeara MIAI
STOVIA	School tot Opleiding van Inlandsche Artsen
TII	Tentara Islam Indonesia
TKR	Tentara Keamanan Rakyat
TNI	Tentara Negara Indonesia
TRI	Tentara Republik Indonesia
WO	War Office

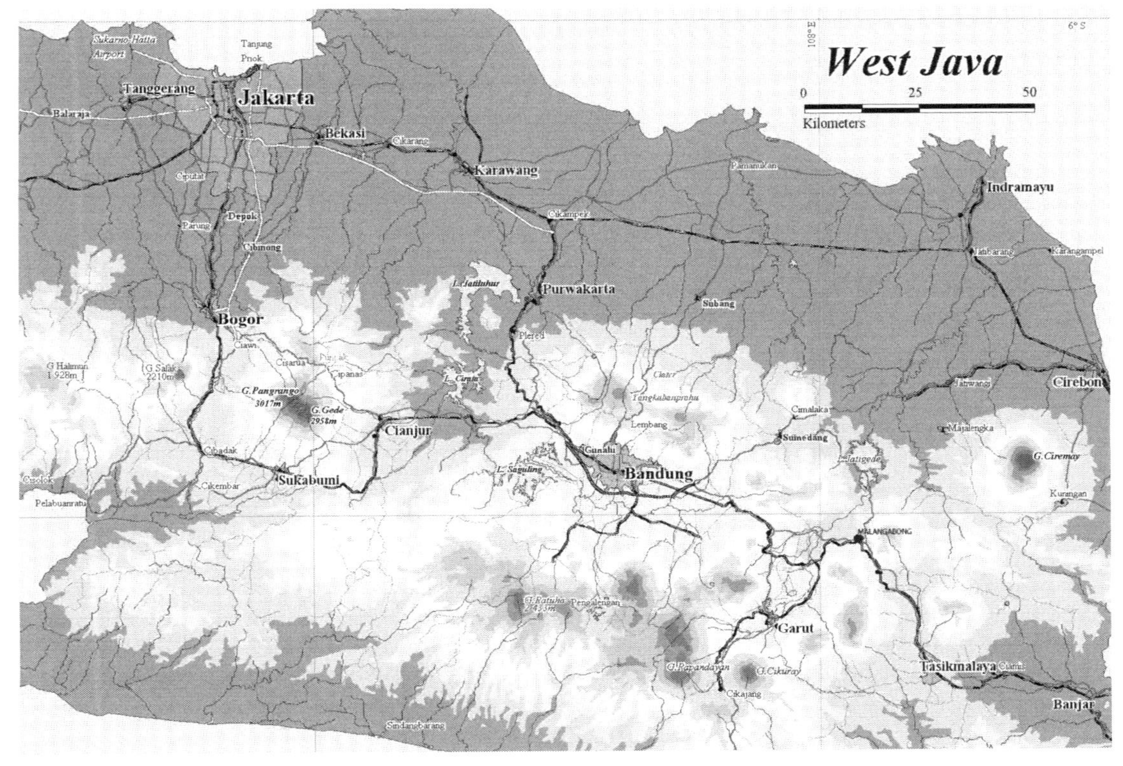
West Java
0
25
50
Kilometers
108° E
6° S
Sukarno-Hatta Airport
Tanjung Priok
Tanggerang
Jakarta
Balaraja
Bekasi
Cikarang
Karawang
Ciputat
Depok
Parung
Cibinong
Pamanukan
Indramayu
Cikampek
Jatibarang
Karangampel
L. Jatiluhur
Purwakarta
Subang
Bogor
Ciawi
Plered
G.Halimun 1 928m
G.Salak 2210m
Cisarua
Cipanas
G.Pangrango 3017m
G.Gede 2958m
L. Cirata
Ciater
Tangkubanprahu
Jatiwangi
Cirebon
Cimalaka
Lembang
Cianjur
Sumedang
Majalengka
Cibadak
Gunahi
Jatigede
G.Ciremay
L. Saguling
Bandung
Cisolok
Cikembar
Sukabumi
Kuningan
Pelabuanratu
MALANGBONG
G.Patuha 2 433m
Pengalengan
Garut
G.Papandayan
G.Cikuray
Tasikmalaya
Ciamis
Cikajang
Banjar
Sindangbarang

Preface
New perspectives on political Islam in twentieth-century Indonesia

No understanding of jihadism in Indonesia is possible without understanding Darul Islam and its very extended family[1]

The idea for this book came from an interest in understanding recent developments in Indonesian Islamism as well as some advice given by my doctoral supervisor, who convinced me that there was little use in analysing the 1970s-1980s jihadist phenomenon without first looking into its roots in the late colonial period. Following this wise advice, in this study I assert the crucial importance of the historical method in understanding the contemporary world.

I do so by treating Islam not as an unchanging theological truth but rather as an element of broader social and political realities that has been influenced by geographical and historical factors. I have made this decision with full awareness of the struggle that scholars face over how much weight to give to the statement that Islam represents the union of *dīn wa-dāwla*, or religion and government, and over whether or not to differentiate between Islam as primarily a set of religious beliefs and Islam as a source of inspiration for politics. The fact that some Muslims consider it a religious duty to pursue the establishment of a government based on Qur'anic precepts makes Islam not so different from communism or secularism, in which followers strive to achieve political victory in order to implement their vision of a 'just' society. This study refers to Islam in its ideological manifestation as Islamism, an ideology that has been just as powerful and politically viable in the process of establishing and consolidating the independent state of Indonesia

1 Sidney Jones, 'Recycling militants in Indonesia: Darul Islam and the Australian embassy bombing', *Asia Report* (Singapore/Brussels: International Crisis Group, 2005), p. 31.

as secular nationalism or communism.[2] In 1926 Soekarno identifies Islam, nationalism and Marxism as the three streams of the Indonesian anti-colonial movement.[3] With the benefit of hindsight I choose the terms secular nationalism and communism instead. On the one hand I argue that 'nationalism' should not be seen only as prerogative of Soekarno's group, and on the other hand left-leaning politicians were more varied in their approaches than dogmatic 'Marxism'.

These premises have encouraged me to see Indonesia's Islamism, including its radical and jihadist branches, as a homegrown phenomenon. Sekarmaji Marjan Kartosuwiryo (1905-1962), a prominent member of the anti-colonial Sarekat Islam party, formed the Darul Islam group in West Java in 1947-1948 with the goal of fighting the Dutch and eventually establishing the Islamic State of Indonesia. Although Kartosuwiryo's motivations lay in domestic politics, these events cannot be analysed in isolation from contemporary developments in the wider Muslim world, from Cairo to India, and his vocabulary and strategies of legitimization found parallels outside of Southeast Asia.

The territorial unity of the *ummah* has been fragmented at least since Genghis Khan's conquest of Baghdad in 1258. During the nineteenth and twentieth centuries, when Muslim lands were ruled by European powers, theologians theorized about the adaptation of Islam to modernity, as well as ideas of 'Islamic nationalism'. In 1924 Mustafa Kemal erased the last vestiges of a transnational Islamic authority by abolishing the Ottoman Caliphate and creating a secular Republic of Turkey. But the ideal of a global caliphate has not disappeared from the Islamist discourse, and it is still the object of much political debate both in the Middle East and in Indonesia (see the Hizb ut-Tahrir movement, for example).

Religiously inspired anti-colonial movements repeatedly swung between pan-Islamism and Islamic nationalism, a fact of history that emphasizes we cannot look at Indonesian Islamism in isolation from the wider Muslim world. Sarekat Islam archival documentation and Kartosuwiryo's own writings from the late 1920s-1930s highlight both this tension and the gradual transformation of pan-Islamism from a goal of the anti-colonial struggle to a tool with

2 Although 'Indonesia' as a political entity was only formed in 1945, Robert E. Elson has amply demonstrated that 'the idea of Indonesia' was already well established in the early 1920s, and it is in this sense that I use the term. See Elson, *The idea of Indonesia: A history* (Cambridge: Cambridge University Press, 2008).

3 Sukarno, 'Nasionalisme, Islamisme dan Marxisme', in *Dibawah bendera revolusi* (Jakarta: Panitia Penerbit Dibawah bendera revolusi, [1926] 1960).

which to achieve national freedom. In the 1950s we witness one further development, as the goal of the Darul Islam's armed struggle against the Republic became articulated as the creation of an Islamic federation encompassing some regions of the archipelago and other Muslim nations.[4]

The Darul Islam movement was terminated only in the mid 1960s, by which time it had turned into a rebellion that challenged the Indonesian Republic and had reached Aceh, South Sulawesi and South Kalimantan. For reasons that will become apparent below, I am here primarily concerned with the Darul Islam in West Java, specifically its ideological foundations as developed by Kartosuwiryo, and the movement's eventual transformation into a rebellion. Despite its name and goals, the group's allegiance to Islam was not evident to an entire generation of colonial administrators and Western scholars. Most works produced between 1949 and the 1980s downplayed the role of religion in Darul Islam's motives for action, highlighting instead its violent turn in later years and its opposition to the established political authority.

This failure to take seriously the importance of Islam in the Darul Islam movement has gone hand-in-hand with a more general marginalization of Indonesia in discussions of political Islam until very recently. Comparative analyses of political Islam and Islamic rebellions, which flourished in the aftermath of the Iranian revolution of 1979, tended to exclude the Indonesian case. It was only with the second wave of interest in political Islam in the early 2000s that Indonesia was brought to centre stage, and in this context the Bali bombings of 12 October 2002 are often interpreted as an aftershock of al-Qaeda's attacks on the World Trade Center in New York.

SCHOLARLY APPROACHES TO ISLAM AND POLITICS

In the past century, everything and its opposite has been written about Islam and its relation to politics, nationalism, and laws in Indonesia. The following paragraphs are far from being a complete review of this literature, as I wish to weave only some threads useful to understanding the scholarly context in which this work is set. Takashi Shiraishi's portrayal of Sarekat Islam and Michael Laffan's investigation into the *Jawi*-Middle East connection in the first quarter of the twentieth century form my starting points. The first work

4 Chiara Formichi, 'Pan-Islam and religious nationalism: The case of S.M. Kartosuwiryo and Negara Islam Indonesia', *Indonesia* 90 (October 2010): pp. 125-46.

has highlighted the key role played by this Islamic organization in the development of the *pergerakan*; the latter has focused on Islam, in particular its ability to adapt to changing circumstances while maintaining an unchangeable and universally recognizable core, as the driving force behind the initial conceptualization of an idea of nation. Bob Elson, however, denies this characterization, placing Islam 'at the margins' of the nationalist discourse.

What they all agree on is that by the mid 1920s, Islam had begun moving slowly towards political inconsequentiality. Locally, Sarekat Islam was weakened by internal splits and colonial repression. And internationally, the aspirations of political Islam were quashed by the failure of post-Ottoman debates on the caliphate and by a surge of nationalism across the Islamic world.[5]

Harry Jindrich Benda's 1958 masterpiece on Islam during the Japanese occupation of Indonesia aptly points to the short-lived prominence granted by the Dai Nippon to the Islamic leadership and the quick turning of the tables that followed in 1945. Recent works addressing the position of Islam in Indonesian politics and law constantly return to the crucial day when Soekarno proclaimed that Indonesian independence was to be founded on the non-confessional Pancasila state philosophy, thereby ignoring the pleas of Islamic parties that requested the inclusion of the Jakarta Charter, a preamble generally interpreted as enforcing the obligation for Muslims to abide by sharia law.

As influential as Soekarno's decision was, there is more to the failure of political Islam than this, and occasionally scholars have addressed some of the other factors involved. Greg Fealy, in his work on Nahdatul Ulama, has given much attention to this party's secession from Masyumi in 1952 and its impact on the overall outcome of the 1955 elections, as well as on future developments of Islam during the Guided Democracy and New Order periods. To a certain extent, and with some confusion, Bernhard Platzdasch has put back on the table the issues related to the delayed formation of a constitutional assembly and Masyumi's decline whilst awaiting elections (due since 1946), but Nadirsyah Hosen and Masdar

5 Elson, *The idea of Indonesia*; Michael F. Laffan, *Islamic nationhood and colonial Indonesia: The umma below the winds* (London: Routledge, 2003); Nikki R. Keddie, 'Pan-Islam as proto-nationalism', *The Journal of Modern History* 41-1 (1969): pp. 17-28; Takashi Shiraishi, *An age in motion: Popular radicalism in Java, 1912-1926* (Ithaca, NY/London: Cornell University Press, 1990). Keddie makes the very interesting point that Pan-Islam came to signify that all Muslim peoples should cooperate with each other in their individual efforts to gain independence from infidel rule, and, possibly (but not necessarily), unite under a single spiritual and political leadership. She defined this as 'proto-nationalism', a movement built upon a mixture of anti-imperialism and Islamic ecumenical sentiments. Kartosuwiryo argued the same in the 1920s and early 1930s.

Hilmy seem to be content with jumping from 1945 to 2000, when President Megawati Sukarnoputri re-opened the constitutional debate on the position of Islam in the legislation.[6] The struggle for the inclusion of religion in the constitutional text and the state's structure is thus commonly considered by most scholars as ending at some point between 1945 and 1955, to be reopened only in 2000.

With few exceptions, the 'new' post-2002 wave of literature addressing Islamic activism and militancy in Indonesia treads the path of looking at external influences to explain domestic events, an approach with foundations in the colonial depiction of Indonesian Islam as a 'thin veneer' coating Hindu and Buddhist beliefs.[7] Accordingly, local Muslims would be 'more tolerant' than their co-religionists across the globe.[8] While rejecting the idea that Indonesian Islam is more tolerant or apolitical because of the historical dynamics that surrounded its spread in the archipelago, my study is also far from suggesting that there is anything inherently violent or intolerant about it.

6 Harry Jindrich Benda, *The crescent and the rising sun: Indonesian Islam under the Japanese occupation, 1942-1945* (The Hague: Van Hoeve, 1958); Greg Fealy, 'Wahab Chasbullah, traditionalism and the political development of Nahdatul Ulama', in Greg Barton and Greg Fealy (eds), *Nahdatul Ulama, traditional Islam and modernity in Indonesia* (Clayton: Monash Asia Institute, 1996), pp. 1-41; Bernhard Platzdasch, *Islamism in Indonesia: Politics in the emerging democracy* (Singapore: Institute of Southeast Asian Studies, 2009); Nadirsyah Hosen, *Shari'a and constitutional reform in Indonesia* (Singapore: Institute of Southeast Asian Studies, 2007); Masdar Hilmy, *Islamism and democracy in Indonesia: Piety and pragmatism* (Singapore: Institute of Southeast Asian Studies, 2010). Also, see Chiara Formichi, 'Review article: Is an Islamic democracy possible? Perspectives from contemporary Southeast Asia', *Journal of South East Asian Research*, 20-1 (2012b): pp. 101-6.

7 Greg Fealy, Martin van Bruinessen and Andree Feillard have advanced 'historical arguments' and explained radicalism as a homegrown phenomenon.

8 See for example Anthony H. Johns, 'Islam in Southeast Asia: Problems of perspective', reprinted in A. Ibrahim, S. Siddique, and Y. Hussain (eds), *Readings on Islam in Southeast Asia* (Singapore: Institute of Southeast Asian Studies, 1985), pp. 20-4 (originally printed in 1976); Merle C. Ricklefs, 'Islamization in Java: Fourteenth to eighteenth centuries', reprinted in Ibrahim, Siddique, and Hussain (eds), *Readings*, pp. 36-43. For the idea of *abangan* ('local, nominal' Muslims) versus *santri* ('orthodox' Muslims), see Clifford Geertz, *The religion of Java* (Chicago/London: The University of Chicago Press, 1960). More recent reformulations have been advanced by Johan H. Meuleman and Azyumardi Azra in numerous publications. Adam Schwarz and Robert Hefner have both pointed to the non-political aspect of Islam until the 1970s-1980s global revival; see Adam Schwarz, *A nation in waiting: Indonesia's search for stability* (St Leonards, NSW: Allen & Unwin, 1999) and Robert W. Hefner, *Civil Islam: Muslims and democratization in Indonesia* (Princeton: Princeton University Press, 2000). The more sensationalist trend, suggesting al-Qaeda's monopoly on militant Islam in Indonesia, is best represented by Bilveer Singh, *Jemaah Islamiyah in Southeast Asia* (Singapore: ISEAS, 2004); Mike Millard, *Jihad in paradise: Islam and politics in Southeast Asia* (Armonk, NY: M.E. Sharpe, 2004); Zachary Abuza, *Militant Islam in Southeast Asia: Crucible of terror* (Boulder: Lynne Rienner Publishers, 2003); and Rohan Gunaratna, *Terrorism in the Asia-Pacific: Threat and response* (Singapore: Eastern Universities Press, 2003) and *Inside al-Qaeda: Global network of terror* (New York: Columbia University Press, 2002).

KARTOSUWIRYO'S MOTIVES

Despite the name and goals of the Darul Islam and despite Kartosuwiryo's long career in the Islamic nationalist movement in the 1920s-1940s, scholars have failed to take seriously the role of Islam – and more specifically, the project of an Islamic Indonesian state – as the main motivation behind this movement's activities. This dismissal, an approach dominant in the 1970s and 1980s, emerged from three considerations: first, that the Darul Islam emerged and gained strength because of the frustration of regional military commanders who were side-lined in the formation of a national army and because of popular discontent towards agrarian reforms and political centralization in Jakarta. Second, that Kartosuwiryo could not have been genuinely committed to the Islamic state ideal because he had not received religious training, and because he was a Sufi, thus his religious understanding must have been apolitical and incompatible with a formalistic view of Islam. And third, that Islam is intrinsically opposed to the idea of 'nation-state', as the concept of 'unity of the Islamic brotherhood' (*ittihad al-ukhuwwa al-Islamiyya*) is paramount over the creation of a territorially discrete entity.

This book intends to bring religion back into the analysis of the Darul Islam, taking Islam not just as a means for rallying popular support or as a rhetorical exercise for gaining legitimacy, but rather as the ideological foundation of Kartosuwiryo's activities.

The first academic book on the Darul Islam, Cornelis Van Dijk's *Rebellion under the banner of Islam*, is representative of the framework described above.[9] This breakthrough study gave Darul Islam the attention it deserved fifteen years after its disbandment by the army, reconstructing the roots of Kartosuwiryo's endeavours while investigating the connections between the West Java Darul Islam and the regional rebellions that swept through the archipelago in the 1950s and 1960s. To the reader familiar with Van Dijk's work, the congruencies and divergences between our two historical reconstructions will be apparent, and I have chosen not to repeatedly refer back to Van Dijk's findings. However, it is evident that dramatically different approaches have informed our analyses. Two points have already been mentioned: Van Dijk places great emphasis on agrarian reforms and social struggles, as well as on arguing that Kartosuwiryo was closer to Sufism than to Islamic modernism and thus

9 Cornelis van Dijk, *Rebellion under the banner of Islam: The Darul Islam in Indonesia*, KITLV Verhandelingen no. 94 (The Hague: Nijhoff, 1981).

did not fit into the Sarekat Islam environment (this latter point is addressed in detail in Chapter 1). Because of the time at which the book was written, and the sources he used (limited to newspaper articles and official army publications), Van Dijk also ignores the impact of Kartosuwiryo and Darul Islam's legacy on Indonesia's political Islam.

Furthermore, in addressing Van Dijk's broader approach to the Darul Islam, what most greatly differentiates our two works is that he analyses this movement as a rebellion and, perhaps more importantly, as a single movement with four or five different embodiments in those regions that wished to secede from Soekarno's Republic. Van Dijk qualifies the limits to, and rationale behind, treating the Darul Islam as a single entity by stressing the importance of finding 'common denominators' and the evidence of contacts between regional leaders. Yet he also admits that the nature of the conflict varied from province to province.[10] The major implication of Van Dijk's claim is thus that joining the Darul Islam-Negara Islam Indonesia project was an afterthought for the leaders of ongoing rebellions in Aceh, Sulawesi and Kalimantan. In this way, Van Dijk is able to consider Islam not as a 'motivation' (motivations were as diverse as the number of rebellions under study) but, rather, as merely a 'justification'. The very title of the book suggests that Islam was used to legitimize the rebellion and to rally popular consensus, and even in his attempt to reassert Islam as a motivating force, the author places the Islamic state ideal back in the picture as a 'rallying point for resistance' rather than as a political project.[11] In my view, the root of Van Dijk's confusion over the role of religion lies in his addressing the Darul Islam as a rebellion, thus removing its early development and goals from his analysis. This approach leads him to turn the question, 'Why did people join the Darul Islam?', into what '*induced people to rise* against the established government?'.[12]

Rebellions in the other regions of the archipelago had their roots in 'the relation between the official Republican Army and the irregular guerrilla units, the expansion of Central government's control [...], changes in landownership, and Islam'.[13] The Republican government's increasing attempts to control the provinces and side-line local guerrilla commanders in favour of 'regular' officers certainly played a key role in fomenting dissent among regional leaders and inspiring a number of full-fledged separatist rebellions.

10 Van Dijk, *Rebellion under the banner of Islam*, p. 340.
11 Van Dijk, *Rebellion under the banner of Islam*, p. 391.
12 Van Dijk, *Rebellion under the banner of Islam*, p. 340; emphasis in original.
13 Van Dijk, *Rebellion under the banner of Islam*, p. 4.

Van Dijk aptly describes Central Java's rebellion as 'an off-shoot' of West Java's; South Sulawesi's as the struggle of the 'disaffected guerrillas'; South Kalimantan's as that of 'the oppressed'; and Aceh's as the 'rebellion of the Islamic scholars'. In so doing, Van Dijk is pointing to the rebels' social revolution against local bearers of authority and their dedication to the Islamic state project. In this argument, Aceh stands out as the only province where the primary motive for rebelling against the Republic in the 1950s was religion.

Edward Aspinall's *Islam and nation* is a new milestone in the literature on Islam and politics in the Indonesian archipelago. Aspinall describes the Acehnese rebellion as embedded in ethnic dynamics and separatist aspirations, yet he also recognizes the Islamic roots of the Darul Islam, the importance of the tensions between regional and national politics, and the complex ties connecting ethnicity, religion and historical circumstances.[14]

Despite the different forces motivating popular mobilizations in South Kalimantan, South Sulawesi, West Java and Aceh, the aura of Islam inspired many inhabitants of the Indonesian archipelago to fight for independence from colonial domination alongside Sarekat Islam, Masyumi and the Darul Islam in name of religion. What is needed, though, is a deeper understanding of the appeal of an Islamic state project during this time. The nuances of this struggle, both in terms of the changing historical context (from colony to independence) and its shifting geographical scope (from nation to province) are crucial in understanding the position of Islam in Indonesian politics throughout the twentieth century and in the first decade of the twenty-first century.

ABOUT THIS BOOK

This book is a historical investigation of the interaction between Islamic groups and government institutions in Indonesia from the late 1910s to today. This effort is aimed at affirming the religious foundations of Kartosuwiryo's Darul Islam and shedding light on the failure of political Islam in the 1950s, when the first elections were held in independent Indonesia, and again in the 2000s, when the country's democratic institutions were fully restored. The thread will be the life, career and legacy of Sekarmaji Marjan Kartosuwiryo (1905-1962), Secretary General of Sarekat Islam in the

14 Edward Aspinall, *Islam and nation: Separatist rebellion in Aceh, Indonesia* (Singapore: NUS Press, 2009).

1930s and Imam of the Islamic State of Indonesia (Negara Islam Indonesia) beginning in 1949.

Kartosuwiryo's Darul Islam has been the eponym for separatist, regional, anti-Republican rebellions, as decades of state propaganda under General Suharto's rule stripped the movement of its religious motives. In more recent times, the same name has been used to rally Islamist sympathizers who aspire for an Islamic state around a well-known, albeit almost mythological, forefather, as militant groups in the pre-Jemaah Islamiyah era hailed from Darul Islam networks and more often than not carried the same name.

The truth lies somewhere in between: Kartosuwiryo and the Darul Islam were neither arch-enemies of the Pancasila Republic, as conveniently argued by the state between the late 1950s and the 1980s, nor were they the ultimate synthesis of Islamic religious piety and political accomplishment, as claimed by Indonesian Islamists today.

In this book, Kartosuwiryo is approached as a journalist and politician who refused to be co-opted by the colonial administration simply because of having received a Dutch education, and who instead reacted to social, economic and political injustice by becoming a prominent figure in the anti-colonial Islamic party and dedicating his efforts to the struggle for independence in religious terms.

STRUCTURE OF THE BOOK

Kartosuwiryo's vision of the anti-colonial movement was framed within the understanding that only through religion – 'with Allah and for Allah' – could the Indonesian people be freed from the physical and ideological oppression of the West, and that the future of Indonesia as an independent nation-state could only be ensured if based on Islam and on sharia law. Islamic groups in Indonesia, as elsewhere in the Muslim world, were influenced by political and theological developments in the Middle East, especially Egyptian modernism. But the movement's activities were dictated by local circumstances, as shown by the alternating fortunes of pan-Islamism and religious nationalism in the 1920s and 1930s, the relation between religious and secularist parties, and Kartosuwiryo's changing approach toward the Dutch in the 1930s and toward Japan in the 1940s.

The first chapter contextualizes Kartosuwiryo's intellectual development in the dynamic landscape of Java during the 1920s, following his move from his native village in the eastern part of the island to Surabaya, Batavia and the rural Priangan in West Java. In this chapter I argue that Kartosuwiryo's reaction to socio-economic injustice and colonial authority in religious terms was the outcome of a Dutch education, Tjokroaminoto and Haji Agus Salim's influence, as well as his involvement with a Sundanese *menak*.

Chapter 2 is set in the 1930s, and here I address the fragmentation and re-shaping of the anti-colonial movement along well-defined ideological lines: communism, secular nationalism and Islamism. Kartosuwiryo has by now smoothly risen to the highest echelon of Sarekat Islam's hierarchy, strengthening his support base in West Java and putting political weight on the promotion of political Islam and non-cooperation with the Dutch. Amidst the shrinking of political space led by the new Governor General Bonifacius Cornelis de Jonge, commitment to the *hijrah* policy will cause Sarekat Islam's isolation and Kartosuwiryo's expulsion. The Japanese occupation, also covered in this chapter, marks the return of Kartosuwiryo on the political stage as well as the rise and fall of Islamic groups as the dominant force in the political sphere.

The end of War World II, and the subsequent turmoil and power contest in Java between Japanese, Allied Forces, Dutch and emerging Indonesian forces, are key to understanding the establishment of the Indonesian state. Chapters 3 and 4 follow the events that took place between Soekarno's proclamation of the Pancasila-based republic in June 1945 and the transfer of sovereignty in December 1949.

I analyse the emergence of Indonesia as a non-confessional state. Soekarno's diplomatic approach towards the Dutch during the revolution years is thus placed in relation with Masyumi's role in Islamizing the struggle by calling for a holy war and making propaganda in favour of an Islamic state of Indonesia. Kartosuwiryo is still a major actor on the stage of formal politics, but the Dutch invasion of West Java in July 1947 instigates radical changes. As Islamic, Republican and Dutch troops confront each other and form loose alliances at the local level, the West Java branch of Masyumi is gradually transformed into a resistance movement aimed at establishing an Islamic state.

Chapter 4 focuses on Kartosuwiryo's initiative to re-organize this regional branch of Masyumi into the Darul Islam group and the party's armed wings into the Islamic Army of Indonesia; the expansion of this group across and beyond West Java; and its relationship with Soekarno's Republic in Yogyakarta. This chapter covers the events that occurred until the proclamation of an independent Islamic state in August 1949, stressing how at this stage the Negara

Islam Indonesia saw itself as a separate state, in no ways competing or challenging the authority of the Republic of Indonesia. This attitude did not prevent opposing sides from engaging in episodes of armed confrontation. The chapter also includes an analysis of the Islamic state's declaration of independence, its constitution and criminal code.

The core argument of Chapter 5, supported by a wide range of archival sources, is that while on the ground republican and Islamic troops often clashed, the republican government held an ambiguous approach to the NII for almost a decade. It was only in 1953 that Soekarno's republic labelled the Darul Islam as an 'enemy of the state' and called for the military repression of the movement; and the Republican Army did not begin organized and systematic operations until 1958-1959.

The political instability of the federal state (and the unitary state since August 1950) emerged in the frequent changes of ministerial cabinets, the antagonism between Masyumi and Partai Nasional Indonesia (PNI, National Party of Indonesia), the continuous power-struggle between the civilian government and the army, and the rebellions that dotted the archipelago. This context led to the lack of a coherent policy towards the Darul Islam-Negara Islam Indonesia. The Islamic groups, spearheaded by Muhammad Natsir and Masyumi in general, were committed to a political solution to 'the Darul Islam problem', but the secular nationalist faction, fearing for the unity of the country, invoked 'the duty to restore peace'. Masyumi's political capital withered: it lost the elections in 1955 and it was dissolved in 1960. Kartosuwiryo was captured, tried and executed in 1962, and by 1965 the army had quashed the Darul Islam from Aceh to Sulawesi.

The last chapter, 'From rebellion to martyrdom', reflects on the changing debates about Kartosuwiryo's motivations and leadership, from the 1950s until the 2010s, and on the legacy of Kartosuwiryo. This second point is also addressed by comparing the different impact of the NII's legal texts in the early 1950s and in the 2000s. I have identified four approaches to Kartosuwiryo's motivations in his struggle for an Islamic state of Indonesia, and I suggest that these portrayals are useful in examining public attitudes towards political Islam in Indonesia in the past sixty years.

The first phase spans from the 1950s to the 1970s, and reflects the Republic's interest in keeping Islam thoroughly separated from politics. In this context, the Soekarno and Suharto governments promoted an official image of Kartosuwiryo as a rebel with no ideological commitment beyond the desire to achieve power for himself – this is what I call the creation of a 'sterile rebel'. The second approach is that of reconciliation, developed amidst the New Order co-optation of Islamic groups and Suharto's gradual embrace of Islamic symbols. This new phase begins in the 1990s, with Suharto's attempt to separate the condemnation of Darul Islam's violent means from expressing sympathy for Kartosuwiryo's desire to establish an Islamic state. After the fall of the regime in 1998 and the reopening of the public and political spheres to Islam, a wide range of literature has emerged 'glorifying' Kartosuwiryo's struggle and framing him as a martyr of Islam. It is only since 2010 that non-politicized authors have made substantial efforts to assess Kartosuwiryo's memory and legacy in contemporary Indonesia, initiating a fourth trend.

A NOTE ON THE SOURCES

Memories of Kartosuwiryo and the Darul Islam were suppressed for decades and altered to fit the needs of the Republican regime. Yet since the end of the New Order regime, the political climate has changed, and historical revisionism has affected the literature on the Darul Islam.

The Darul Islam and Kartosuwiryo himself have been defined as terrorists, bandits and rebels by Indonesian officers, the press and Western observers alike. But Kartosuwiryo has also been described as a hero and a martyr by revisionist historians and veterans. These representations and descriptions are all part of the story, and what I aim at is a balanced account and assessment of Kartosuwiryo's role in shaping the relationship of Islam and politics in Indonesia over the past century. I do so making use of official sources as well as oral recollections and the movement's own materials. Each of these sources bears its own biases, which one must contextualize.

Approaching Kartosuwiryo as a politician and thus going beyond the crystallized dichotomy between rebel and martyr has been possible only by analysing sources produced by many different actors on the stage of Indonesian history, both at the time of the events and in the following decades. The material referred to in this book draws on colonial government files stored at Het Nationaal Archief (NA, National Archives of the Netherlands), The Hague; Dutch colonial newspapers and Darul Islam-Negara Islam Indonesia pamphlets found at the Koninklijk Instituut voor Taal-, Land- en Volkenkunde (KITLV, Royal Netherlands Institute of Southeast Asian and Caribbean Studies), Leiden; Indonesian newspapers and magazines stored at the Perpustakaan Nasional Republik Indonesia

(PNRI, National Library of the Republic of Indonesia), Jakarta; and official documentation produced by the Indonesian government in the 1940s found in the Arsip Nasional Republik Indonesia (ANRI, Indonesian National Archives), Jakarta, and the Indonesian army in the 1940s-1960s (or, at least, those files that were made available to me at the Military Archives, Museum ABRI [Angkatan Bersenjata Republik Indonesia], Ruang Dokumentasi, Jakarta). Data on the short SEAC interim period were collected at the National Archives of the United Kingdom (NAUK) in Kew. Both Dutch and Indonesian archival files include several documents produced by the Darul Islam and NII organizations throughout the years, and some of Kartosuwiryo's pamphlets and 'announcements' have been recently republished as individual publications or appendices to books.

This book is a substantial revision of my doctoral dissertation, submitted to the History Department of the School of Oriental and African Studies, University of London, in September 2009. The related research was conducted between 2006 and 2009 in Indonesia, the Netherlands and the United Kingdom, under the committed and attentive guidance of my supervisor, Professor William Gervase Clarence-Smith.

1

Planting the seeds
Java, the nationalist movement and Kartosuwiryo in the 1920s

In 1918 Kartosuwiryo was a dear friend. We worked side by side with Tjokro[aminoto] for our country. In the '20s in Bandung we lived, ate, and dreamed together. However as I [Soekarno] progressed on nationalistic principles, he worked solely along Islamic principles.[1]

FROM DESA TO KOTA: A NATIONALIST LEADER IN THE MAKING

Colonial perspectives

The beginning of the twentieth century was marked by deep changes in the social structure and political configuration of colonial Indonesia. The emergence of a new administrative local elite, the increase in urbanization, the formation of workers' unions and the reforms in the religious sphere all contributed to the rise of what Takashi Shiraishi has defined as the *pergerakan*, or 'movement', of the indigenous population towards achieving social, cultural, economic and political advancement.

Sekarmaji Marjan Kartosuwiryo was born in 1905 in Cepu, a small town between East and Central Java. Kartosuwiryo's family belonged to what in the early twentieth century was called the 'low-*priyayi*' class, a status earned through employment in the colonial administration rather than through aristocratic birth. His father was an opium trade supervisor. Kartosuwiryo, educated in the Dutch system from primary school to the tertiary level, is representative of a new social group in the Indies that emerged from the government-promoted 'Ethical Policy'.

During the 1800s, the Dutch colonial administration had maintained a system of indirect rule, in which 'Europeans' and

1 Cindy Adams, *Soekarno: An autobiography* (Indianapolis: Bobbs-Merrill, 1965), p. 272. The date mentioned by Soekarno might be wrong.

'Natives' were separated. However, after a hundred years of domination, the central government in The Hague had called for a new approach, what they called 'Ethical Policy'. Aimed at uplifting the indigenous population, the Ethical Policy promoted education, tackled irrigation challenges and encouraged migration to relieve over-populated areas of the archipelago. A major outcome of the expansion of Western-style schooling promoted by the Ethical Policy was the dissemination of European history, politics, culture and values among local elites. Dutch advocates of this policy promoted the pursuit of higher education in the Netherlands (especially in Amsterdam and Leiden), further exposing this new generation of indigenous intelligentsia to ideas about self-determination, nationalism, workers' rights and student organizations.[2] The anti-colonial nationalist awakening which in the mid-twentieth century would eradicate colonial domination had emerged from within this circle of Western-educated elites. Nonetheless, Western ideals were not solely responsible for motivating these anti-colonial efforts.

While some sectors of the population in the Netherlands inveighed against the capitalist system and other Europeans engaged in anti-imperialist debates, Muslims in Mecca and Cairo discussed the issue of independence from 'infidel' colonial rule and the possibility of establishing a transnational Islamic state. The debates in Europe were considered innocuous by colonial governments, who saw these as a source of intellectual enrichment for indigenous populations.[3] Yet at the same time, the pilgrimage to Mecca and the spread of pan-Islamism were perceived by the authorities as threats, fostering fears of a pan-Islamic anti-colonial movement. This resulted from the fact that Java and Sumatra were integral part of trans-oceanic networks of Islamic authority, education and political activism.

Advances in seafaring greatly increased the numbers of *Jawi* visiting the holy places of Islam. *Jawi*, the collective name used in the Middle East to describe Southeast Asian Muslims, had been undertaking the journey to the Arabian Peninsula for centuries, and by the late 1800s *Jawi* constituted the largest group of pilgrims.[4] It was a long-established tradition that pilgrims would extend their stay in

2 R. van Niel, *The emergence of the modern Indonesian elite* (The Hague: Van Hoeve, 1960), Chapter 2. This is still the most exhaustive treatment of the Ethical Policy and the formation of an indigenous intelligentsia in the early twentieth century. Specifically on *Ethici* and Islam, see Laffan, *Islamic nationhood.*

3 Van Niel, *The emergence,* p. 57.

4 R. Michael Feener, 'New networks and new knowledge: Migrations, communications, and the refiguration of the Muslim community in the nineteenth and early twentieth centuries', in Robert Hefner (ed.), *The new Cambridge history of Islam,* vol. 6 (New York, NY: Cambridge University Press, 2010), p. 63.

the region to meet other Muslims who came from different corners of the world, to exchange experiences and opinions, and to share their knowledge about religious matters. For centuries Mecca had been the destination *par excellence* for religious studies when, at the turn of the twentieth century, Cairo made its appearance on the map of Islamic learning. At this time, Muhammad 'Abduh (1849-1905) and Rashid Rida (1865-1935) developed an innovative discourse engaging both religion and modernity, which would soon be described as 'Islamic reformism,' attracting increasing numbers of students to al-Azhar University.

Though at the end of the 1800s approximately 5,000 *Jawi* were based in Mecca,[5] Egypt's appeal was slowly increasing. In 1912 there were only twelve *Jawi* in Cairo,[6] in 1919 there were roughly fifty or sixty Indonesians, and by 1925 more than two hundred Southeast Asian students were living in the Egyptian capital.[7]

Although it is at the juncture of Western education and Islamic networks that we find most leaders of the religious nationalist movement in the Indies, including Tjokroaminoto (1882-1934), Muhammad Natsir (1908-1993), Ahmad Hassan (1888-1958), Hadji Agoes Salim (1884-1954), and several others who received both secular and religious education,[8] Kartosuwiryo was a product of the Indies' Dutch schooling and society. When in the late 1920s he expressed concerns about the weakness of the Indies' independence movement, Kartosuwiryo pointed to the negative effects of Dutch educa-

5 Zamakhsyari Dhofier, 'The intellectualisation of Islamic Studies in Indonesia', *Indonesia Circle* 58 (1992): p. 21.

6 Michael F. Laffan, 'An Indonesian community in Cairo: Continuity and change in a cosmopolitan Islamic milieu', *Indonesia* 77 (April 2004): p. 7.

7 William R. Roff, 'Indonesian and Malay students in Cairo in the 1920s', *Indonesia* 9 (April 1970): p. 74. On the impact of al-Azhar Islamic reformist movement on Indonesia see Azyumardi Azra, *The origins of Islamic reformism in Southeast Asia* (Honolulu, HI: University of Hawai'i Press, 2004). M.C. Ricklefs's *Polarizing Javanese society: Islamic and other visions (c. 1830-1930)* (Singapore: NUS, 2007), pp. 57-60, offers a valid overview of the dynamics and data related to the *hajj*, whilst the formation of a self-conscious religious intelligentsia in Java and Sumatra resulting from this network has been thoroughly examined in Laffan's *Islamic nationhood.*

8 Tjokroaminoto, Muhammad Natsir, Ahmad Hassan and Hadji Agoes Salim are all further discussed at various stages in this book. It is important to keep in mind that they all had key roles in shaping Islamic views in Indonesia in the 1920s-1960s, and substantially interacted with Kartosuwiryo. Tjokroaminoto and Salim were Kartosuwiryo's teachers within Sarekat Islam, whilst he came in contact with Natsir and Hassan through Persatuan Islam (Persis) in Bandung. As Persis gathered most of the religious-oriented nationalist intelligentsia in Bandung, Ahmad Hassan soon became a close friend and peer of Kartosuwiryo. Natsir, who was already a member of the Jong Islamieten Bond (JIB) in Sumatra, moved to Bandung and joined the local youth branch before entering the more active Persis. In more recent years, Natsir has admitted that it had been Kartosuwiryo who had introduced him to the 'Negara Islam' and 'Darul Islam' terminology in the 1930s (in 'Mereka yang dikecewakan', *Panji Masyarakat*, 24 November 1997, p. 20.)

tion on the Indonesian youth: it alienated them from their original social and cultural contexts.

Kartosuwiryo compared the indigenous elite to 'a locomotive pulling the carts from far ahead', as the leaders had been separated from society and were unable to act 'for the people' and to 'mix with them'.[9] It is from this perspective that we should consider Kartosuwiryo's choice to write in Malay and to give his speeches in local dialects, even though at times it entailed the employment of a translator, as in October 1929. But as soon as June 1930 Kartosuwiryo delivered his first speech in Sundanese. Thirty years later, Van Niel and Benda would suggest a similar idea, commenting that these elites acted as an 'isolated social group',[10] a group of intellectuals removed from indigenous society and only representing their own interests and aspirations.[11]

In 1911 Kartosuwiryo entered the Tweede Klasse Inlandsche School (Second-Class Native School), and after four years there he was admitted to the Hollandsch-Inlandsche School (Dutch Native School). This kind of institution had existed since 1914 for the children of natives employed within the colonial administration. Classes were taught in both Malay and Dutch, and attendance gave its pupils access to Dutch secondary schools. After following his father to Bojonegoro, in 1919 Kartosuwiryo enrolled at the Europeesche Lagere School (European Elementary School). Attending this school was considered a high privilege, as here European and high-status native pupils sat in the same classes.[12]

Thanks to this curriculum, at eighteen Kartosuwiryo succeeded in being admitted to the Surabaya Medical School, the Nederlandsch-Indische Artsen School (NIAS), commonly known as Sekolah Dokter Jawa.[13] There is no information available about this period of Kartosuwiryo's life. What is known is that he attended the medical school until 1927, when he was expelled under uncertain circumstances, possibly for his involvement with communism. This was not the only time Kartosuwiryo would be linked to communism, as various accusations were made throughout the 1940s-1960s. However,

9 Kartosuwiryo, 'Politiek djadjahan dan igama IV', *Fadjar Asia*, 14 June 1928. All translations from Indonesian and Dutch languages are my own.

10 Van Niel in Harry Jindrich Benda, 'Non-Western intelligentsias as political elites', *The Australian Journal of Politics and History* 6 (1960): p. 96.

11 Benda, 'Non-Western intelligentsias': p. 97.

12 For more details on Western-style education in Java and Madura, including statistics, see Shiraishi, *An age in motion*, pp. 28-9.

13 Pinardi, *Sekarmadji Maridjan Kartosuwirjo* (Jakarta: Badan Penerbit Aryaguna, 1964), pp. 20-1, 35. The data on Kartosuwiryo's life until 1923 are based on Pinardi's book, as no other source is available.

these charges seem unfounded and largely aimed at discrediting his commitment to creating a social and political order that conformed with Islamic values.[14]

Reflecting the complexities of Islamic belief in Java, Kartosuwiryo's religiosity has been depicted in many, often contrasting, ways. He has been perceived both as a 'fundamentalist', because of his commitment to Islamic politics, and as a Sufi, because of his propensity towards mysticism and popular beliefs. Others have argued that Kartosuwiryo used religion as nothing more than a thin veil masking his ambition for political power. If on the one hand Islam emerges in the sources as the core of his political ideology and as his main strategy to achieve independence and establish a post-colonial state, on the other hand Kartosuwiryo's individual religious experience can only be understood through such contested representations. These representations are addressed later in this chapter to further illustrate his leadership patterns, and then again in the last chapter of this book.

Surabaya

By the early twentieth century, Surabaya had become one of the major cities in Java – and, by default, of the Indonesian archipelago. Between 1900 and 1914, Surabaya underwent a sudden increase in industrial employment, with colonial statistics suggesting that by 1915 there were at least ten thousand workers employed in industrial establishments across the city and its residency. World War I pushed the colony to change its production patterns, and the manufacturing of materials that had typically been destined for the export market – like sugar, tobacco and textiles – was largely replaced by the metallurgical, machinery and building-materials sectors. All told, these industries employed around twenty to twenty-five thousand workers in 1920.[15]

14 This point is further discussed in Chapter 6. Pinardi mentions that whilst attending NIAS, Kartosuwiryo was boarding with his uncle Marco Kartodikromo, and claims that it was Marco who initiated Kartosuwiryo to politics, thus leading to his expulsion from NIAS in 1927 (Pinardi, *Sekarmadji Maridjan*, p. 21). Marco was an early member of the reformist movement, who soon shifted from pan-Islamism to communism. He had entered the Semarang Sarekat Islam branch with Semaoen in 1917 and had steadily gained authority in 'red' SI circles to the point that in 1924 he was nominated chairman of the Surakarta PKI and 'red' SI branches. It must be mentioned, though, that between 1923 and 1927 – the years that Kartosuwiryo spent in Surabaya – Marco was first based in Surakarta; then, after the 1926 communist revolts, he was exiled to the Boven Digoel prison, from which he never returned (Shiraishi, *An age in motion*, pp. 81, 299). This timeline indicates that Kartosuwiryo could have not possibly been living with Marco.

15 Howard Dick, *Surabaya, city of work: A socioeconomic history, 1900-2000*, Research in International Studies (Athens, Ohio: Ohio University Press, 2002), pp. 262-70.

In Soekarno's often-quoted words, 'In 1916 Surabaya was a bustling, noisy port town, much like New York. [...] [A] key industrial area with [...] a large influx of mariners and merchantmen who brought news from all parts of the world. [...] The town was seething with discontent and revolutionaries.'[16] It is partly because of its overwhelmingly proletarian population and partly because of its distance from the colonial administration that Surabaya became host to a lively intellectual (mostly socialist) anti-Dutch movement, in much the same way that Bandung would in the 1920s-1930s for the Islamic movement.

In 1912, Oemar Said Tjokroaminoto transformed Surabaya's batik traders' union, the Sarekat Dagang Islam, into a political organization known as Sarekat Islam (SI, Islamic Union). Together with Boedi Oetomo, Sarekat Islam constituted the groundings for the anti-colonial movement. Though Boedi Oetomo is generally considered the first nationalist organization in the Indies, the group had originally been an association advancing Javanese cultural values. Van Niel has described it as the first Indonesian organization structured along Western lines, but, as it was aimed at representing the interests of one particular cultural group, this organization had 'no pretensions about establishing a nation'.[17] Boedi Oetomo, literally meaning 'beautiful' or 'noble' endeavour, was established in 1908 under the leadership of STOVIA (School tot Opleiding van Inlandsche Artsen, Training School for Native Doctors) alumnus and village aristocrat Dr Wahidin Soedirohoesdo in Weltevreden, which is now known as Menteng, in central Jakarta. Aimed at the advancement of both Javanese aristocrats and the Javanese people (*bangsa Jawa*) in the fields of education and culture, Boedi Oetomo's only nationalist aspiration was at the ethnic level.[18]

The desire to see the natives advance to the same level as the Europeans was to take different forms. For the colonial establishment, this advancement was to be achieved through education and integration into the administrative system. For some local aristocrats, progress involved the promotion of ethnic culture and values. For others, especially those who in the long run would become advocates of the nationalist movement, mobilization was aimed at social and political change. Raden Mas Tirto Adhi Soerjo (1880-1918), who founded the Sarekat Priyayi (Priyayi Union) in 1906, soon joined Boedi Oetomo, hoping that this group would be a

16 Adams, *Soekarno*, p. 34.

17 Van Niel, *The emergence*, p. 56.

18 M. Balfas, *Dr Tjipto Mangoekoesoemo, demokrat sedjati*, Seri Tjermin Kehidupan (Jakarta: Penerbit Djambatan, 1952), pp. 36, 46.

better vehicle for inducing radical change in the Indies. Tjipto Mangoenkoesoemo was of a similar mind. However, their efforts to transform Boedi Oetomo into a socialist party dedicated to improving the masses failed, as they found the Boedi Oetomo environment too entrenched in Javanese aristocratic values. Tirto and Tjipto then took separate paths in their common efforts. Tirto, betting on the dynamism of the Muslim trading class, established the Sarekat Dagang Islam (Islamic Trading Union) together with Hadji Samanhoedi. Tjipto joined the socialist Indische Partij (Indies' Party) in 1911.[19]

The Sarekat Dagang Islam was the first embodiment of what would later be known as Sarekat Islam. It originated as an organization whose main stated aim was the economic protection of Muslim batik traders against the powerful Chinese textile industry.[20] In a statute submitted to the Dutch authorities, Tirto portrayed Sarekat Islam as 'an association of Muslims working for *progress*', in which Islam, as Shiraishi has argued, was the signifier of nativeness.[21] As Laffan has shown, this group soon developed as the political organization that 'formed the true basis for the nationalist movement'.[22]

In its early years, Sarekat Islam's strength lay in Tjokroaminoto's ability to create a bridge between socialism and Islam. From a mixed *santri-priyai* background, Tjokroaminoto succeeded in reaching farmers, coolies and intellectuals alike, addressing issues of social and economic inequality as well as pointing to Islam as the foundation of society. Tjokroaminoto assumed leadership in 1912 and retained it until his death in 1934. He had attended the Opleidingsschool voor Inlandsche Ambtenaren (OSVIA, Training School for Native Officials) in Magelang and the Burgerlijke Avondschool (Civil Evening School) in Surabaya, where he became proficient in the English language and at the same time received a religious education. As long as Tjokroaminoto led the group, Sarekat Islam was primarily concerned with advancing the socio-economic conditions of the widely exploited Javanese peasantry.

19 Bob Hering, *Soekarno: Founding father of Indonesia*, KITLV Verhandelingen n.192 (Leiden: KITLV Uitgeverij, 2002), pp. 32-4; Van Niel, *The emergence*, pp. 58-9.

20 For different reconstructions of the origins of Sarekat Islam, see Safrizal Rambe, *Sarekat Islam: Pelopor nasionalisme Indonesia, 1905-1942* (Jakarta: Yayasan Kebangkitan Insan Cendekia, 2008), pp. 2-3. Benda, *The crescent and the rising sun*, p. 42; Ruth Thomas McVey, *The rise of Indonesian communism*, (Singapore: 1st Equinox ed., 2006), p. 8; Van Niel, *The emergence*, p. 90; Natalie Mobini-Kesheh, *The Hadhrami awakening: Community and identity in the Netherlands East Indies, 1900-1942* (Ithaca: Cornell University Southeast Asia Program, 1999); Shiraishi, *An age in motion*, pp. 41-3; Laffan, *Islamic nationhood*, p. 167.

21 Shiraishi, *An age in motion*, p. 43.

22 Laffan, *Islamic nationhood*, pp. 166-7.

Despite the fact that Tjokroaminoto's socialism had its philosophical foundations in Islam, thereby rejecting Marx's theory of historical materialism, he was still able to ensure close cooperation between Sarekat Islam and the Indische Sociaal-Democratische Vereeniging (Indies' Social-Democratic Association). Charisma and political strategy allowed Tjokroaminoto to attract those elite factions concerned with the economic and social conditions of the Indies, as well as the disaffected masses. Shiraishi describes the fascination and excitement surrounding the peasants' experience at the rallies, and interestingly reverses the traditional understanding of Tjokroaminoto as the Just King: people did not 'flock to the SI out of their "millenarian" and "messianic expectations"', but 'rather the unusual and strange experiences people had [...] generated the language of the Ratu Adil'.[23]

Tjokroaminoto was soon aided by Hadji Agoes Salim, also a Dutch-educated intellectual, whose religious understanding had been influenced by his cousin Ahmad Khatib, a Shafi'i *imam* in Mecca. Hadji Agoes Salim had joined Sarekat Islam in 1915 as an informant for the colonial secret police, but he soon converted to the cause, becoming the party's religious soul and second only to Tjokroaminoto in the party structure. Salim's influence on the young recruit Kartosuwiryo is undeniable, and it emerges with particular clarity when considering Salim's dedication to the pan-Islamic ideology. Working at the Dutch consulate in Jeddah had shaped both Salim's religious piety and his way of interacting with the colonial authorities. On the one hand, he should be seen as the figure who most significantly contributed to the Islamization of Sarekat Islam's policies, and on the other hand, as the one who favoured cooperation with the colonial authorities.

In the late 1910s, as the Indies' manufacturing industry was booming, increasing the number of industrial workers as well as accelerating urbanization, Sarekat Islam rapidly expanded across and outside of Java. Pointing to the violence sparked in Central Sulawesi and West Java in the name of Sarekat Islam's struggle for economic justice, and to the colonial authorities' reaction, Shiraishi sees 1919 as a turning point for Tjokroaminoto's decline and eventual failure to reconcile the communist and religious souls of Sarekat Islam.[24] During Tjokroaminoto's jail term, Salim took control of the 1919 Congress, and capitalizing on his familiarity with both the colonial and religious elites, he pushed SI towards

23 Amelz, *H.O.S. Tjokroaminoto: Hidup dan perdjuangannja* (Jakarta: Bulan Bintang, 1952), vol. 1, pp. 48-111; Shiraishi, *An age in motion*, pp. 66-7.

24 Shiraishi, *An age in motion*, pp. 113-6.

Islam and away from communism. The 1923 Madiun Congress proclaimed 'party discipline' against members of the Partai Komunis Indonesia (PKI, Communist Party) and changed the organization's name to Partai Sarekat Islam-Hindia Timoer (Islamic Union Party-East Indies), marking the beginning of its existence as an explicitly Islamic party.

In the early 1920s, the party was increasingly Islamized. Tjokroaminoto's attempts to maintain a focus on the socio-economic empowerment of the indigenous population were overpowered by the impact of Mustafa Kemal's decision to abolish the Caliphate in March 1924. The activities of the Khilafat movement in India had stirred admiration across the Muslim world in general, and in Java in particular, such that in 1925 the al-Islam Congress in Yogyakarta decided that an envoy would be sent to India to establish relations with the Central Khilafat Committee. In 1924, Sarekat Islam party leaders had already established a Central Comite Chilafat in Surabaya, and later that year the same city hosted the al-Islam Congress to discuss how to approach the Caliphate question. Tjokroaminoto attended the Meccan Moe'tamar 'Alam Islami (International Islamic Congress) in 1926, and Hadji Agoes Salim was sent as the Indies' delegate in 1927.[25] The al-Islam movement would re-emerge in 1930, but with a different aim (see Chapter 2).

As the Middle East was hit by the internal dismantling of the caliphal institution and the external fragmentation of the Ottoman Empire, pan-Islamism was also losing support in favour of pan-Arabism and nationalism. Yet it is at this historical juncture that Muslims 'at the periphery' of the Islamic world began to play a crucial role in the revival of the caliphate ideal.[26] The fact that the Caliphate question began to gain support in the Dutch Indies only in the 1920s, when the rest of the Islamic world was shifting from pan-Islamism to nationalism, should be analysed in conjunction with the state of political activism in the archipelago. Hadji Agoes Salim first asserted the centrality of religion as the founding principle of Sarekat Islam with the establishment of the al-Islam Congress in 1923. On this same year Salim had reoriented Sarekat Islam's approach to the colonial administration by pushing for the approval of the non-cooperation *hijrah* policy.[27]

25 Amelz, *H.O.S. Tjokroaminoto*, pp. 163-51, 174. For an extensive investigation of the Indies' Muslims' reaction to the abrogation of the caliphate, see Martin van Bruinessen, 'Muslims of the Dutch East Indies and the Caliphate question', *Studia Islamika* 2-3 (1995): pp. 115-40.

26 For more on the Khilafat movement, see A.C. Niemeijer, *The Khilafat movement in India, 1919–1924* (The Hague: Nijhoff, 1972); and S. Oliver-Dee, *The Caliphate question: The British government and Islamic governance* (Lanham, MD: Lexington Books, 2009).

27 McVey, *The rise*, pp. 76-104; Rambe, *Sarekat Islam*, pp. 90-145.

Before the 1920s the Indies' anti-colonial movement had not yet been ideologically defined. I suggest that the Indonesian nationalist movement emerged as a result of a transformation that took place in the 1910s. Accepting the fact that the first organizations to advocate independence from colonial rule were Boedi Oetomo and Sarekat Dagang Islam, I argue that the nationalist movement emerged from fractures within, and reorganizations of, these two groups, a reshaping that occurred along ideological lines.

This process of moving away from a general idea of 'indigenous advancement' towards the formation of well-defined Islamic, communist and nationalist parties, with agendas molded according to domestic needs and international models, passed through a transitional period in which each organization had multiple political souls. Sarekat Islam had split into a socialist and an Islamic wing in the mid 1920s. In following years, the caliphate issue, the Islamic state ideal and the pan-Islamic project would quickly become important elements in rallying support among the Indies Muslims, and in further widening the chasm between the various groups. Appeals to a transnational network of alliances based on Islam strengthened Sarekat Islam's position against Soekarno's nationalism and Semaoen's socialism. The case for independence from colonial rule as part of a transnational religious movement was made even stronger by the argument that striving for the unity of the *ummah* was a religious duty.

The abrogation of the Caliphate, together with the Saudi conquest of Mecca in the Arabian Peninsula and the already heated Palestinian question, dominated political debates in Indonesia as in other Muslim countries. These became powerful elements to rally Muslims' sympathies and channel them into the anti-colonial struggle, but the goals of the religious groups were to gradually shift away from the creation of a transnational caliphate and instead towards the establishment of an independent nation-state.

Scholars of colonial Indonesia have argued that by the mid 1920s, political Islam in the Dutch East Indies was in steep decline, with communism and secular nationalism taking its place among the indigenous population. I contend, however, that although Sarekat Islam had been seriously weakened by its internal division, and by the soaring enthusiasm for Soekarno's Perserikatan Nasional Indonesia, the Islamic party did not decline but, instead, entered a new phase. The party's focus was no longer on relieving the indigenous population from colonial mistreatments, but on laying out the platform for an independent state of Indonesia based on Islamic precepts.

Amidst these events Kartosuwiryo moved to Surabaya in 1923. It is unclear how he entered the Sarekat Islam circle, but it is likely that during his days at the medical school, his interest in politics brought him to the steps of Tjokroaminoto's house. In the 1910s and early 1920s Tjokroaminoto's residence also functioned as Sarekat Islam's office and was a known hub for socio-political discussions. Soekarno would recall his boarding days at Tjokroaminoto's in 1915-16 as crucial to his political formation.[28] In 1962, Kartosuwiryo reportedly stated that it had been during a trip with Tjokroaminoto to Cimahi, north of Bandung, West Java, that he had first met Soekarno in 1927.[29] This meeting could be connected to Kartosuwiryo's presence at the Pekalongan Congress discussed below, a congress in which both Tjokroaminoto and Soekarno participated. The congress would also explain Kartosuwiryo's presence in Batavia in early 1928, soon after Tjokroaminoto's moving there and establishing *Fadjar Asia*'s office in Weltevreden in November 1927.[30]

Batavia

What Kartosuwiryo did in the aftermath of his expulsion from medical school in 1927 has not been recorded. However, by March 1928 he was in Batavia, dedicating much of his time to Sarekat Islam activities. It is possible that he served as General Secretary at the 12th PSI Congress held in Pekalongan between 28 September and 2 October 1927, as a Dutch account reports a 'Kartodiwirjo' fulfilling this position, a name that does not appear before or after this congress and could have been a misspelling of 'Kartosuwirjo' by the Dutch administrator.[31]

This congress highlighted Tjokroaminoto and Salim's differences over what to prioritize within the wider context of the anti-colonial struggle. Salim's speech focused on Islam, Islamism and nationalism, as well as on the party's organization and its connection with the international anti-imperialism league, while Tjokroaminoto highlighted the relevance of the unfair economic conditions of the Indonesian people in the fight for political free-

28 Amelz, *H.O.S. Tjokroaminoto*, p. 55.

29 Kartosuwiryo's confession letter to Kodam Siliwangi VI in Pinardi, *Sekarmadji Maridjan*, p. 34.

30 Amelz, *H.O.S. Tjokroaminoto*, pp. 172-7.

31 'Programma van het XIVe Congres der Partij Sarekat Islam Oost-Indie to Pekalongan vanaf 28 September tot 2 October 1927' [1927], Archief van het Ministerie van Koloniën, 1900-1963 [hereafter AMK]: Geheime Mailrapporten [hereafter GMr], no. 52, Het Nationaal Archief [hereafter NA], The Hague.

dom, stating that 'the intellectuals should not be oriented towards capitalism'.[32] It seems that Kartosuwiryo did not participate in two events on the Sarekat Islam agenda in January 1928. These were the Cianjur open meeting and the al-Islam Congress. While the former was a local event,[33] the latter involved 150 delegates representing more than forty branches across Java. As Salim had requested at the 1927 congress in Pekalongan,[34] Salim and Tjokroaminoto established the Majelis Oelama (Assembly of Islamic Scholars) as an institution representing the *ulil amri* as a form of Islamic consultative and judicial authority.[35]

Documentary evidence marks Kartosuwiryo's first unequivocal participation in the party's activities in March 1928, when his name appears in *Fadjar Asia* as a donor to the 'Indonesian Students' Mutual-Help Committee', and then again on 2 April when his first article was published. From then on, he would be a regular contributor to the party's daily newspaper.[36] In his early articles, Kartosuwiryo reported news of socio-political relevance and wrote about religious-political issues, but his focus gradually shifted towards Islam, Islamic nationalism and Islamic law.

Kartosuwiryo's interest in Islam as a political instrument soon attracted the Dutch authorities' attention. They started reporting news about this young journalist's 'religious fanaticism' and commenting on his articles in the pages of their press overviews.[37] This attention began in August 1928 and continued for several months, with the authors of the *Overzicht van de Inlandsche (Maleisisch-Chineesche en Arabische) Pers* even suggesting that publishing Kartosuwiryo's opinions and giving him too much space was compromising Sarekat Islam Party's leadership.[38] Kartosuwiryo was described as a young anti-European journalist who was fanatical in his religious views and behaviour.[39]

32 'Het congres der Partij Sarekat Islam te Pekalongan van 28 September – 2 October 1927' [1927], pp. 23, 26-7, AMK GMr, no. 53, NA.

33 'Verslag der openbare P.S.I. Vergadering te Tjandjoer op 22 Januari 1928' [1928], AMK GMr, no. 57, NA.

34 Amelz, *H.O.S. Tjokroaminoto*, p. 175.

35 'Islam Congres' [1928], AMK GMr, no. 57, NA.

36 *Fadjar Asia* is stored at the Perpustakaan Nasional Republik Indonesia (PNRI) in Jakarta, where continuous issues are available from 8 November 1927 until 31 July 1930 with a gap between 15 November 1929 and 1 January 1930. For a list of Kartosuwiryo's contributions, see the Appendix.

37 See the General Overview of the Indigenous (Malay-Chinese and Arab) Press, *Algemeen Overzicht van de Inlandsche (Maleisisch-Chineesche en Arabische) Pers*, and the weekly Overview of the Indigenous and Malay-Chinese Press, *Overzicht van der Inlandsche en Maleisisch-Chineesche Pers.*

38 *Algemeen overzicht*, August 1928.

39 *Algemeen overzicht*, August 1928 and October 1929.

Kartosuwiryo made his first official appearance at the second Youth Congress, held in Weltevreden on 27-28 October 1928. On this occasion, representatives from several youth organizations and newspapers – including Jong Java, Jong Batak Bond, Jong Islamieten Bond, and the Chinese daily *Keng Po* – issued a pledge, the *Sumpah Pemuda*, affirming their commitment to the establishment of an Indonesian nation in which the unity of the homeland would prevail over different ethnic and linguistic communities. The *Sumpah Pemuda* was a milestone on the road towards the formation of a politically conscious youth and future political elite who were attempting to articulate an anti-colonial discourse in terms broader than ethnicity or religion. The conclusion of the pledge, signed by Kartosuwiryo and others, stated: 'We, young men and women of Indonesia, accept to belong to one motherland, Indonesia; we, young men and women of Indonesia, accept to belong to one nation, Indonesia; we, young men and women of Indonesia, hold high one language, Indonesian.'[40]

Kartosuwiryo, however, could not refrain from pointing to Islam as a necessary element of the anti-colonial discourse in Indonesia. He later reported on *Fadjar Asia* that

> this writer, as a child of Indonesia, and especially as a child of Indonesia who embraces Islam, meaning the religion of the Indonesian nation (*kebangsaan Indonesia*), [reminds you] that because this is the religion embraced by a large part of the Indonesian people in general, and also the religion that functions as a bond between several groups and peoples that have settled in our homeland Indonesia, it is because of that that it is appropriate and not far from the truth to say that if in this meeting [the Youth Congress] we want to talk, our opinions should be exclusively based on Islam and Islamization.

His speech was interrupted soon after he started it, as the chair of the congress argued that, 'Certainly unity does not demand religion, especially not Islam'. To this statement, Kartosuwiryo answered: 'Even foreigners see the truth of this, that Islam is an important and big issue – if not the biggest – in our motherland,

40 Suswadi, and Endang Pristiwaningsih (eds), *Sumpah Pemuda: Latar sejarah dan pengaruhnya bagi pergerakan nasional* (Jakarta: Kementerian Kebudayaan dan Pariwisata Indonesia, 2003), pp. 87, 100. For a discussion of the significance of this pledge and the congress in the pre- and post-independence periods, see Keith Foulcher, '*Sumpah Pemuda*: The making and meaning of a symbol on Indonesian nationhood', *Asian Studies Review* 24-3 (2000): pp. 377-410.

especially in relation to colonization politics [...] Why, then, do those youth still not see it?'[41]

Two months later, Kartosuwiryo represented the party at the Jong Islamieten Bond Congress in Bandung (22-26 December 1928).[42] The Islamic Youth League had been established in 1925 as an off-shoot of Jong Java, with the explicit mission to 'Islamize educated people' and breed future cadres for the religious nationalist movement.[43] According to a Dutch press report, on this occasion Kartosuwiryo called for 'peace through religion'.[44] However, his speech seemed far from peaceful, as the only available excerpt quotes him accusing the colonial government of implementing policies of Christianization with the specific intent of weakening the Islamic political movement.[45]

Throughout 1929, Kartosuwiryo was extremely active in *Fadjar Asia* as well as in the Jakarta branch of PSI. On 1 March, the party announced the creation, under Kartosuwiryo's initiative, of a *Komite Zakat-Fitrah*,[46] a committee for the collection of Islamic tax, which can be considered a prototype for the Japanese-era *bait al-mal* (Islamic treasury). More than a decade later, during the occupation, Kartosuwiryo would create this treasury within the structure of the Majelis Islam A'la Indonesia (MIAI, Islamic Superior Council of Indonesia).[47] As Agoes Salim organized his journey to Geneva to attend the International Labour Conference, which was hosted by the League of Nations in July 1929, the editorial team of *Fadjar Asia* was restructured, and on the eve of Salim's departure aboard the *Prins der Nederlanden*, Kartosuwiryo became editor.[48]

41 Kartosuwiryo, 'Lahir dan bathin', *Fadjar Asia*, 29 October 1928. On the second day of the congress, he was also reported as replying to Anta Permana's speech on the need to abolish polygamy so hastily that the congress chairman felt it necessary to ask participants not to discuss issues linked to religion; see Kholid Santosa, *Jejak-jejak sang pejuang pemberontak: Pemikiran, gerakan & ekspresi politik S.M. Kartosuwirjo dan Daud Beureueh*, 2nd ed. (Bandung: Sega Arsy, 2006), p. 64.

42 'Adviseur voor Inlandsche Zaken Verslag van het 4e congres den JIB gehouden te Bandung' [1929], AMK GMr, no. 384x/29, in Abdurrahman, 'Jong Islamieten Bond, 1925-1942 (sejarah, pemikiran, dan gerakan)' (thesis, IAIN Sunan Kalijaga, 1999, p. 139). I have not seen the original document.

43 For more details on JIB, see Deliar Noer, *The modernist Muslim movement in Indonesia, 1900-1942* (Singapore: Oxford University Press, 1973) and Yudi Latif, *Indonesian Muslim intelligentsia and power* (Singapore: Institute of Southeast Asian Studies, 2008), pp. 203-11 (quote on p. 204).

44 *'Vrede door religie'*, in *Algemeen overzicht*, 22 December 1928.

45 Abdurrahman, 'Jong Islamieten Bond', pp. 139-40.

46 Kartosuwiryo, 'Seroean oemoem komite zakat fitrah', *Fadjar Asia*, 1 March 1929.

47 See Chapter 2.

48 *Algemeen overzicht*, July 1929 and *Fadjar Asia*, 30 April 1929. Salim's journey was announced by Tjokroaminoto and Kartosuwiryo, 'Ma'loemat Loedjnah Tanfidhijah P.S.I. Indonesia', *Fadjar Asia*, 20 April 1929 and Kartosuwiryo, 'Selamat djalan', *Fadjar Asia*, 2 May 1929.

From then on, Kartosuwiryo's contributions appeared in the newspaper almost every day, providing a clear picture of his activities and the development and reception of his ideas in 1929 and 1930. As Kartosuwiryo was gaining attention on the political scene, his statements became part of journalistic debates, as *Darmokondo*, *Bintang Timoer* and *Oetoesan Hindia* often reacted to his writings.[49]

BACK TO THE DESA: BUILDING LOCAL NETWORKS

West Java

In mid August 1929, Kartosuwiryo was in Garut at the West Java Provincial Congress acting as Secretary of the party's executive committee (a position he had held since March).[50] On this occasion Tjokroaminoto changed the party's name to Partai Sarekat Islam Indonesia (PSII, Party of the Islamic Association of Indonesia) to further stress the party's nationalist stance and its vision of a future Indonesian nation.

The August provincial congress, which marked Kartosuwiryo's entry to the West Java branch of the party, was attended by 800-1,200 representatives of Islamic as well as secular organizations, including some who in later years would become prominent figures in local Islamic politics. In the absence of the West Java chairman, Abdoelmoetallib Sangadji, the congress was opened by Tjokroaminoto and Kadar, who was president of the Jakarta branch, and was chaired by Aroedji Kartawinata, the director of the PSII school in Garut who in the 1940s would become a military commander in the Tasikmalaya area. Among those who participated were Kiyai Ardiwisastra (president of PSII-Malangbong), Kiyai Joesoef Taoeziri (chairman of the Garut branch of the Majelis Oemmat Islam [MOI, Council of the Islamic Ummah]), Kiyai Hadji Moestafa Kamil (national MOI leader) and the PSII-Garut women's organization, along with vari-

49 It is on one of such occasions that Kartosuwiryo's disgruntled comments on Dutch attempts to establish a National Bank of Indonesia (Bank Kebangsaan Indonesia) were picked up and used as an example of his unwillingness to cooperate, and his 'fixation' with linking nationalism to Islam. *Bintang Timoer* excerpt republished in Kartosuwiryo's 'Lagi tentang persatoean I', *Fadjar Asia*, 12 March 1929; Kartosuwiryo, 'Naik tiang pengantungan', *Fadjar Asia*, 25 July 1929; 'Oentoek collega S.M.K. I', *Darmokondo*, 9 July 1929 and 'Oentoek collega S.M.K. II', *Darmokondo*, 10 July 1929. The content of the articles and the nature of the dispute are analysed in the last section of this chapter.

50 'Klachten gehuit [*sic.*] tydens de provinciale congressen van de PSII' [1929], AMK GMr, no. 70, NA. The congress was held on 16-19 August 1929.

ous members of Persis (Bandung), the Majelis Ahli's-Soennah and Persatoean Oelama (Madjalengka). In addition to these Islamic nationalists, also in attendance were Soekarno and Gatot Mangkoepradja from the Bandung branch of PNI, Mirza Wali Ahmad Bey of the Yogyakarta-based Lahori Ahmadiyah, and the Perserikatan Chauffeurs (Drivers' Union).

It is interesting to note that despite the conflict between Sarekat Islam and PNI leadership on the establishment of PPPKI (discussed below), Soekarno participated at this congress. The most notable absentee was, in fact, Muhammadiyah.[51] In 1925 Tjokroaminoto had begun translating into Malay the English version and commentary of the Qur'an made by the Ahmadi scholar Maulvi Muhammad Ali. The project – and the Ahmadi group of Yogyakarta in general – had been initially supported by Muhammadiyah's Kiyai Haji Mas Mansur. However, as this particular instance of the Qur'an's translatability was brought to the attention of Rashid Rida in Cairo, Muhammadiyah felt compelled to withdraw its support and comply with its own alignment to Cairene modernism. Rashid Rida's legal opinion against this translation was published in *al-Manār* in July 1928, yet in September the Sarekat Islam council allowed Tjokroaminoto to continue his work, which was published later the same year.[52]

Sarekat Islam, then, reaffirmed its character as a modernist, yet Indonesia-centred, Islamic organization, of which Kartosuwiryo was an exemplary representative. In April 1928, in his effort to deconstruct the misperception of Islam as an element foreign to the Indies' culture, Kartosuwiryo argued that the Qur'an speaks to all peoples, at all times and in all languages, and that a Malay translation would have been a step in the direction of the consolidation of nationalism, while at the same time strengthening individual piety.[53]

At the 1929 provincial congress, speeches addressing socio-economic issues related to rural life went hand-in-hand with pow-

51 Muhammadiyah was established by Ahmad Dahlan upon his return from Mecca, in 1912; this organization had the stated goal of 'purifying' Indonesian Islam from innovation and local traditions.

52 Nur Ichwan has looked at this instance of Qur'an translation to conclude that Rashid Rida's objection to a Malay (English, Dutch or Turkish) Qur'anic text was a marker of 'the attitudes of Arabic-speaking Muslims towards non-Arabic-speaking Muslims'. The absence of such debates in Indonesia, Nur Ichwan continues, should then not be seen as a deviation from Islamic modernist thought, but rather as a practical implication of the fact that most Muslims did not speak Arabic. See Moch Nur Ichwan, 'Differing responses to an Ahmadi translation and exegesis: The Holy Qur'ān in Egypt and Indonesia', *Archipel* 62 (2001): pp. 143-61.

53 Kartosuwiryo, 'Bertoekar fikiran: Agama dan politiek II', *Fadjar Asia*, 4 April 1928.

erful speeches on the Islamic basis of nationalism and recitations of Qur'anic verses accompanied by *takbir*. Notably, Kartosuwiryo's contribution stands out for its lack of references to nationalism and Islam, focusing instead on problems of irrigation and land ownership. Beginning with a complaint about the contamination of waterways, which had caused the death by malaria of about 90 people in the Cianjur area, Kartosuwiryo then swiftly moved to criticize the granting of agricultural land to Indo-Europeans at advantageous premiums. Kartosuwiryo pointed to local and national implications of these policies: on the one hand villagers from Lampung, afraid of government authorities and the police, had fled their villages, burning houses and trees, and on the other hand he was concerned that once independence was achieved, this land still would not belong to the Indonesian people.[54] Kartosuwiryo's words suggest that he saw Indo-Europeans as more European than Indonesian. The issue of the relationship between ethnicity and citizenry would become an important aspect of the nationalist debate, as Indonesian Chinese and Arabs were gradually pushed out of the picture as 'foreigners'.

Gatot Mangkoepradja and Soekarno delivered their speeches in Malay rather than Sundanese, and the content – as well as the medium – shows how PNI gatherings would usually address an urban audience. They focused on the Russo-Japanese war, labour workers, and the necessity of overcoming differences in the name of cooperation. It is only in looking at the political milieu of these congresses that we can understand the balancing act attempted by Tjokroaminoto, who in his concluding speech mentioned the evils of imperialism and capitalism, comparing them to Gog and Magog, at the same time invoking the blessing of the One and Only God.

At the aftermath of this congress, Kartosuwiryo spent some time in West Java, and between August and October 1929, he often visited the Priangan region to represent the central executive committee.[55] Nonetheless, it is evident that he was still based

54 'Aanbieding van verslagen van Provinciale PSII congressen in Midden-Java van 2 tot 5 Augustus en in West-Java van 16 tot 1[9] Augustus' [1929], AMK GMr, no. 69, NA. This issue is also discussed in Kartosuwiryo, 'Perkara tanah: Bangsa mendjadi oekoeran hak', *Fadjar Asia*, 16 August 1929. Another aspect of Dutch policies mentioned in his speech is colonial expansion through religion, land and trade. The adviser for internal affairs, Gobee, commented on Kartosuwiryo's speech, saying that 'even though this case might be important, the speech was useless because of the unbelievably incorrect one-sided view of affairs'. See also *Politiek-politioneele overzichten van Nederlandsch-Indië* [hereafter PPO], August 1929, pp. 184-5.

55 *Fadjar Asia*, 13 August 1929. Kartosuwiryo is sent to Cianjur together with other party officers to solve unspecified 'party problems'; in *Fadjar Asia*, 5 October 1929 and 8 October 1929, Kartosuwiryo is representing the Ladjnah Tanfidziyah (executive committee) of PSII at a propaganda meeting in Nagrek (Cicalengka).

in Jakarta, where he was active in the youth group. In August he established the Taman Marsoedi Kasoesastran, an educational institution that held classes on subjects ranging from science and English to Dutch and Arabic, and which also had a bookshop.[56] During these months Kartosuwiryo regularly lectured members of the Sarekat Islam Angkatan Pemoeda (SIAP, SI Youth Group) in Jakarta, cultivating these youngsters' morals and strengthening their debating skills.[57] Every Thursday night, his house would host educational *tabligh* sessions, during which he focused on the fundamental principles of Islam, the sciences, and the youth movement in general.[58]

We can see the importance Kartosuwiryo placed on the youth branch through his own eyes: when introducing the new Solo-Surabaya PMI (Pemoeda Moeslimin Indonesia, or Indonesian Muslim Youth) branch, which was another local youth wing of Sarekat Islam not appreciably different from SIAP,[59] Kartosuwiryo explained that Islamic youth groups had great potential to combine strong religious dedication, a deep desire to act for the benefit of the people, the nation and religion, and a thirst for knowledge of Islam, general sciences and speech-giving. All this, he argued, would eventually create a group of 'perfect Muslims', whose minds would be filled with faith and knowledge and whose actions would be fully dedicated to the implementation of Islam.[60]

Malangbong

The complicated nature of local network politics during this time is evident in Kartosuwiryo's connection to Malangbong, a village situated on the busy winding road that connects Bandung to Ciamis and Banjar in the heartland of the Priangan region in the mountainous province of West Java.

The Jakarta branch of PSII, where Kartosuwiryo was actively involved, established a women's wing in late August 1929. The Sarekat Islam Bagian Isteri (SI Women's Group) was, in a way, led by 'party wives', as its chairwoman was Siti Roehati, wife of the PSII Jakarta vice-president, and its vice-secretary was Siti Kalsoem, iden-

56 *Fadjar Asia*, 15 August 1929, 16 September 1929 and 26 September 1929.

57 *Fadjar Asia*, 18 September 1929: *untuk mendidik budi pekerti*, the same expression later used to describe the Soeffah Institute.

58 *Fadjar Asia*, 22 October 1929.

59 Kartosuwiryo, 'Pergerakan pemoeda dan politiek', *Fadjar Asia*, 19 April 1929.

60 Kartosuwiryo, 'Halangan PMI Solo', *Fadjar Asia*, 28 June 1929.

tified as Kartosuwiryo's wife.[61] In a society in which socio-political networks dictated one's fortune and misfortune, such a marriage was quite likely to represent an alliance between Kartosuwiryo and PSII in West Java, as Siti Kalsoem was the daughter of Kiyai Ardiwisastra, chairman of the party's Malangbong branch.

A second important aspect related to this union is the social status brought along by Kiyai Ardiwisastra's position as a representative of an important aristocratic (*menak*) Sundanese family and a revered Islamic scholar. These two elements played an important role in transforming Kartosuwiryo into a bearer of traditional authority in the years that followed, as well as in the deepening of his own religious knowledge.

Reportedly, Kartosuwiryo used to spend long hours with local *kiyai*, among whom were party leaders Moestafa Kamil and Joesoef Taoeziri, mentioned above.[62] Moestafa Kamil (born 1884) was himself the son of a well known *kiyai* in Garut and had long studied in *pesantren* in West and East Java and also in Mecca. It was in Mecca that he first encountered Hadji Agoes Salim, and first heard of Sarekat Islam. Upon his return to Garut, Moestafa Kamil joined the ranks of the local branch and soon became a prominent political figure who was also often imprisoned by the colonial police.

Joesoef Taoeziri (died 1982), too, was renowned for his religious knowledge and was among the early members of the Sarekat Islam branch in Ciparay. Both *kiyai* were arrested with Tjokroaminoto in relation with the Cimareme *Afdeeling B* affair in 1919, during which the Dutch authorities suspected some Sarekat Islam members of having established a 'section B' of the party aimed at exterminating all Europeans and Chinese in Java.[63]

Taoeziri entered the Party Central Board in 1931 and left in 1938, one year before Moestafa Kamil became a member. Where these two politicians differed was in their approach to Islamic politics during the Japanese occupation. In the 1940s Moestafa Kamil was recruited as a lecturer for West Java's armed wing of the Islamic

61 *Fadjar Asia*, 29 August 1929. This seemed to happen quite often. See also the women's wing of PSI in Sungai Batang, Meninjau, Sumatra, in *Fadjar Asia*, 1 August 1929. *Pandji Poestaka* reported that the initiative of creating a women section of PSI had been spearheaded by Tjokroaminoto's wife, and that this group's leadership reflected that of the general Sarekat Islam party. 'Kroniek Hindia', *Pandji Poestaka* no. 72, 6 September 1929, p. 1144.

62 Pinardi, *Sekarmadji Maridjan*, pp. 24-5, and an interview conducted by the author in Malangbong, 6 February 2008.

63 On *Afdeeling B* see Else Ensering, 'Afdeeling B of Sarekat Islam. A rebellious islamic movement', in Dick Kooiman, Otto van den Muijzenberg, and Peter van der Veer (eds), *Conversion, competition, and conflict: Essays on the role of religion in Asia* (Amsterdam: VU Uitgeverij, 1984); William A. Oates, 'The Afdeeling B: An Indonesian case study', *Journal of Southeast Asian History* (March 1968).

party, the Hizboellah (literally 'Party of God') troops, and after the capitulation, he joined Kartosuwiryo's Darul Islam. Taoeziri, on the other hand, rejected military intervention and established his own school in Ciparay, *pesantren* Daroel Salam (Abode of Peace), dedicating his full attention to teaching.[64]

Islam, authority and leadership in the Priangan

In 1925, Adviser for Domestic Affairs (Inlandsche Zaken) R.A. Kern observed that the Dutch East India Company's takeover in West Java had increased the religious authority of the *bupati* (regents), as they were called *imam* or *khalifa* and considered substitutes of the kings of Mataram, the sixteenth-century Islamic empire of Central Java.[65] More recently it has been suggested that in rural West Java the local aristocracy – the *menak* – had been transformed into a political elite by the Mataram Empire and kept as such by the Dutch East India Company and the colonial government. Herlina Lubis has argued that this phenomenon eventually resulted in the merging of the roles of *bupati* and *ulama* (religious scholar), as the *menak* succeeded in maintaining both the political power bestowed upon them by the Dutch and the people's recognition as bearers of traditional authority.[66]

Ardiwisastra was not only a member of the *menak* aristocracy and a *kiyai pesantren*, but also the local PSII chairman, and the vice-*bupati*. By marrying his daughter, Kartosuwiryo strengthened his political standing in Sarekat Islam and gained a position within traditional patterns of authority. In the 1970s, Karl Jackson argued that Darul Islam followers joined in the rebellion because of networks of authority. However, he referred to individual village *kiyai*, while downplaying Kartosuwiryo's role as the movement's leader.[67] What

64 Biographic data for Moestafa Kamil are from Ismail, 'Perjuangan K.H. Mustofa Kamil pada masa penjajahan dan kemerdekaan di Garut antara tahun 1914-1945' (thesis, IAIN Sunan Gunung Jati, 1998). For Joesoef Taoeziri, see Dudung, 'Peristiwa Cipari' (thesis, Universitas Padjadjaran, 1987) and Wahyudi, 'Aktivitas K.H. Yusuf Tauzirie dalam mengembangkan syiar Islam di desa Cipari kecamatan Wanaraja kabupaten Garut (1926-1981)' (thesis, UIN Sunan Gunung Jati, 2006). On Moestafa Kamil as *dewan partij* member, see *Berita Priangan,* 17 July 1939.

65 Letter from R.A. Kern, 9 June 1925, p. 12, in Mohammad Iskandar, *Para pengemban amanah: Pergulatan pemikiran kiai dan ulama di Jawa Barat, 1900-1950* (Yogyakarta: MataBangsa, 2001), p. 66.

66 Nina Herlina Lubis, 'Religious thoughts and practices of the *kaum menak*: Strengthening traditional power', *Studia Islamika* 10-2 (2003): pp. 5-7.

67 Karl D. Jackson, *Traditional authority and national integration: A study of Indonesian political behaviour* (Berkeley/London: University of California Press, 1980 [1971]). His argument is further analysed in the concluding chapter to this book.

I am suggesting, instead, is that traditional networks of authority worked to the advantage of Kartosuwiryo's career, allowing him to start creating a following well before the rebellion began.

Herlina Lubis develops her argument from the observation that Priangan society displayed several examples in which the link between local aristocracy and Islam is embodied in members of the *menak* group who were also *ulama*, as in the cases of Hadji Hasan Moestafa of Garut (1852-1930) and Raden Hadji Moehammad Moesa (1822-1886). While recognizing the exceptionalism of these figures, Lubis nonetheless concludes that 'all *kaum menak* were required to make Islam a factor in their political thoughts and practices'. The *kaum menak* obtained religious legitimation by closely aligning their social and political life with Islamic values and institutions. For example, they often attended and sponsored the building of *pesantren*, thereby creating strong bonds with local *ulama*. A body of legends claiming that *kaum menak* families descended from the Sultan of Pajang – an extension of the Demak Sultanate in sixteenth-century Java – or from Prabu Siliwangi of Pajajaran – the pre-Islamic Sundanese Empire – also served to further strengthen their connections with traditional religious and political authority.

More relevant to Kartosuwiryo's case, the political authority embodied by this elite was founded on local concepts of power, described as *pulung* in Javanese or *wahyu* in Arabic, a term that also indicates a 'divine revelation'. These local ideologies tended to identify authority as something bestowed either from a previous king or a *bupati*, or directly through God's blessing. When considered alongside the fact that a *bupati* who could display religious knowledge and understanding was held in higher regard than one who could not, it can be concluded that the adoption of Islamic values in *kaum menak*'s traditions was pursued in favour of their own political interests.[68]

Villagers often perceived these *bupati* as 'holy people', from whom blessings could be obtained because of their alleged supernatural abilities and connections with the world of magic. Nonetheless, among these *ulama-bupati* aristocrats there was still a strong tendency towards orthodoxy and towards the implementation of sharia law. Material testimony of Priangan *menak*'s syncretism can be found in the maintenance of their heirlooms, which usually consisted of *keris* (daggers with undulated blades deemed to possess spiritual essence), spears, swords, books, puppets, and the like. These were deemed to possess magical powers, but at the same time were considered religious symbols, as they often featured Qur'anic inscriptions, and were

68 Lubis, 'Religious thoughts': pp. 10-8.

used in Islamic ceremonies, such as the Prophet's birthday (*Maulid Nabi*).[69] This characterization of Sundanese *menak* as bridge between the supernatural world of magic and Islamic orthodoxy fits well with later tales of Kartosuwiryo's charismatic leadership.

In his first biography, published in 1963, just one year after his capture and execution, Kartosuwiryo was presented as having a complex character. He was described as a mystic, believed by his followers to practice the *ilmu Joyoboyo* ('science of prophecy', see footnote) and to be the *Imam Mahdi* (Islamic messianic figure) or *Ratu Adil* (Just King).[70] In this biography, much attention is dedicated to the accounts of Kartosuwiryo's followers, some of whom maintained that God had chosen him as their leader through divine revelation. Others claimed that he had received the *wahyu Cakraningrat Sadar*, which among all the *wahyu* is the only one bestowed upon kings, and that he had been invested with the title of *Kalifatullah seluruh ummat manusia*, or representative of God to the entire Islamic community. It was said that he owned amulets (*jimat*) that protected him even from bullets, as well as a *keris* and a *cundrik* (a small *keris* with a straight blade). Put simply, his followers deemed him to have *sakti* (divine power).[71]

This representation of Kartosuwiryo as both a fanatical Muslim and a mystic quickly became predominant in the literature, especially as writers made increasing use of tales recounted by Darul Islam/Tentara Islam Indonesia (DI-TII) members. Pinardi, the author of Kartosuwiryo's other major biography, reports the comment of one TII militiaman, who recalled Kartosuwiryo as

> a very fanatical religious man with strong mystical beliefs. To several of his followers he once admitted to be the reincarnation of Raden Patah, one of the most famous men of religion and the first sultan of Demak, the first Sultanate of Java. He told his devotees that for long he had desired to establish the NII [Negara Islam Indonesia] and that only he could become the leader, or *imam*, because he had been predestined for that by God [...] Kartosuwiryo once said he had received the *wahyu Cakraningrat Sadar* from God, this was like a beam of bright light from the sky down onto him.[72]

69 Lubis, 'Religious thoughts': pp. 18-20, 26.

70 *Joyoboyo* (or *Jayabaya*) is, generally speaking, a mystical foretelling (*ramalan*). Nancy Florida describes *Joyoboyo* texts as follows: 'texts of this genre turn on historical periodization, political symbology, and, especially, prophecy.' Florida, *Writing the past, inscribing the future: History as prophecy in colonial Java* (Durham, NC: Duke University Press, 1995), p. 273.

71 Amak Sjariffudin, *Kisah Kartosuwirjo dan menjerahnja*, 3rd ed. (Surabaya: Grip, 1963), pp. 7, 20-1. This text contains several biographical mistakes; nonetheless, it is still worth discussing its approach to the character of Kartosuwiryo.

72 Pinardi, *Sekarmadji Maridjan*, p. 41.

The story goes that whilst Kartosuwiryo was in the jungle, a ray of light appeared in front of him and an 'essence' (*zat*) drew the *kalimat shahadat* (Islamic profession of faith) on his forehead. Pinardi concluded that this aura of mystery, mysticism and fanaticism was Kartosuwiryo's key 'leadership skill', or *seni kepemimpinan.*[73]

In the mid 1970s, the idea of mysticism as an aspect of Kartosuwiryo's leadership was reaffirmed in the pages of his psychological evaluation:[74]

> Kartosuwiryo's intelligence is great, [...] Intuition has empowered him as a leader, [...] and has also induced his interest in mysticism and metaphysics. At the same time, his rationality was so developed that his objective critical capacity was dominant, and it has become representative of his thinking and actions. His mystical activities were neither essential nor fundamental to him, and he approached them in a critical way. So the mystical path that he might have experienced was maybe something meaningful on a personal level. His mystical activities – the little available news on these – were used as a tool to strengthen the implementation of his ideas. Thus, he used mysticism as a tool neither essential nor crucial to him, but rather as an element of authority in the face of the masses he led.[75]

Hiroko Horikoshi, in her study of Darul Islam's following, takes a similar approach. In explaining the initial success of the Darul Islam, she places the appeal of Kartosuwiryo's charisma on the same level as the failure of national Islamic parties, and the parallel military and historical circumstances. Horikoshi ultimately concludes that Kartosuwiryo succeeded in gathering support as a result of the combination of military-political circumstances, Islamic politics, and personal characteristics:

> He evidently possessed the invaluable quality, typical among Java's *jago* (champions) of being *gagah* (translated in a colloquial sense as 'having guts') [...] Men who are *gagah* fear nothing but God and are strongly convinced of their cause (*yakin*). They tell the truth

73 Pinardi, *Sekarmadji Maridjan*, p. 45.

74 This investigation examined intelligence, emotional behaviour, motivation, personal development since 1950 and prognoses for the future. It is interesting to note that the doctors explicitly stated that Kartosuwiryo's motivation for pursuing the rebellion was rooted in childhood developments and therefore impossible to assess at that point in time.

75 Dinas Sedjarah TNI, *Penumpasan pemberontakan D.I./T.I.I., S.M. Kartosuwiryo di Jawa Barat* (Bandung: Dinas Sejarah Tentara Nasional Indonesia Angkatan Darat, 1982 [1974]), p. 35, quote p. 33.

> even to the authorities without any fear of the consequences. Such a charismatic man inspires awe (*segan*) in his followers. [...] Where *gagah* behavior is associated with a high cause, it commands great respect and obedience. In rural Java high causes have traditionally been based on the values of communal peace, prosperity, and social justice, and expressed either in indigenous (*Ratu Adil*) or Islamic (*Imam Mahdi*) idioms.[76]

Mysticism and 'uncompromising advocacy of Islamic ideals' are the markers of Kartosuwiryo's success, an ideal combination for being recognized as a leader in Java.[77] It is surprising that subsequent scholars have not taken this suggestion more seriously, focusing instead on either belittling Kartosuwiryo's commitment to the establishment of an Islamic state or sanctifying his endeavours while erasing his charisma and mysticism. I further address this point in the concluding chapter of this book. To Horikoshi's analysis, I would add that Kartosuwiryo's becoming part of a *menak bupati-ulama* family in the early stages of his career in West Java further enhanced his appeal as a successful leader in the Priangan.

DEVELOPING AN ISLAMIC NATIONALIST IDEOLOGY

Within the first four months of beginning to contribute to *Fadjar Asia*, Kartosuwiryo had already addressed the major topics that would constitute his ideology: criticism of colonial policies, socio-economic injustice, abuse of power by police, governmental interference in religious matters, religious and political neutrality, the internal nationalist debate, Islam's modernity and the international dimensions of the nationalist struggle.

Kartosuwiryo's articles appeared in *Fadjar Asia* between April 1928 and May 1930 and show a coherent, if somewhat fragmented, picture of how he viewed the state of the indigenous population and its relation both to the colonial administration and to the international anti-colonial and anti-capitalist movements. In April 1929 Kartosuwiryo lamented that

> in politics, economics, but also society, the world still searches and gropes in the dark. The strong ones inevitably rule, and the weak

76 Hiroko Horikoshi, 'The Dar-ul-Islam movement in West Java (1942-62): An experience in the historical process', *Indonesia* 20 (1975): p. 73.

77 Hiroko Horikoshi, 'The Dar-ul-Islam movement', p. 73.

> are governed, the rich accumulate material things and the poor fail to do so, and every day the burden to be carried increases. Hundreds of thousands of traders and businessmen fail in their trades. Hundreds of thousands are the old farmers who don't own any land anymore because it has been bought off by someone else, and they are now transformed into labourers, [dragged] deep into slavery and humiliation.[78]

Kartosuwiryo applied his understanding of socio-economic oppression, which emerged from his direct experience in Java, to similar situations across the world and history. The examples he produced were from Russia, China, and France, but his heart and mind were in Sukabumi, where taxes and the cost of living had increased to the point that local farmers were forced to sell their land to pay current expenses, and then to rent back smaller pieces of their own *sawah* paddy field to sustain their families.

The absence of, and quest for, justice is at the centre of more than twenty articles, in which socio-economic injustice takes several different forms in various aspects of the indigenous population's life. In addition to focusing on the constant economic harassment by the colonial administration at the local and national levels, Kartosuwiryo dedicates considerable attention to police intrusions at political activities and religious gatherings. Sarekat Islam party members were jailed, party cadres questioned and prayer sessions broken up with little apparent reason other than creating difficulties for the *gerakan*, in the rural areas as much as in Batavia.

Such occurrences were lessons Kartosuwiryo would use to enlighten his readership on the party's political strategy and on the reasons Islamic nationalism offered a more solid foundation upon which to build an anti-colonial movement than did secular nationalism, which professed neutrality towards religion.

The very first article Kartosuwiryo wrote for *Fadjar Asia* was titled 'Religion and politics', and it imagines a fictional debate between a 'modern' Muslim, and a pious 'conservative' Muslim.[79] The figures are opposed to explain how being pious does not mean being 'traditional', but rather means looking at the socio-political prob-

78 Kartosuwiryo, 'Keber'atan ra'iat', *Fadjar Asia*, 27 April 1929.

79 This debate between *kaum muda* and *kaum kolot* (or *kaum tua*) was also often featured in *Taman Pewarta*; however, here the modernized man works within the framework of the colonial policy, whilst the 'traditional' man is the one that fears the loss of his Javaneseness because of the Dutch-ification of customs, rather than his religious values. See Paul Tickell, 'Taman Pewarta: Malay medium-Indonesian message', in *The Indonesian press: Its past, its people, its problems*, Paul Tickell (ed.), Annual Indonesian Lecture Series (Melbourne: Monash University, 1987).

lems of the Indies' through the lens of religion. The pious man addresses the modern man, saying,

> Maybe, then, you don't know that religion embodies rules, rules for this world and the hereafter. Hence, religion is political. Aren't you aware that in the history of Islam there are Islamic empires, Islamic wars, and so forth? Colonial politics itself is founded on religion, especially the Christian religion; there is a policy named *Kersteningspolitiek*, aimed at Christianizing the Indonesian population. Hence, religion is an important factor in colonial politics.

Upon hearing this statement, the modern Muslim, who works for the Dutch administration, is easily convinced and sets aside the common, secular understanding of religion as a private matter. He replies: 'If that is so, Islam is also political.'[80]

Throughout Kartosuwiryo's writings, the focus is on the need to obtain freedom, independence, *merdeka*. Achieving independence, however, is not important for its own sake, but rather for the sake of creating an environment favourable to the implementation of Islamic laws and the establishment of a government based on Islam.[81] In this understanding, the way out of oppression and poverty is religion:

> Hold on to the ties connecting the Islamic *ummah*! Hold on to Islam truly! Follow the orders of Allah, and stay away from that which He forbids. Clearly this is the noble way to obtain freedom for the people and the motherland in a more encompassing and true sense, liberated from all forms of slavery, humiliation and subjugation, which are still now affecting us Indonesians in general and Muslims in particular.[82]

But these are not just empty words of propaganda, aimed at rallying the support of disenchanted peasants; this is a political platform, in which 'Islam' and 'the orders of Allah' are to be translated into a free, independent, sovereign Islamic state:

> We must prioritize and put our deepest efforts into establishing and building such [Islamic] government, so that we can succeed in becoming one *ummah*, holding its laws, implementing such laws

80 Kartosuwiryo, 'Bertoekar fikiran: Agama dan politiek', *Fadjar Asia*, 3 April 1928.
81 Kartosuwiryo, 'Faham koeno dan faham moeda', *Fadjar Asia*, 12 September 1928.
82 Kartosuwiryo, 'Keber'atan ra'iat', *Fadjar Asia*, 27 April 1929.

> independently, and having sovereignity over our own land. In short: [we have to do this] so that we can follow Islamic sharia law in its most perfect and complete way, in all matters.[83]

Such a bold statement, made in May 1930, must be seen in relation to the repeated intrusions of the colonial government in the activities of the Sarekat Islam Party and in its religious gatherings in Malangbong. His claim should be read in light of the debate on the government's supposed 'neutrality' towards religion, a stand that, according to Kartosuwiryo, had been broken when the government requested that each mosque obtain official permission to hold congregational prayers on Fridays.[84]

This concept of being 'neutral' towards religion was first formulated by Snouck Hurgronje, who, according to Kartosuwiryo, had suggested that

> the government must be careful on matters relating to Islam. On Islamic understanding, the government must be *neutraal.* Never make a comment on the Caliphate question, especially on pan-Islamism [...], educate Indonesian children, and give them classes on all subjects but religion [...], seek friendship between Holland and Indonesia on matters of politics and nationalism, but do not envisage friendship in religion.

This effort towards establishing 'neutral education' is defined by Kartosuwiryo as 'associationist' and an attempt to westernize not just education but, ultimately, the Indies' population by stripping it of its nationalist sentiment.[85]

Himself the product of Dutch schooling, Kartosuwiryo felt that the imposition of higher education in the language of the colonial administration was part of the Dutch policy to 'divide and rule', ultimately aimed at fragmenting the unity of the Indonesian people. It is along these lines that Kartosuwiryo argued in favour of the use of Malay for intellectuals and nationalist leaders.[86]

Neutrality soon became the core issue of the debate within the nationalist movement. However, the exact meaning of 'neutrality' was far from clear. Secular nationalists took it to mean a rejection of religion as a political ideology in favour of 'nationalism'. For

83 Kartosuwiryo, 'Lagi tentang oelil amri', *Fadjar Asia*, 24 May 1930.

84 Kartosuwiryo, 'Boepati dan agama Islam', *Fadjar Asia*, 21 April 1930.

85 Kartosuwiryo, 'Politiek djadjahan dan igama IV', *Fadjar Asia*, 14 June 1928.

86 Kartosuwiryo, 'Bangsa dan bahasa', *Fadjar Asia*, 8 May 1928, and Kartosuwiryo, 'Politiek djadjahan dan igama V', *Fadjar Asia*, 16 June 1928.

many religious organizations, including Muhammadiyah, 'neutrality' entailed safeguarding their own survival by stepping out of the political arena entirely, and concerning themselves only with social activities without opposing those organizations that involved themselves with it. For Kartosuwiryo, neither attitude made sense, nor could either lead to success.

In another fictional conversation, Kartosuwiryo presents the 'modern' man as employed in the colonial bureaucracy and convinced that only by being 'neutral' can he keep his position. For him, neutrality means 'not mixing with Indonesian political organizations', especially Sarekat Islam.[87] It was this very audience, the Indonesians employed in the colonial administration and fearful of political-religious involvement, that Kartosuwiryo targeted when explaining that it is impossible to be neutral. To those who argued that the principle behind their organizations is 'only Indonesian nationalism' – as did Jong Java and Pemoeda Indonesia – Kartosuwiryo answered that the 'neutral effort' was an 'empty effort': 'Our measures are the Qur'an and the *hadith* [prophetic traditions]. Instead they have... science, intelligence, and whatever else. But most people would admit that science changes and expands, depending on theories; in a word, science is not constant'.[88]

To Kartosuwiryo, those who based their nationalism solely on their love of the motherland without recognizing any higher unchanging principle were doomed to become political 'chameleons'.[89] Similarly, when commenting on the nationalist anthem, *Indonesia Raya,* which refers to the motherland as *Ibu* and *Dewi,* Kartosuwiryo deplored this form of nationalism as 'chauvinistic' and easy to 'turn into capitalism and imperialism'.[90]

Where Kartosuwiryo interpreted the Dutch 'divide and rule' approach as an attempt to fragment indigenous society and one that might have been countered, for example, by using the Malay language, Soekarno instead saw it as the ideological fragmentation of the anti-colonial front from within, which could only be overcome through internal collaboration. Following on his early attempt to merge the nationalist, religious and socialist movements into one, which he expressed in his 1926 *Islamisme, nasionalisme, dan Marxisme* pamphlet, in 1927 Soekarno succeeded in establishing the Permoefakatan Perhimpoenan Politik Kebangsaan Indonesia (PPPKI, Agreement of Indonesian People's Political Associations).

87 Kartosuwiryo, 'Pertjakapan di dalam kereta api', *Fadjar Asia,* 15 May 1928.

88 Kartosuwiryo, 'Sambil laloe: Soeara baroe! Model lama', *Fadjar Asia,* 4 May 1929.

89 Kartosuwiryo, 'Faham koeno dan faham moeda', *Fadjar Asia,* 12 September 1928.

90 Kartosuwiryo, 'Indonesia Raja dan... kerbau', *Fadjar Asia,* 6 August 1929.

This federation was the outcome of the collaborative efforts of Soekarno, Tjokroaminoto and Salim, and was an attempt at unifying the nationalist front.

For the first two years Sarekat Islam argued that PPPKI was just a federation of parties and not a union (*persatuan*), and therefore allowed participating organizations to maintain their autonomy. In March 1929, however, Sarekat Islam took a stronger position against PPPKI and its attitude of cooperation with the colonial authorities (a point further discussed in the next chapter), and it gradually distanced itself from the federation. As several branches of PSII had not obtained permission from the party's executive committee to participate in the August 1929 PPPKI congress, a rumour began circulating in secular circles that Kartosuwiryo had influenced the decision to exclude these groups in support of his anti-cooperationist approach. *Fadjar Asia* responded to this accusation by explaining that the decision had been made on financial grounds. To this official response, Kartosuwiryo added his personal perspective on the issue of 'unity', stating that a true and genuine union can only be based on Islam, as any other form of *persatuan* would only be based on fear of the enemy.[91]

Kartosuwiryo took the idea that genuine unity could only be obtained within the frame of Islamic groups and extended it to the international dimensions of the anti-colonial struggle. As Tjokroaminoto had already pointed out in his *Islam dan sosialisme*, socialism and Islamism both relied on international networks for the achievement of their socio-political goals. However, where Tjokroaminoto and Soekarno had used this commonality to bridge differences, Kartosuwiryo used it to prove Islam's superiority over secular ideologies.

Even though it might appear to conflict with the nationalist objectives of the Sarekat Islam party, what follows shows that the shifts between Islamic nationalism and pan-Islamic transnationalism cannot be understood apart from their historical contingencies, an approach that I also apply to understanding this same phenomenon in the 1930s-1950s period.[92]

91 On PSI and PPPKI see Kartosuwiryo, 'Sambil laloe: Lagi tentang persatoean', *Fadjar Asia*, 12 March 1929; 'Sambil laloe: Lagi tentang persatoean II', *Fadjar Asia*, 15 March 1929; 'Kongres P3KI kedoea', *Fadjar Asia*, 10 August 1929; 'Liga, Perhimpoenan Indonesia dan kita', *Fadjar Asia*, 31 August 1929; 'Boekan merintangi, melainkan tidak toeroet', *Fadjar Asia*, 4 September 1929; 'Sambil laloe: Pikiran sehat', *Fadjar Asia*, 7 September 1929; 'Soe'al persatoean', *Fadjar Asia*, 10 September 1929; 'Warta bagi pers', *Fadjar Asia*, 13 September 1929. See also PPO, August 1929, p. 177.

92 An earlier draft of this section has been published in Formichi, 'Pan-Islam and religious nationalism'.

Kartosuwiryo first raised the issue of Islamic transnationalism in July 1928. Arguing for the primacy of Islam, Kartosuwiryo pointed to the socio-political dimensions of the *hajj* pilgrimage as a physical manifestation of Islamic brotherhood, crossing boundaries of ethnicity, language and nationality.[93]

The term pan-Islamism appears for the first time in late September 1928. When commenting on the colonial authorities' mismanagement of justice, Kartosuwiryo calls for Indonesian Muslims to 'wake up' and join the one organization, PSII, that defends the people and is ready to sacrifice itself to ensure its top priority, pan-Islamism: 'Our movement dedicates each and every bone of its body to *pan-Islamisme*.'[94] At this point in time Kartosuwiryo saw pan-Islamism not as a goal *per se*, but rather as a political tool, an orientation that became clearer in subsequent articles.

I am not suggesting that Sarekat Islam was instrumentalizing pan-Islamism as an element of its political propaganda, but rather that the idea of a global community united by the same religious beliefs and striving for the same freedom from foreign domination was considered a powerful rallying point for political action. It would only be in the 1950s that Kartosuwiryo developed a vision of pan-Islamism as the final goal of his struggle. This he would represent as the creation of a transnational political entity, namely, a state based on Islamic laws that unified the *ummah* worldwide. Despite the existence of several secular political parties that claimed to be inter-Asiatic, Kartosuwiryo believed that only Islam called for pure and genuine cooperation across borders, untainted by political opportunism.

Showing how difficult it was to balance nationalism and pan-Islamism intellectually, Kartosuwiryo added that an additional function of Islamic internationalism – which he also referred to as inter-Islamism – was the creation of a network of Islamic countries that desired to cooperate with one another on the road to nationalism.[95] This apparent contradiction, which recalls the ideological shift in the Indian Khilafat movement, soon attracted the attention of the Chinese-Malay newspaper *Keng Po*. In November 1928 its lead article argued that, 'In Islam there is neither nationalism nor internationalism'. But this polemic, instead of harming the Islamic faction, became an ideal platform for *Fadjar Asia* to further enlighten its readership about the political duties of Muslims.

93 Kartosuwiryo, 'Perdjalanan ketanah soetji', *Fadjar Asia*, 20 July 1928.
94 Kartosuwiryo, 'Aniajaan dan siksaan', *Fadjar Asia*, 26 September 1928.
95 Kartosuwiryo, 'Pertjaja kepada diri sendiri dan ...', *Fadjar Asia*, 31 October 1928.

Kartosuwiryo's argument was twofold. On the one hand he demonstrated Islam's commitment to nationalism by invoking the Prophet's alleged saying, 'Love for the homeland is a part of faith'. On the other hand, he identified the struggle to become one unified Muslim nation as the political implication of the religious concept of *ummah*, and pointed to the duty to perform pilgrimage as the 'broadest, purest, and holiest' manifestation of this struggle. Kartosuwiryo thus concluded that secular nationalists did not fully understand the complexity of Islamic nationalism, which was aimed not at the freedom and promotion of one people, one race or one kingdom, but was instead pursued for the prosperity of 'the One God, One belief, One Prophet, One flag' of Islam.[96]

Kartosuwiryo's articles published in 1929 focused on domestic politics, but as the debate among indigenous parties intensified, Kartosuwiryo offered his reflections on the different characteristics of nationalist ideologies in the Indies. In 'Islam dan nasionalisme', Kartosuwiryo succeeded in balancing his warnings that national pride might result in international confrontations together with his effort to preserve the notion that one should love the motherland. To avoid this potentially 'deviationist attitude', Kartosuwiryo argued that patriotism should follow the model of monotheism, and thus should be directed towards what he called '*Mono-Hoemanisme*', a term here used to described 'the unity of the human race to become one *ummah*' (*persatoean manoesia mendjadi satoe Oemmat*). Islam is 'not just a way to establish relations between humans and God', but it can guide relations between humans and organizations. As such, it can help shape a wider concept of nationality (*kebangsaan*) that is not limited to its 'usual understanding'.[97] A couple of months later Kartosuwiryo explained these differences, contributing to the vigorous public debate over how nationhood should be perceived under colonial rule. For Boedi Oetomo, nationalism is 'Javanese nationalism'; for Soekarno's PNI, it is 'pan-Asianism'. But for Kartosuwiryo and the PSII, *kebangsaan* was not to be linked to worldly desires nor was it limited by any territorial boundary. It was wide and broad, and connected only to religious affiliation and to the unity of Islam: Islamic nationalism was solely committed to the prosperity of God.[98]

96 Kartosuwiryo, 'Islamisme, nasionalisme dan internasionalisme I', *Fadjar Asia*, 3 November 1928, and 'Islamisme, nasionalisme dan internasionalisme II', *Fadjar Asia*, 7 November 1928. Quote from *Keng Po* and Qur'anic verse (in Indonesian) included in: Kartosuwiryo, 'Islamisme, nasionalisme dan internasionalisme I'.

97 Kartosuwiryo, 'Islam dan nasionalisme', *Fadjar Asia*, 24 May 1929.

98 Kartosuwiryo, 'Berekor pandjang (pers dan politiek)', *Fadjar Asia*, 2 July 1929.

CONCLUDING REMARKS

Born in a low-*priyayi* family and educated in the Dutch system, Kartosuwiryo was to become a prominent political proponent of anti-colonialism and anti-Western ideologies. He soon gained the attention of authorities for his work as a journalist and the attention of Tjokroaminoto for his political engagement. And while the former accused him of fanaticism, the latter reared him as a godson.

Gradually shifting his attention from socio-economic concerns towards Islamic modernism, from condemning the colonial state for ignoring the importance of religion in Indonesians' lives to accusing secular nationalists of doing the same in politics, Kartosuwiryo's own development mirrored the changes in the Sarekat Islam party. Initially incorporating socialists and Islamists and embodying this double soul in its leader, Tjokroaminoto, Sarekat Islam had clearly defined itself as an Islamic political party in opposition to Soekarno's secularism and Semaoen's socialism by the end of the 1920s. Exposed to international dynamics originating both in Europe and the Middle East, regional and ethnic cultural organizations were transformed into political parties that were increasingly defined by their founding ideologies.

Kartosuwiryo's dedication to gathering popular support in the countryside, fostering the urban youth as 'perfect Muslims', and creating new family connections in order to be recognizable as a bearer of local and traditional authority were all key elements in his leadership in subsequent decades. As the Dutch curbed political activities, the anti-colonial front became increasingly fragmented, with each party further radicalizing its position.

2

Political Islam in changing times Sarekat Islam and Masyumi under the Dutch and Japanese occupations (1930-1945)

Djadi, berdiri di luar, bukan berdiam diri!!

(So, we stand outside, we are not staying silent!!)[1]

The same forces that had ensured economic growth and prosperity in the 1920s were, a decade later, pulling the Indies down the road towards stagnation. The Great Depression that hit the West inevitably reached the colonies, stalling exports of manufactured goods and crop production. Schools were producing thousands of unemployable graduates, and trained clerks were forced to take up menial jobs, while older employees were fired to make room for younger (cheaper) workers. Nonetheless, in urban Java real wages increased, socio-economic conditions were no worse than usual and the general economic distress did not stir political discontent, much to the surprise of colonial authorities and nationalist leaders alike.[2]

The 1930s were characterized by the further fragmentation of the nationalist movement, which experienced external pressure from the heavy-handed colonial authorities, as well as internal pressure from the movement's own inability to find solid common ground for a unified front. For Partai Sarekat Islam Indonesia, this decade marked its isolation from mainstream politics, as the party pulled out of PPPKI's 'brown front',[3] rejected any form of cooperation with the Dutch and, under Kartosuwiryo's guidance, became increasingly concerned with Islamic politics.

Sarekat Islam's commitment to non-cooperation is often considered an earthquake second in damage only to the split

1 Kartosuwiryo, *Sikap hidjrah PSII*, 1936.

2 John Ingleson, 'Urban Java during the depression', *Journal of Southeast Asian Studies*, 19-2 (September 1988): pp. 292-309.

3 Soekarno had begun to refer to a 'brown front' in late 1927, in opposition to Dutch talks of establishing a *blank front* (white front) under the leadership of the hardliner H.C. Zentgraff; see Hering, *Soekarno: Founding father*, pp. 134-4.

between the 'red' and 'white' wings that occurred in 1923, as membership dropped, leaders were expelled and splinter parties mushroomed.

Yet, as anticipated by the changes in the party statutes in December 1929, the 1930s should also be seen as a time when the religious soul of the party gained prominence, 'freed' as it was both from the controlling hand of Tjokroaminoto, who died in 1934, and from diplomatic efforts to establish a common strategy with the secularists. Even as Japan took over Java and Sumatra in 1942, effectuating major changes in the independence movement, the two groups were to remain separated, each with its own ideological and strategic concerns.

KARTOSUWIRYO: A RISING STAR?

In January 1930 the Dutch authorities welcomed Kartosuwiryo's disappearance from the pages of *Fadjar Asia*, praising the editorial board for 'coming to its senses' and realizing the threat presented by his 'fanatical' and 'intense' articles. The *Overzicht* also voiced its disapproval of the party's choice to keep Kartosuwiryo within the leadership cadres.[4] Kartosuwiryo had only been appointed in mid November 1929, as Agoes Salim had embarked for Geneva to attend the International Labour Conference meeting in December, but the brevity of his appointment was not tied to his ideas, as the Dutch had instead assumed.[5]

Kartosuwiryo continued to hold tight his position in the party; if anything, the immediate future saw his influence on shaping PSII policies increase. This holds true for the period between the 1930 Yogyakarta Congress, when the non-cooperation *hijrah* policy became central to the party, and 1936, when the party's sturdy commitment to this approach led to the deterioration of relations between Kartosuwiryo and Agoes Salim, a rift that ultimately resulted in the fragmentation of the leadership.

It is likely that Kartosuwiryo's withdrawal from the editorial board was related to Salim's return to Batavia and to his own bad health, rather than to changing winds in the party. *Fadjar Asia* advertised Kartosuwiryo's presence at a PSII-Jakarta meeting on 5-6 January 1930, mentioning that he had participated 'although he has now [9 January] retreated to the mountains near Malan-

4 *Algemeen overzicht*, January 1930.

5 Hadji A. Salim, 'Ma'loemat', *Fadjar Asia*, 14 November 1929.

gbong due to health problems'.[6] These health concerns faded by mid 1930 and did not prevent Kartosuwiryo from retaining his rank in the party. This early January meeting, as well as the subsequent party congress in Yogyakarta at the end of the month, were pivotal in shaping Sarekat Islam's future strategies, especially in relation to the secular nationalist movement represented by Soekarno, his PNI and the PPPKI federation. The initial attempt to set aside differences over the role of religion and the level of cooperation with the colonial authorities was doomed to fail, thus pulling PSII out of the 'brown front' and radicalizing the Islamic and non-cooperative attitudes of its members.

While in Malangbong, in April 1930 Kartosuwiryo started once again to write for *Fadjar Asia*. The following year, further affirming his stronghold in the Priangan, he was nominated Garut editor of a new Sundanese newspaper, *Sora Ra'jat Merdika*, whilst Tjokroaminoto was its editor in Bogor. Kartosuwiryo began travelling across the region on propaganda tours in May. He headed a PSII-Garut branch meeting to organize political action against the 'wicked and evil' requirement of *corvee*.[7] Along with Moestafa Kamil, Joesoef Taoeziri and other local leaders, Kartosuwiryo chaired an open meeting of the Garut MOI to expound his political views, and his choice of topics ranged from the impact of the plague epidemic that had affected the region since February, to the duty to follow Islamic law. This meeting was attended by some 3,500 people, and Kartosuwiryo delivered his speech directly in Sundanese, an indication that he had already spent some time in West Java.[8] It should be remembered that Kartosuwiryo had already been married to Siti Kalsum since August 1929, at least. On 10 June 1930, he addressed the party constituency in Cilame on the right to assembly for Friday prayers, and on 14 June he was in Leles at the local MOI meeting.[9]

Under Tjokroaminoto's protection, Kartosuwiryo was reaching the highest echelons of the party, as evidenced by his recurrent invitations to lead propaganda campaigns[10] and to chair party conferences outside of Java.[11]

6 *Fadjar Asia*, 9 January 1930; Pinardi also mentions health problems for Kartosuwiryo around 1929. Pinardi, *Sekarmadji Maridjan*, p. 23.

7 *Fadjar Asia*, 7 May 1930.

8 *Fadjar Asia*, 4 June 1930. At a previous propaganda meeting in October 1929, a local representative of PSI-Cicalengka acted as translator; see *Fadjar Asia*, 8 October 1929.

9 *Fadjar Asia*, 10 June 1930 and 14 June 1930. On *Sora Ra'jat Merdika*, see *Algemeen overzicht*, July and August 1931, p. 14.

10 *Overzicht*, 18 June 1932, 10 September 1932 and 26 October 1935 report his many trips across West Java.

11 *Overzicht*, 22 December 1934 and 11 May 1935.

REDEFINING PARTAI SAREKAT ISLAM INDONESIA'S PRIORITIES

Pan-Islamism and non-cooperation

The 1930 party congress in Yogyakarta held in late January marked the height of the friction between PSII and the PPPKI federation. Despite Tjokroaminoto's conciliatory tone and his efforts to revoke past criticisms, Kartosuwiryo's position was gaining stronger support, as his new role as commissar for West Java and member of the executive committee gave him increased space to influence the membership. What was at stake in these debates was Sarekat Islam's integrity as an Islamic party, as the condition for affiliation with PPPKI was that members must be 'Indonesian' and thus affirm the group's identity as an 'Indonesian' party, while PSII (despite having recently added the second 'I' to its name) was open to Muslims from all over the world.[12]

This conflict was more than a mere matter of principle or theology; it sheds light on the implications of being an Islamic party that could not limit itself to a geographically defined area. This position would be formalized on 28 December 1930 with Sangadji's statement that PSII, as an Islamic party, could no longer be part of the Indonesian federation PPPKI, nor could it cooperate with a despotic foreign ruler. A few months later, at the party congress, Soekiman, who had initially co-founded the PPPKI with Soekarno, concluded that 'without any doubts, the PPPKI is imperialistic!',[13] a claim that marked the final rupture.

The new party statute, as published in *Fadjar Asia* in mid January 1930, shows a change in priorities and a complete shift from being

12 PPO, January 1930, pp. 291, 293. The PSII Congress was held in Yogyakarta from 24 to 27 January 1930; 'Verslag van het 16de congres der PSII, gehouden op Jogjakarta op den 24sten tot den 27sten Januari 1930' [1930], AMK GMr, no. 230x, NA, suggests that Kartosuwiryo was the executive committee's member for agriculture. The party board was represented by Tjokroaminoto, Salim, Soerjopranoto, K.H. Anwaroedin, Wondosoedirdjo, Pardikin and Kadar, whilst the other members of the executive committee were Soekiman and Kiyai Taoefiqoerachman, commissars for finance and for sharia and *'ibada*, respectively; Kiyai Taoefiqoerachman later, in 1945, signed Masyumi's call for *jihad* against the Dutch. Major points of discussion at this congress were hereditary property, the *poenale sanctie* and *guru ordonnantie*, as well as opium consumption, prostitution and gambling; these issues were specifically mentioned in an action programme released on this occasion and named *programma van actie (jihad)*. The 1945 call for *jihad* is further investigated in Chapter 3.

13 'Verslag van de op 28 December 1930 te Batavia delegde [*sic.*] vergadering der PSII' [1931], AMK GMr, no. 327x, NA; 'Verslag van het 17de Congres der Partai Sarekat Islam Indonesia' [1931], AMK: Kabinet Verbaal Geheim [hereafter KVG] no. 5, NA. The congress was held between 16 and 22 March 1931.

an Islamo-socialist organization to becoming an Islamic party committed to pan-Islamism. The PSII executive committee now added a new first article titled 'unity in the Islamic community' (*persatoean dalam oemmat Islam*), which stated that the unity of Indonesian Muslims was 'a step towards the unity of the Islamic community across the world'. This goal was more important – at least as a matter of principle – than 'national freedom', which became the second article of the party's 'foundation statement' (*keterangan asas*). This concept, that Indonesian Muslims' unity was a stage in the development of a worldwide unity of the *ummah*, was then repeated in the first and second articles of the constitution, titled *persatoean pergerakan dan organisatie* ('unity of the movement and organization') and *toedjoean* ('aims'), respectively.[14]

In harmony with such a redefinition of aims and strategies, in March 1931 Tjokroaminoto opened the party's 17th congress with a quote from the leading member of the British Indies' Khilafat movement, Maulana Muhammad Ali: 'It is a wrong conception of religion that you have, if you exclude politics from it; it is not [just] dogma, it is not [just] ritual.' While this congress was strongly oriented towards the state of Muslims abroad, particularly the Berbers of Morocco and the Palestinians, it also sought and received affirmation of the Indies' position on the global map of Islam, as Tjokroaminoto received a telegram from the Mufti of Jerusalem, Sayed Amin al-Husayni, that discussed the situation in Palestine and, more significantly, condemned Soekarno's PNI for its secularism.[15]

A couple of months later, Tjokroaminoto began to promote the creation of a permanent al-Islam Committee, to be based in Surabaya under the leadership of Wondoamiseno. The committee's broader aim was to advocate and promote pan-Islamism via local publications, like the new magazine *al-Djihad*, and building an Islamic Union (*Islam-bond*) together with foreign organizations, such as the British-Indian Muslim Association. This committee was also charged with tackling the anti-Islamic feelings that had surfaced in secular circles.[16]

14 'Persatoean oemmat Islam se-doenia', *Fadjar Asia*, 21 January 1930. The statute was edited between October 1929 and January 1930.

15 'Verslag van het 17de Congres der Partai Sarekat Islam Indonesia' [1931], AMK: KVG no. 5, NA.

16 Soetomo's Persatoean Bangsa Indonesia (Association of the Indonesian Nation) had been generic in its anti-Islamic propaganda, but the Surabaya Studieclub, for example, had attacked the pilgrimage to Mecca (belittled *vis-à-vis* banishment to the Dutch penal colony in Boven Digul, Papua), and nationalist women groups condemned polygamy. 'Oprichting "Centraal Comite al-Islam"' [1931], AMK GMr, no. 716x, NA.

The first al-Islam meeting gathered in Batavia in October 1931, and the second in Malang in April 1932. Neither of these meetings made any progress in connecting Muslims in the Indies with the rest of the *ummah.* However, the committee succeeded in pulling together political and non-political Islamic groups under the banner of the Pergerakan al-Islam Indonesia (Indonesian al-Islam Movement), which reached a total membership of around 4,000 individuals in 1931-32.[17]

First established in the 1920s in the aftermath of Mustafa Kemal's abolition of the Ottoman Caliphate, the al-Islam committees were tasked with suggesting ways to bring about a new worldwide Islamic order. Nevertheless, it would be a mistake to see the significance of these committees in the 1930s in this same light. Attempts to recreate a global caliphate had long since been abandoned, and even in the British Indies, where the Khilafat movement was more persistent and dedicated, the focus and priorities of the movement had shifted away from the caliphate and towards nationalism. The caliphate as the basis of a political platform reappears only in more recent times, with Kartosuwiryo's call for a federation of Muslim nation-states in 1950, and later with Jemaah Islamiyah's propaganda for a transnational Islamic state in the 2000s.[18]

The 1930 Yogyakarta congress and the discomfort that emerged from participation in the PPPKI are representative of the issues at the core of the party and, more generally, of the debates dominating this decade. On the one hand, there was opposition to secular nationalism and commitment to religiously informed politics; on the other hand, there was the issue of (non-)cooperation. Both had been central concerns for Kartosuwiryo since his early days as a journalist, and his growing influence on the executive committee resulted in Partai Sarekat Islam's policies being increasingly determined by his views. Partai Sarekat Islam Indonesia had thus begun shaping itself along these two projects of Islamic politics and non-cooperation. However, as political winds in the Indies changed, this redefinition had to be halted.

17 'Vergadering van het al-Islam-comite te Batavia op den 11den October 1931' [1931], AMK GMr, no. 939x, NA; and 'Verslag van het 2e al-Islam congres in de maand April 1931 te Kalang gehouden' [1932], AMK GMr, no. 472x, NA. The latter congress was held between 16 and 18 April 1932.

18 Jacob M. Landau, *The politics of pan-Islam: Ideology and organisation* (Oxford: Oxford University Press, 1994); Formichi, 'Pan-Islam and religious nationalism'. On the impact of the abolition of the Ottoman Caliphate in 1924, see Chiara Formichi, 'Mustafa Kemal's abrogation of the Ottoman Caliphate and its impact on the Indonesian nationalist movement', in al-Rasheed, Kersten and Shterin (eds), *Demystifying the caliphate: Historical memory and contemporary contexts* (London: Hurst Publishers; New York: Columbia University Press, 2012a), pp. 95-115.

Within two years of his appointment as Governor General in 1931, the conservative Bonifacius Cornelis de Jonge had dramatically reduced the political space in the Indies, and by 1933 only openly cooperative organizations and parties were allowed to operate freely in the political sphere. Sarekat Islam's 18th congress, held in Bandung at the end of 1931, was mostly concerned with local economic and social issues. Salim focused on new press limitations, Soekiman invoked social legislation, Sangadji complained about agrarian reforms, and Tjokroaminoto attacked the *cultuurstelsel* as a manifestation of 'capitalism's baneful influence'.[19] This 'cultivation system' had been in place for a century, with the Dutch government determining what crops Javanese peasants had to produce in order to ensure the steady supply of tropical products in which the trading company was interested.[20]

The Islamic movement and secular nationalism

It is often mentioned that in the 1930s the Islamic movement was deeply fragmented, having neither a strong leadership nor a clear strategy, and that these two factors together were crucial to the decline of PSII's influence at the national level. The same holds true also for the secularists.

Following Soekarno's arrest in December 1929, Sartono – who had taken up the leadership of the movement – dissolved the PNI to establish, in 1930, the more accommodating Partindo (Partai Indonesia, Indonesian Party). This new party did not satisfy all of the old PNI membership, so in late 1931 the Study Clubs merged into a 'new' PNI, the Pendidikan Nasional Indonesia (PNI Baru, Indonesian National Education). When Soekarno was released from prison in December 1931, Soetan Sjahrir and Mohammad Hatta had already returned from the Netherlands, and Sartono was holding tight his leadership of Partindo. Their contrasting approaches resulted in a splintered movement, and the shattering of Soekarno's achievements in unifying the movement in the previous decade.[21]

19 'Verslag van het 18de PSII congres te Bandoeng gehouden sinds December 1931' [1932] AMK GMr, no. 518x, NA. The congress was held between 25 and 27 December 1931.

20 For more on the *cultuurstelsel*, see Cornelis Fasseur, *The politics of colonial exploitation: Java, the Dutch, and the cultivation system* (Ithaca, NY. Cornell University Southeast Asia Program, 1992).

21 John David Legge, '*Daulat Ra'jat* and the ideas of the Pendidikan Nasional Indonesia', *Indonesia* 32 (October, 1981): pp. 151-68.

The fragmentation of the nationalist front was not simply a matter of leadership and power, but, rather more significantly, a matter of strategy about how to strengthen the movement and how to relate to the colonial authorities. On the first count, Hatta, Sjahrir and the new PNI believed in forming highly educated and intellectualized cadres, whilst Partindo and Soekarno focused on stirring mass agitation. On the second count, Hatta and Soekarno differed on the issue of cooperation: in 1929 Hatta announced that 'non-cooperation is the only correct weapon' in the current colonial relationship between Indonesia and the Netherlands, and in 1931 he criticized Soekarno for using non-cooperation only to provoke the masses, but not to educate them about the ongoing political battle. But by 1932-33 the tables had turned, with Hatta's acceptance of the candidacy for the Dutch parliament as a member of the Onafhankelijke Socialistische Partij (Independent Socialist Party). Soekarno declared that 'non-cooperation is not only struggle, it is also a principle of that struggle', thus accusing Hatta of betrayal for participating in the Dutch parliament. Yet, when he was arrested again in November 1933, Soekarno abandoned Partindo and non-cooperation, an act that Hatta described as the 'Soekarnoist tragedy': 'it was not yet ten months since Soekarno had beaten his breast and cried out that non-cooperation excluded cooperation with the masters in every field, and had called for unremitting struggle'[22] when he decided instead to accept the Dutch hand.

The arrest of Soekarno was followed by those of Hatta and Sjahrir in February 1934. Soekarno – probably in exchange for softening his political rhetoric – was sent to Flores, but the more radical Hatta and Sjahrir were exiled to Digul until the Japanese invasion of Java and Sumatra in 1942. The colonial government's treatment of Soekarno, Hatta and Sjahrir proved to most nationalists that non-cooperation was no longer politically viable, and thus that they needed to change strategy.

After Partindo abandoned non-cooperation in December 1934, nationalist groups tended to be generally 'cooperationist', in the sense that they agreed to participate in the Volksraad to advance their demands for increased autonomy, as Susan Abeyasekere

22 Hatta's quote from *Indonesia Merdeka*, in Greta O. Wilson (ed.), *Regents, reformers, and revolutionaries: Indonesian voices of colonial days* (Honolulu: University Press of Hawaii, 1978), p. 136; Bernhard Dahm, *Soekarno and the struggle for Indonesian independence* (Ithaca and London: Cornell University Press, 1969), Chapter 4. Soekarno's quote from *Dibawah bendera revolusi*, in Dahm, *Soekarno*, p. 161; Hatta's quote from *Daulat Rakjat* 30 November 1933, in Dahm, *Soekarno*, p. 168.

points out. This 'People's Council' had been established in 1917 as an elected proto-parliament, where Europeans, 'Foreign Orientals' and 'Indigenous' members could voice 'independent opinions'. Because of the electoral policies implemented, however, the council was not representative of the indigenous population, nor did it have any decision-making powers. In 1925 the council was transformed into a semi-legislative body, and in 1929 for the first time European members were the minority.

One example of the nationalists' cooperationist tendencies is Soetomo's decision to merge his Persatoean Bangsa Indonesia (Union of the Indonesian People) with Boedi Oetomo to form a new organization, Partai Indonesia Raja (Parindra, Great Indonesia Party). Protected by their immunity, several of the Volksraad members – especially those belonging to Mohammad Hoesni Thamrin's political wing in Parindra – made radical statements, as they appeared to be coming to terms with their participation in the councils only so far as doing so was an avenue to independence. Yet, their grudging support for the councils did not translate into their support for gradual reforms. The Soetardjo petition of 1936 requested a conference to discuss the possibility of autonomy from the Netherlands. However, not only did the petition fail to gather the votes of the nationalist movement (as this proposal had emerged from a moderate and assorted group), but it was also rejected by the Dutch government in November 1938.[23]

In December 1936 Partindo dissolved, leaving Parindra as 'the chief political organization' until Amir Sjarifuddin's founding of Gerakan Rakjat Indonesia (Gerindo, Indonesian People's Movement) in 1937. Though it represented the left wing of the nationalist movement and was 'inherently militant', Gerindo took an overall cooperationist attitude,[24] thus making Sarekat Islam the only remaining party practising non-cooperation, a commitment that came with a high price.

23 Susan Abeyasekere, 'The Soetardjo petition', *Indonesia* 15 (April 1973): pp. 80-108; the petition was signed by Soetardjo Kartohadikoesoemo (a *patih*), Ratu Langie (a Christian representative of the Minahasa Union), Kasimo (the Javanese president of the Political Association of Indonesian Catholics), Datoek Toemenggoeng (a Minangkabau aristocrat) and two representatives of ethnic minorities, a Chinese and an Arab. Susan Abeyasekere, 'Partai Indonesia Raja, 1936-42: A study in cooperative nationalism', *Journal of Southeast Asian Studies*, 3, 2 (September, 1972): pp. 262-76. Since 1931 the composition of the Volksraad had been half Dutch and half Indonesian, with one third of its members nominated, and the rest elected from amongst the civil servants.

24 George McTurnan Kahin, *Nationalism and revolution in Indonesia* (Ithaca: Cornell Southeast Asia Program Publications, 2003 [1952]), pp. 95-6.

THE CONSEQUENCES OF NON-COOPERATION

Maintaining its commitment to non-cooperation was no easy task. For one, it resulted in radical changes in the PSII party leadership. The first purge occurred in March 1933, when Soekiman – at that point vice-president of the executive committee – and Surjopranoto – leading member of the *dewan partij* – were expelled.[25] The official reason for their expulsion was related to mismanagement of funds, yet it is not far-fetched to suggest that it was also connected to the anti-cooperation contingent's gaining strength. After their forced exit from PSII, Soekiman and other former party members formed a new cooperationist party, the Partij Politiek Islam Indonesia (Partii, Indonesian Islamic Political Party), which in 1938 added several Muhammadiyah members and re-organized as Partai Islam Indonesia (PII, Islamic Party of Indonesia).[26]

In the meantime, PSII continued its double-track policy of promoting non-cooperation and upholding Islamic politics. Under the guidance of Agoes Salim, for example, it established a commission to solve the conflict between traditional *adat* and Islamic law. The commission suggested the replacement of *adat* with sharia, with particular attention to the realm of family law, a motion strongly backed by Tjokroaminoto at the 1934 congress, just a few months before his passing.[27]

Tjokroaminoto's death left the leadership vacant, and the whole party in shock. Kartosuwiryo, Salim and Abikoesno now led the directorate and took charge of the transition.[28] Without Tjokroaminoto, the fragile balance within the leadership could not hold, and by January 1939 Dutch authorities reported that if PSII members had lost interest in their party, it was mostly because of a loss of authority at the leadership level.[29]

At the Malang congress of July-August 1935, Salim took Tjokroaminoto's place as president of the *dewan partij*, while Sangadji sat as chairman of the executive committee. Abikoesno took Soekiman's place as president of the executive committee, and Kartosuwiryo maintained his position as secretary. The party's branches had withered from 140 in 1934 to 90 at the time of the congress,

25 PPO, March 1933, pp. 268-9; *Overzicht*, 8 April 1933.

26 Rambe, *Sarekat Islam*, pp. 251-2.

27 'PSII congress te Bandjarnegara in 1934' [1934], AMK GMr, no. 756x, NA. The congress was held between 20 and 26 May 1934.

28 'Maklumat H. Agoes Salim, Abikoesno, dan Kartosowirjo, Ma'lumat No. 33', Ladjnah Tanfidzjah PSII kepada terhormat seluruh Ladjnah Afdeeling PSII, Jakarta, 17 December 1934 in Amelz, *H.O.S. Tjokroaminoto*, pp. 146-8.

29 PPO, January 1939, vol. 4, pp. 256-7.

even as they still counted a total membership of around 45,000. The youth, divided between Pemoeda Moeslimin Indonesia and SIAP, had an overall membership of 5,000, and the women's section had 6,000 members scattered across 34 branches.[30]

Throughout the year, the latent disagreement between Salim and Kartosuwiryo on the *hijrah* policy grew into an open conflict. Salim asked the executive committee to revise the policy, concerned that the government would further limit the party's activities if it did not assume a more moderate attitude. Salim also asked permission to re-join the Volksraad, where he had been a member from 1921 to 1924. Nevertheless, the 1936 congress shows that Kartosuwiryo's position, which was seconded by Abikoesno, was not even questioned by the remainder of the leadership and was instead actually reinforced as the party's official policy. The politics of PSII were rooted in Islam, and non-cooperation was 'the best way' to further the interests of the Islamic community.

Salim was ousted, and by the time the party convened for the Jakarta congress, the leadership had already been changed. The *dewan partij* was presided over by Wondoamiseno and Kartosuwiryo, who had brought along several members from the West Java branch to fill positions in the executive committee. Amongst its members were Latief, Moestafa Kamil, Toha, Kamran, and Joesoef Taoeziri; Abikoesno was nominated as president and Kartawinata as secretary.[31]

These changes meant that PSII was not to pursue independence by cooperating with the colonial government, as Salim had recommended, but that it would instead fight for it. In propagandist terms, this reorientation was articulated in the drafting, by the central party leadership, of a *Brosoer sikap hidjrah PSII* ('Pamphlet on PSII's non-cooperation policy', discussed below). At the end of the congress, the task of articulating the party's goal in this way was handed over to Kartosuwiryo, who had the assignment of 'clarifying, explaining and giving his opinion' on the origins of the party's non-cooperation policy. In the words of *Pandji Islam*, which reviewed the booklet in mid-September, 'For the Islamic struggle of Indonesia, there should be more books on political Islam, like this one, published and distributed among the people of our nation'.[32] To Kartosuwiryo this pamphlet represented the political platform

30 'Congres van de Partij Sjarikat Islam Indonesia te Malang van 31 Juli tot 4 Augustus 1935' [1935], AMK GMr, no. 963x, NA.

31 *Overzicht*, 18 July 1936; *Soeara PSII*, 25 April 1937. The congress was held in Jakarta between 8 and 12 July 1936.

32 'Pertimbangan Boekoe', *Pandji Islam* no. 36-37, 15 September 1936, p. 9391.

for a new era of the Partai Sarekat Islam Indonesia,[33] but for Salim this marked the end of his career in the party.

Agoes Salim responded to Kartosuwiryo's brochure with a series of articles published in the periodical *Pergerakan*, which in August of the same year became a pamphlet in its own right.[34] In his *Pedoman politiek* ('Political directive'), Salim stated that he was no longer prepared to work within a party that continued to seek conflict with the colonial government.[35] Salim still desired to return to the Volksraad. After his request to do so had been rejected by both Kartosuwiryo and the executive committee's chairman, Sabirin,[36] he felt increasingly marginalized in his cooperative efforts, and eventually left the party in 1937. Salim was followed by Sangadji, Mohammed Roem and Wibisono, amongst others. On 17 February, they held the first meeting of the Komite Penjadar PSII (PSII Awareness Committee), which was attended by some 500 people, including several members of Muhammadiyah, Persis and PMI.[37]

At the Bandung congress of 1937, Kartosuwiryo and Wondoamiseno were still advocating the *hijrah* policy as a political and economic strategy, although throughout the year at least 21 branches had made known their discontentment with this approach, with some even moving their allegiance to Salim's Komite Penjadar.[38] It was reported that at Bandung, out of a total of 131 PSII branches, only 70 participated, and that of the party's 40,000 members, at least 200 had moved to the Penjadar faction.[39] Although this was quite a rescaling of PSII's attendance, comparing these numbers to secular nationalist followers shows that Sarekat Islam still garnered much broader support.[40]

33 Kartosuwiryo, *Sikap hidjrah PSII*, Introduction.

34 'De PSII brochures "Hidjrah"' [1937], AMK GMr, no. 101x, NA.

35 *Overzicht*, 22 August 1936.

36 *Overzicht*, 11 January 1937.

37 'Vergadering van het "Comite Penjadar Barisan PSII" te Batavia op Februari 1937' [1937], AMK GMr, no. 227x, NA.

38 *Overzicht*, 30 January 1937. The 21 branches were: Batavia, Bandung, Kebarongan, Sidareja, Cilacap, Banyuwangi, Serono, Tempeh, Probolinggo, Pasuruan, Malang, Bululawang, Surabaya, Babat, Ngronggot, Paree, Kota Bumi (Sumatra), Biaro (women's wing), Bukittinggi, Dangung-Dangung (women's wing), and Surau Pinang Biaro. In early January the provincial congress of Sulawesi, in Gorontalo, had issued a press release voicing its disappointment over the *hijrah* policy. See also PPO April-October 1937.

39 'Congres PSII te Bandoeng Juli 1937' [1937], AMK GMr, no. 703x, NA. The 23rd congress was held between 19 and 23 July.

40 In mid 1933 Partindo counted around 20,000 members, and at the same time the new PNI barely had 1,000 members. The old PNI, at the height of its popularity, gathered 10,000 supporters. Parindra, instead, jumped from 3,200 in 1936 to 19,500 in 1941.

At Bandung, Kartosuwiryo focused on two of the issues of major concern for the Islamic party: the new limitations imposed on the authority of the religious courts, and the *hijrah* policy. These limitations were seen as yet another means to control the indigenous population and their religious affairs, as they revoked the relative autonomy granted to Islamic courts since 1882 in family- and inheritance-related matters. With the support of Muhammadiyah, Nahdatul Ulama and Persis, PSII passed two motions against the new regulations, recommending the establishment of a temporary *majelis ulama* (assembly of scholars) to settle conflicts arising from inheritance problems and a *majelis syari'* (sharia assembly) to officiate at weddings. More importantly, the motion prohibited PSII members from making use of the Landraad, the colonial civil courts set up for indigenous Indonesians.

Anticipating the subject of his speech for the 1938 Majelis Islam A'la Indonesia congress, at Bandung Kartosuwiryo questioned the appropriateness of the government's intervention in religious matters, as he believed religious affairs should be self-regulated by the Muslim population. Kartosuwiryo also blamed the community for referring to the colonial authorities rather than to local leaders when seeking solutions to their daily problems.[41] In this system, inheritance-related matters were reassigned from Islamic courts to the Landraad, and all of the former's decisions had to be approved by the latter's president. Kartosuwiryo, voicing his disapproval of this system, returned to these issues at the first MIAI al-Islam congress, held in February 1938. This federation of Islamic organizations, modernist and traditionalist alike, had been established in September 1937 with the aim of forming an Indonesian parliament based on Islamic legislation,[42] possibly as a reaction to the Soetardjo petition of 1936.

Using his vigorous oratorical skills, Kartosuwiryo, representing PSII, tackled the problem of implementing Islamic law from two sides: on the one hand, he blamed the Indonesian *ummah* for not following Qur'anic precepts, and on the other hand, he accused the Dutch of not abiding by their pledge to maintain religious neutrality and to grant freedom of religious expression. This

41 'Congres P(artij) S(jarikat) I(slam) I(ndonesia) te Bandoeng, Juli 1937' [1937], AMK GMr, no. 830x, NA.

42 'Letter of Ladjnah Tanfidzijah Partij Sjarikat Islam Indonesia Batavia-Centrum 2044/L.W. Sidang Congres Majelis-Islam-A'laa-Indonesia di Soerabaja, LT-PSII [executive committee] Vice-President S. Latif and 2nd Secretaris H.Tjokroaminoto' [1938], Archief van de Procureur-Generaal [hereafter APG], no. 1007, NA. On MIAI see *Overzicht*, 9 December 1939.

was an easy opening for Kartosuwiryo to stress the importance of harmonizing political and judiciary systems. The sole solution to ensure full adherence to Islam, he argued, was a satisfactory implementation of Islamic law, which by itself would only be possible through the combination of religious judges (*hakim*) and religious authority (such as the *wali-al-amr*, *amir-ul-mu'minin* or *ulil amri*).[43]

Once the conflict with Salim had been settled by his withdrawal from the party, the *hijrah* remained the key point on PSII's agenda, but also something that Kartosuwiryo felt compelled to clarify and justify at every given occasion. In Bandung he reiterated its 'multidimensionality' as a socio-economic as much as a religious and political effort. To further reinforce the membership's consciousness of its value, the party established an *Oesaha hidjrah* committee with Kartosuwiryo as chairman, which was tasked with the compilation of the *Daftar oesaha hidjrah*, a pamphlet that was finally released in 1940,[44] even though a first draft had already been approved at the Surabaya congress in 1938.

THE BROSOER SIKAP HIDJRAH PSII AND DAFTAR OESAHA HIDJRAH

In the *Brosoer sikap hidjrah PSII* and *Daftar oesaha hidjrah* pamphlets, Kartosuwiryo focused at length on the origins and aims of the non-cooperation policy. He first identified its roots in Tjokroaminoto's decision to withdraw from the Volksraad in 1923, and then labelled all subsequent attempts to join any colonial representative body or to cooperate with the Dutch as manifestations of an 'accommodationist' approach; he referred explicitly to Salim and Soekarno. Notably there was no reference to the Indian Khilafat's movement constitution, drafted in 1919.

As a figurative migration from the 'Indonesian Mecca to the Indonesian Medina', the *hijrah* marked the transition from a regime of *adat* to a religious ideological framework articulated

43 'Preadvies tentang Raad Agama dan Mahkamat Islam Tinggi, berhoeboeng dengan pemindahan hak-waris dari Raad Agama kepada Landraad, dihidangkan pada Al-Islam-Kongres jang ke-10 di Soerabaja, pada tg. 28 Februari menghadap 1 Maart 1938' [1938], APG no. 1007, NA.

44 Kartosuwiryo, *Daftar-oesaha hidjrah PSII bagian muqaddima* (Malangbong (SS W/L)) (Java: Poestaka Dar-oel-Islam, March 1940) in Al Chaidar, *Pemikiran politik proklamator negara Islam Indonesia S.M. Kartosoewirjo: fakta dan data sejarah Darul Islam* (Jakarta: Darul Falah, 1999), pp. 461-76. 'Pertimbangan Boekoe', *Pandji Islam* no. 36-37, 15 September 1936, p. 9391, indicates Daroel Oeloem as the publisher.

as the *darul Islam*, an ideal Islamic state.[45] This transition was a priority in the party's political platform, and could only be made possible as a result of *jihad*. To realize the pan-Islamic project was as important as the Islamization of Indonesian politics (as opposed to its Westernization), the education of Indonesian Muslims or the establishment of contacts with other Muslim communities outside of the archipelago. Ultimately, Kartosuwiryo declared that PSII was neither communist nor fascist and inspired by neither Arabism nor 'Indonesianism', as its foundation was only Islam.[46]

The *Sikap hidjrah* pamphlet, arranged in two parts, was published under Kartosuwiryo's signature in September 1936 following deliberations by the Party's 22nd Majelis Tahkim. The *Sikap hidjrah* was conceived as a new manual for all members of the party, who had the duty to understand and implement the 'Supreme Directives' of the party's non-cooperation. Abikoesno and Kartawinata admitted that its content might have sounded like 'new stuff' to readers, yet they nevertheless were confident that it would rapidly become an exemplary model for Islamic politics. The pamphlet aimed at illustrating the religious foundations of the party's non-cooperation policy by focusing on the theology and history of the Prophet's migration as much as on its political implications. However, Dutch officials saw the pamphlet in isolation from its context, claiming it was purely the outcome of Muslims' unwillingness to cooperate with *kafir* (infidel) rule.[47]

The first part of the pamphlet is mostly concerned with laying the historical and theological foundations for the second part. It begins with the events surrounding Muhammad's migration from Mecca to Medina in 622, before considering the following eight years of his leadership, the structure of the first Islamic institutions in Medina and the political outlook of this first 'Islamic state'.

Throughout most of the first part, the discussion does not stray from standard theological teachings. However, at the end of each section, Kartosuwiryo skilfully connects these principles to PSII's politics. In explaining the relations between the Creator and His creatures (*khalik* and *makhluk*), for example, Kartosuwiryo argues that it is because of this strong and enduring relation that Islam

45 Here, '*dar al-Islam*' and '*dar-ul-Islam*' refer to the principle of 'house of peace', or 'territory of Islam', its spelling depending on the source; '*darul Islam*' refers to the ideal of an Islamic state in Indonesia. 'Darul Islam', in capital letters and set in roman, refers to Kartosuwiryo's group.
46 'PSII congres 1938 te Soerabaja' [1939], AMK GMr, no. 1170x, NA. The congress was held between 30 July and 7 August 1938.
47 'De PSII Brochures 'Hidjrah'' [1937] AMK GMr no. 101x, NA.

> offers directions in all aspects of life: both in this world and in the afterlife, to individuals as well as communities, one nation and the whole of humanity, for glory in this world and happiness in the next. In short, all the rules needed for internal and external conduct can be found in Islam, from the smallest to the biggest.

In this way, the Qur'an and the Prophet are portrayed as the models of behaviour in social and economic life.

As humans can be divided into three categories depending on their proximity to God, so can the history of PSII be organized in this same way: first, the party had a 'materialistic' existence (*hidup hissy*)[48] from its establishment in 1912 until the Madiun congress of 1923. Then, the expulsion of communist members had ensured a deeper concern for the afterlife (*hidup ma'nawy*). But it was not until the 1930 congress in Yogyakarta that the PSII shifted its focus from 'pure action' to 'belief'. The party had subsequently promoted the further elevation of the party to a life freed of material concerns and in perfect harmony with Islam (*hidup ma'any*).

The main engine behind this shift – from focusing on a materialistic existence to rooting itself in pure belief – is identified in members' adherence to Islamic precepts, fear of God, faith in Allah and His One-ness, and complete surrender (*tawakkal Allah*). This surrender, however, must not translate into inertia, but rather should result in *isti'anah* (the act of seeking help) and *istiqamah* (knowledge that help will come from God), thus instigating *istitha'a*, or the power and willingness to act. In political terms, this meant that party members would abide by God's laws, involving themselves in the anti-colonial struggle and believing in the sole efficacy of not cooperating with the Dutch.

As Muhammad and his followers had left Mecca and migrated to ensure the supremacy of justice over evil, and of monotheism over polytheism, so Partai Sarekat Islam Indonesia had to seek happiness (*falah*) and victory (*fatah*) by pursuing its own *hijrah* and starting a new era. It is on these reflections that part two of the pamphlet is opened, explaining how in this context Mecca is not a dot on the map of the Middle East, but instead represents the metaphorical situation of oppression and ignorance that can be found in every kampong and country of the world, and thus a situation that needs to be (figuratively) abandoned in favour of Medina-

48 The Islamic term *hissy* can also be translated as 'sensationalist' or 'sensuous'. However, as here it is opposed to lives inspired by deep concern for the afterlife or lives conducted in full harmony with Islam, I chose to translate the term as 'materialistic', suggesting a life grounded in worldly matters and goals.

Indonesia, where the law of God rules and the *ummah* is happy and victorious.

Where the second part surpasses the first is in its focus on PSII's strategies and aims. Above all, the *hijrah* to Medina-Indonesia – and hence to an Islamic state – is marked by three steps: *jihad, iman* (faith) and *tauhid* (unity). This path is well trodden, as it places Kartosuwiryo in an intellectual and strategic tradition that connects al-Ghazali (1058-1111), Ibn Taymiyyah (1263-1328), Hasan al-Banna (1906-49), Abu 'Ala Maududi (1903-79), Sayyed Qutb (1906-66) and contemporary Islamist militants.[49] As mentioned in the Preface, I see Kartosuwiryo's radicalization as a development strictly correlated with domestic political and social dynamics. However, it would be erroneous to consider developments in Indonesia in isolation from events occurring in the Middle East. I will explore this point further in the next section.

Kartosuwiryo dedicates several pages to explaining the meaning of *jihad, iman* and *tauhid,* making generous use of Qur'anic quotations and bringing forward their practical implications for the political struggle. Having established that in the Qur'an there is no *hijrah* without *jihad,* Kartosuwiryo is careful to explain that the 'positive' struggle is the *jihad* of the tongue and the heart (the *jihad al-akbar,* led by *iman*), and not that of the sword – the *jihad al-asghar,* defined instead as negative and destructive. The *Program djihad partij,* or 'programme of action', issued by the Yogyakarta congress in 1930, should therefore be understood as a 'progamme of the greater *jihad*'.

Reconnecting with the earlier discussion of the relation between God and His creatures, Kartosuwiryo blames the West for severing the ties linking religious duties to believers' daily activities, thereby breaking the unity of religion and politics (*agama dan kerajaan*) and shifting the *hijrah* unto the realm of *'ibada* (worship). Nevertheless, Kartosuwiryo emphasizes that the *jihad ubudiyah,* based on faith in unity, has to be complemented by the *jihad ijtima'iyah* which embodies the social, economic and political dimensions of *hijrah* and *jihad,* and represents the foundation of PSII. Politically it calls for Islamic politics; economically, for cooperatives and self-reliance (for which Kartosuwiryo uses the Indian term *swadeshi*); and socially, for the benefit of public interest (*maslaha*).

The last section of the pamphlet is fully dedicated to the party's agenda, which is summarized as 'achieving the implementation of the laws of God, on the way of God, because of God'. In essence,

49 John L. Esposito, *Un-holy war: Terror in the name of Islam* (Oxford: Oxford University Press, 2002), pp. 49-64.

this agenda was the implementation of sharia law and the creation of a society in which it was possible for all Muslims to conduct fully Islamic lives.

What had been generally defined as 'Islamic politics' was expounded in three clear points: the propagation of Islamically interpreted knowledge and politics amongst PSII members in particular and amongst Muslims in general; the establishment of relations with Muslims across the world to work towards the realization of pan-Islamism as the unity of the Islamic *ummah*; and the dissociation of PSII actions from colonial bodies and policies.

The *Daftar oesaha hidjrah*, printed in 1940, complemented the *Sikap hidjrah* by illustrating the anticipated *Program djihad partij*. This short pamphlet laid out the necessary steps for the transformation from 'Mecca-Indonesia' to 'Medina-Indonesia', a goal that could only be achieved through *jihad*. Weaving together the threads laid out in the past decade, Kartosuwiryo argued that PSII should direct its efforts towards improving the status of the Indonesian population (meaning the natives) by expanding the reach of the *dar-ul-Islam* and thus widening the constituency of the Muslim society. Loyal only to God, and thus dedicated to the implementation of sharia on an individual (*shakhsiyah*) as well as a social (*ijtima'iyah*) level, the party and the members of this Islamic society were committed to pursuing pan-Islamism – here also referred to as 'the unity of Islam and oneness of God' (*al-ittihad-oel-Islam dan wahdanijat Allah*)[50] beyond the borders of the Indonesian archipelago, implementing sharia law, and reuniting *agama dan dunia* (religion and government), the link between which had been severed by Western colonial domination.[51]

REFLECTING ON THE 'MIDDLE EAST' FACTOR

In the previous chapter, I mentioned that the connections between the Middle East and Southeast Asia were kept alive by the circulation of pilgrims, students and printed material, which stimulated a vibrant exchange of ideas across these regions. I also showed that debates within Sarekat Islam often touched upon issues involving the wider Muslim world. As far as Kartosuwiryo himself is con-

50 Arabic grammar dictates that the article of the first noun is dropped when followed by a second qualifying noun. The mistake (*al-ittihad-oel-Islam* instead of *ittihad-oel-Islam* or *al-ittihad-oel-Islamiyah*) might indicate a low level of familiarity with Arabic, or even an over-correction.
51 Kartosuwiryo, *Daftar-oesaha*.

cerned, there is not much evidence of direct contact with Middle Eastern modernists or activists. However, there is enough evidence to suggest a degree of influence that goes beyond 'parallel development', as instead argued by Howard Federspiel in the case of Persis leader Ahmad Hassan and Hasan al-Banna, for example.[52] In this section, I do not suggest any causality or a direct reproduction of Middle Eastern patterns in Indonesia, but simply wish to highlight instances in which foreign developments were brought to bear upon Kartosuwiryo's ideas since the late 1920s.

It is worth noting that C.A.O. van Nieuwenhuijze, in his *Aspects of Islam in post-colonial Indonesia*, mentioned that whilst he was in Egypt at a meeting with Muslim Brotherhood leaders, in 1950 he was questioned on the Darul Islam movement of West Java. Van Nieuwenhuijze defined their enquiries as an interest

> supported by a good deal of rather detailed information, it seemed. In fact, would it not be surprising if no relations existed between movements, each so well settled – even though not legally – in its own society?[53]

In more abstract terms, Boland also suggested possible influences from the Muslim Brotherhood and Abu Ala Mawdudi on the Darul Islam.[54]

I could find no indication of Mawdudi's influence on Kartosuwiryo. However, some evidence of direct contact between Hasan al-Banna's group and the Indonesian community in Cairo can be found in the existence of the post-independence group named, in Arabic, Lajnatul-Difa'i'an Indonesia (Committee for the Defence of Indonesia, in Indonesian: Panitia Pembela Indonesia). It appears that Hasan al-Banna participated in its establishment, together with other Brotherhood leaders and the Palestinian leader Muhammad Ali Taher in October 1945. Further, when in April 1946 the Indonesian Republic's delegation visited Cairo, the delegates were received by al-Banna and dozens of Brotherhood members.[55]

52 Howard M. Federspiel, *Islam and ideology in the emerging Indonesian state: The Persatuan Islam (Persis), 1923-1957* (Leiden: Brill, 2001), p. 121.

53 C.A.O. van Nieuwenhuijze, *Aspects of Islam in post-colonial Indonesia: Five essays* (The Hague/ Bandung: Van Hoeve, 1958), p. xi.

54 B.J. Boland, *The struggle of Islam in modern Indonesia* (The Hague: Nijhoff, 1982), p. 147.

55 Rizki Ridyasmara, 'Yang pertama kali mendukung kemerdekaan Republik Indonesia 1945', *Majalah Saksi* 4-21 (18 August 2004), http://hensyam.wordpress.com/2006/08/18/yang-pertama-kali-mendukung-kemerdekaan-republik-indonesia-1945 (accessed 5 May 2009).

The military publication *Penumpasan pemberontakan D.I./T.I.I., S.M. Kartosuwiryo di Jawa Barat*, itself a collection of Darul Islam documents' reproductions, as well as accounts produced after Kartosuwiryo's capture, report that in the 1950s Kartosuwiryo's intention was to first consolidate his authority on the archipelago, and then to build relations on the international level with Malaysia, Pakistan and Egypt. Once linked with movements like the Muslim Brotherhood, the Indonesian Islamic state would have been able to establish a pan-Islamic *dewan Khalifatullah fil'ardi* (Council of God's Caliphate on Earth), which would assume a federal structure with a rotating leadership of two-year terms.[56]

Finally, I would like to add some reflections on Kartosuwiryo's use of one specific term, *sji'ar Islam*, between 1929 and the mid 1940s. As explained below, this has a wide range of meanings. Although at first glance 'Nasib ra'iat Tjitjoeroek' (published in *Fadjar Asia* on 11 May 1929) might seem no different from other articles in which Kartosuwiryo invoked Islam as the solution to all social problems, it is worth noting that he uses the word *sji'ar*. In traditional *fiqh* (jurisprudence), this term was used to define the mark of sacrificial animals, pilgrimage 'stations', and sumptuary laws. Though the use of this word has been increasingly common in Islamist circles since the 1970s, it had not been present in the Indonesian context in the preceding decades, leading scholars to believe that it had been introduced only during the Islamic revival period. I have, however, encountered the term on several occasions, from this 1929 article to the *Sikap hidjrah* pamphlet, and the *Soeara MIAI* magazine during the Japanese occupation. In its contemporary usage and in Kartosuwiryo's understanding, the term indicates a complete implementation of Islamic precepts, equating the expression *Islam kaffah*. What is most relevant to this study is that it appears that Egypt's Muslim Brotherhood was using this sense of the term *sji'ar* Islam in their early days.[57]

Kartosuwiryo's weakening support and withdrawal from politics

Between 1937 and 1938, no significant shrinking of the party's constituency was recorded, and at the Surabaya congress of 1938 Karto-

56 Dinas Sejarah TNI, *Penumpasan pemberontakan*, pp. 80-1.

57 For the above information on *sji'ar Islam* I am indebted to Michael Feener, who is researching this subject.

suwiryo was still vice-president of the board. Yet, just one year later, he would be expelled from the party, mostly as a result of his non-cooperationist approach. Kartosuwiryo's conflict with other party leaders was aggravated by the clash of his *hijrah* policy with Abikoesno's decision, in early 1938, to join Soetomo in forming the Gaboengan Politik Indonesia (GAPI, Indonesian Political Federation).[58]

The GAPI embraced 'cooperative nationalism', and set itself the task of creating a united national front. As nationalist leaders' requests for self-government were becoming entangled with developments in Europe, GAPI agreed to cooperate with the colonial authority on two levels: internationally it would help to fight Fascism, and nationally it would contribute to establishing a democratically elected Indonesian parliament (the movement was commonly referred to as *Indonesia ber-parlemen*).[59] But Germany's occupation of Holland in August 1940 resulted, insofar as the Indies were concerned, in the Dutch government having a strong reason to stall any structural reform until the end of the war. This uncommitted approach to Indonesia's independence was further stressed in Queen Wilhelmina's London speech in May 1941, in which she promised to revisit the relations between Indonesia and the Netherlands after the war, but gave no indication that independence as such would be discussed.[60]

At the same time as relations between Kartosuwiryo and the leaders of other Indonesian parties were worsening on account of their disagreement on the issue of cooperation, the central board of PSII came under the impression that Kartosuwiryo had pursued a wide campaign to propagate mystical teachings. Members of the executive committee argued that Kartosuwiryo's *Sikap hidjrah* pamphlet contained the building blocks of a Sufi *tarekat*, which they saw in full opposition to the principles of PSII in particular, and of Islam in general. It was suspected that these teachings had spread across the region, and mass expulsions were led in Garut and beyond.[61] The party's leadership became concerned

58 The first organizational meeting was held in March 1938 and was led by Abikoesno and Soetomo. However, as Soetomo died in May 1938, the leadership shifted to Thamrin. The first gathering of GAPI was held in May 1939, and it was joined by Parindra, Pasoendan, Gerindo, PSII, PII and several other smaller parties.

59 'Actie in Nederlandsch-Indië voor een volwaardig parlement' [1939], AMK GMr, no. 101x, NA.

60 Susan Abeyasekere, *One hand clapping: Indonesian nationalists and the Dutch, 1939-1942*. Monash Papers on Southeast Asia 5 (Clayton, Australia: Centre of Southeast Asian Studies, Monash University).

61 PPO, January 1939, p. 257. None of the sources explain which elements of the *Sikap hidjrah* pamphlet indicated an alignment with the *tarekat* movement, and I could not detect any such indications from my reading of the text.

that the interests of Sarekat Islam had been compromised, and as Kartosuwiryo refused to stop the re-printing of the brochure, he was eventually expelled too.[62] A later issue of the *Overzicht* suggested that in addition to the conflict over the non-cooperation policy, there was also a theological one on the nature (*sifat*) of the Qur'an. This statement is, however, left unexplored by the sources.[63]

Kartosuwiryo was not the only victim of this purge: several other leading figures, together with the entire memberships of the Malangbong and Tejamaya (Tasikmalaya region) branches[64] and of eight other branches (including some in Central Java), incurred the same fate.[65] In late January 1940 Wondoamiseno declared that the party had 'long since abandoned the non-cooperation policy' and had changed its strategy from *hijrah* to *tauhid*, joining in the wider cooperative effort to establish an Indonesian parliament.[66]

Kartosuwiryo's activities between mid 1939 and early 1940 are unknown, but the suggestion that he had established a new party – a third PSII splinter group – was first aired at the 1939 PSII congress and later publicized by several newspapers between late January and early February.[67] A more detailed account appeared later in April in a report by Statius Muller, *Adviseur voor Inlandse Zaken*, explaining how after a few months of inactivity – or, more likely, of preparation – on 24 March 1940 Kartosuwiryo had formed a new party headquartered in Malangbong.

The Komite Pertahanan Kebenaran-PSII (KPK-PSII, Committee for the Defence of the Truth-PSII) was labelled by the Dutch a sect rather than a party, and was supported by around 1,500 members originating from 21 different PSII branches, including those in Padang Panjang (West Sumatra) and Manado (North Sulawesi).[68] The Malangbong branch, at the centre of this new splinter party, held a public meeting to discuss the decision of the Palembang congress to expel Kartosuwiryo in May 1940. They decided, first, that the central board's expulsion was against the

62 *Overzicht*, 17 June 1939.

63 *Overzicht*, 3 February 1940.

64 PPO, January 1939, p. 257.

65 *Overzicht*, 17 June 1939.

66 *Overzicht*, 3 February 1940.

67 These were *Pewarta Deli* (25 January), *Sinar Sumatra* (26 January), *Pertja Selatan* (27 January) and *Penjebar Semangat* (3 February) – all mentioned in *Overzicht*, 10 February 1940 – and *Overzicht*, 3 February 1940.

68 'Oprichting van een nieuwe politiek-godsdienstiege [*sic.*] partij door het KPK-PSII' [1940], AMK GMr, no. 529x, NA.

party's principles, and second, that the KPK-PSII would autonomously continue to work along PSII lines, even keeping the same flag and name.[69] The *Daftar oesaha hidjrah* (discussed above) was printed in March 1940 by Kartosuwiryo in Malangbong, and thus the absence of any comments in the pamphlet on the split could be read as a marker of this desire for continuity or, even, as a manifestation of self-perceived authenticity and commitment to the true PSII aims.

In his report, Statius Muller also made a note about an educational institution, the Soeffah. Through the development of intellectual capacities and character building, members of the Soeffah were seen as forming the core of an 'Islamically perfect' society. While this was the same aim that Kartosuwiryo had set for the Batavian Taman Marsoedi Kasoesastran in 1929, what he intended to do in his enterprise in Malangbong by referring to it as a Soeffah was to reconnect his efforts with Muhammad's dual role as political leader and teacher. In Medina, the Prophet used to expound Islamic teachings in a sheltered corner of the mosque (in Arabic called *suffah*), which at night also functioned as makeshift home for the newly arrived migrants, the *muhajirin*.[70]

To Kartosuwiryo the prophetic *suffah* represented the place where *syariat Islam* – the way of Islam – was taught in Medina and where the *muballighin* practiced their teaching skills.[71] In the memories of one of his associates, life in this institution was conducted in complete fulfilment of the Qur'an and the *sunnah* of the Prophet. According to one of Kartosuwiryo's grandsons, whose house today still faces the lot where the Soeffah once stood, this was a place where around one hundred religious teachers were trained at any given time in what was still considered Tjokroaminoto's political strategy for achieving independence: *persiapan, kemerdekaan, Negara Islam* (preparation, independence, Islamic state).[72]

It is difficult to date the end of the KPK-PSII and the Soeffah. According to the *Overzicht*, Kartosuwiryo's PSII splinter group was still active in mid January 1942[73] and a Dutch military report from January 1948 mentions that Kartosuwiryo's Soeffah was active

69 PPO, May-June 1940, p. 341.

70 An alternative explanation could be in reference to the *Ikhwān as-Saffā*; I am grateful to Michael Laffan for pointing this out to me.

71 Kartosuwiryo, *Sikap hidjrah PSII*, IV/5 and V/3.

72 Interviews conducted by the author in Bandung, 16 January 2008, and in Malangbong, 6 February 2008.

73 *Overzicht*, 17 January 1942.

before the military campaign of July 1947.[74] Oral sources provided inconsistent information, as one stated that the Japanese bombed its mosque, school and houses soon after the invasion, whilst another remembered that the destruction of the Soeffah occurred at the hands of the Dutch in 1947, thus triggering Kartosuwiryo to move to Ciamis.[75]

NEW REGIME, NEW APPROACH: DAI NIPPON AND ISLAMIC POLITICS

The Japanese landing on Sumatra in February 1942 and their invasion of Java the following month occurred at a time when relations between colony and motherland were strained, as exemplified in August 1941 by the Indonesian nationalists' boycott of the bill on native militias. The Dutch authorities in Java and Sumatra quickly surrendered to the new occupier, which meant that significant changes had to be made to ensure the survival, if not the success, of the nationalists' aspirations to independence.

Exiled nationalist leaders returned to the centre of the struggle, boundaries between cooperationists and non-cooperationists shifted, and the Japanese-led mobilization of the Indonesian population all had consequences for the nationalist movement. Though at first Japan had promoted the religious wing of the nationalist movement, by the time Japan capitulated, Soekarno and the secularists had gained the upper hand.

As short-lived as it was, the Japanese occupation was a formative experience for the Indonesian political leadership, as it gave a structure to what until then had been just hopes, dreams and visions of an independent state. Even more significantly, in the beginning it strengthened politicized Muslims' expectations for an Islamic state.[76] Japan sought to gather support for its anti-Western Greater Asia Co-Prosperity Sphere by appealing to the anti-colonial movement and the Islamic nationalists, and it is in this framework that Japan had propagandized its support for Islam and its victories against European powers for decades.

74 'Overzicht en ontwikkeling van de toestand 1 Jan 1800 uur tot 5 Jan. 1800 uur', Territorial ts. Troepencommandant West Java [1948], Ministerie van Defensie [hereafter MD]: Archieven Strijdkrachten in Nederlands-Indië [hereafter AS], no. 2224, NA.

75 Interviews conducted by the author in Malangbong, 6 February 2008, and in Jakarta, 7 February 2008.

76 The importance of the Japanese invasion and occupation of Southeast Asia has been explored by Harry Jindrich Benda, 'The structure of Southeast Asian history: Some preliminary observations', *Journal of Southeast Asian History* 3 (1962).

Japan also reversed the Dutch attitude of 'regarding Indonesian politics as a troublesome irritation',[77] and along with re-organizing the bureaucratic apparatus at the local and national levels, it proceeded to substitute all existing political parties with broader mass organizations. These two trajectories led, first, to the unintentional politicization of the rural population, as traditional structures of power were replaced by new organizations whose leadership was entrusted to physically strong, administratively able and highly cooperative youth.[78] Second, it provided urban Indonesians with ready-made mass organizations, thus facilitating the formation of an Indonesian national identity beyond the regional and ideological lines that had characterized the anti-colonial movement since the 1910s.

The first such organization was the Gerakan Tiga A, which hailed Japan as leader, protector and light of Asia. The group was established within weeks from the Japanese arrival, as early as April 1942. As all pre-invasion organizations and parties had been abolished, the Triple A Movement was to include members of both nationalist parties and government officials without distinction. The first sign that Japan was not going to sideline, but instead would emphasize, the role of the Muslim leadership was the formation of an Islamic sub-division of the Triple A Movement, the Persiapan Persatoean Oemmat Islam (Preparation of the Unification of the Islamic Community), entrusted to Abikoesno in July 1942.[79]

Japan's arrival in March had been welcomed by all constitutencies,[80] and the Islamic leadership was particularly enthusiastic. Their enthusiasm was demonstrated, for example, by Wondoamiseno's comment in August 1942 that the Japanese arrival was an event to be thankful to God for, as 'the brave sacrifice of the Dai Nippon' had freed the Indonesian people of 340 years of Dutch colonization and 'had lifted it from the mud of subjugation and humiliation [...]; now there is no more ethnic differentiation,

77 M.A. Aziz, *Japan's colonialism and Indonesia* (The Hague: Martinus Nijhoff, 1955); Benda, *The crescent and the rising sun*. For additional details on the bureaucratic transition, see Shigeru Sato, *War, nationalism, and peasants: Java under the Japanese occupation, 1942-1945*, Asian Studies Association of Australia (St. Leonard's, Australia: Allen & Unwin, 1994), pp. 22-45; on mobilisation, see Sato, *War, nationalism, and peasants*, pp. 36-59 and Benedict R.O'G. Anderson, *Java in a time of revolution: Occupation and resistance, 1944-1946* (Ithaca, NY/London: Cornell University Press, 1972), pp. 16-34; quote from Anderson, *Java in a time of revolution*, p. 31.

78 Kurasawa Aiko, 'Japanese occupation and leadership changes in Javanese villages', in Jurrien van Goor (ed), *The Indonesian Revolution: papers of the conference held in Utrecht, 17-20 June 1986* (Utrecht: Rijksuniversiteit Instituut voor Geschiedenis, 1986), pp. 57-78.

79 Benda, *The crescent and the rising sun*, pp. 112-4.

80 Aziz, *Japan's colonialism*, pp. 147, 149, 173.

everyone is equal, and this is the blessing of the leadership and protection of our brother Japan'.

Wondoamiseno also suggested to the party's local leaders in Sulawesi that they follow the Japanese request to dissolve the party, as it was expected that Japan would soon create an Islamic organization independent from the Triple A Movement. There was no reason to upset the new regime, argued Wondoamiseno, as it seemed committed to strengthening the Islamic movement by providing it with a united organization. Until then Sarekat Islam was to focus on education (*tabligh*) and economic initiatives.[81] The following month Japan re-established MIAI, entrusting its leadership to Harsono Tjokroaminoto and Wondoamiseno, who at that point were seen as the most cooperative elements of PSII.[82]

Driven by the idea that Islam could be a viable way to penetrate Indonesians' souls, and thus help their effort to gain popular support, in 1943 the Japanese begun to co-opt *kiyai* and *ulama* by training them in pan-Asian ideology, hoping that this would be integrated in their pan-Islamic vision.[83]

In March 1943 the Triple A Movement experiment was terminated, and Japan created Putera in its stead (Pusat Tenaga Rakjat, Concentration of the People's Power). Putera brought together all political and non-political nationalist organizations to work towards establishing a form of self-government. Although in the hands of secular nationalists - its directorate included Soekarno, Hatta, and Ki Hadjar Dewantoro of the Taman Siswa - Putera also gave a leading role to the former chairman of Muhammadiyah K.H. Mas Mansur. In its attempt to seal a partnership with Islam, Japan went as far as calling upon the Indonesian people to fulfil their 'duty to defend themselves as an Asiatic race, to defend the religion, the sovereignty, and justice as Muslems [*sic*], and to support the realisation of *Hakko Itjoe* [Japanese for 'the world as

81 'Letter of Ladjnah Tanfidzijah Partij Sjarikat Islam Indonesia Batavia-Centrum 2044', APG, no. 1007, NA.

82 *Soeara MIAI* [hereafter SMIAI], 1 January 2603 JIY/1943 CE.

83 The Japanese administration in 1943-44 established obligatory courses for religious teachers. 'Kiai-Cursus', Archief van de Algemene Secretarie, 1944-1950 [hereafter AAS], nos. 5236, 5237, includes several exercise notebooks that show the high level of indoctrination on themes such as pan-Asianism and the Co-Prosperity Sphere these teachers were subjected to. *Kiyai* were also asked to answer questions such as 'in which practical ways do you expect to cooperate with the *Dai Nippon*?'. Also very interesting are the archives containing the registration modules of participating *kiyai*. These offer extensive information on their family history and education, and often also on the titles of the texts studied and taught.

one house'] as ordained by Allah'.[84] The honeymoon between the Japanese authority and the Islamic movement would only last until late 1944, when Japan's favour was transferred to the secular nationalists, a shift that led Soekarno to cry: 'to live and die with Japan'.[85]

Kartosuwiryo was just as enthusiastic about the change of regime, and he was ready to fight for the supremacy of Japan along with other Islamic leaders. Returning to journalism, he became a regular contributor to the bi-weekly magazine *Soeara MIAI* from its inception in March 1943 until it dissolved at the end of the same year.[86] Kartosuwiryo promoted a profoundly cooperative attitude towards the foreign authority, marking a dramatic change from his earlier pieces published in *Fadjar Asia.*

Kartosuwiryo pledged support to Japan – which he described as 'earnestly endeavour[ing to advance] the common welfare and prosperity of Greater East Asia' – and stated that his own 'modest contribution' to the war effort was, 'whether one liked it or not,' cooperation. Nonetheless, Kartosuwiryo also reminded his readers that the duty to participate in building a Greater East Asia under Japanese leadership was not to eclipse Muslims' religious duties: Indonesian Muslims had to persevere in their belief in the afterlife and maintain patience in meeting their individual and communal obligations through *iman* and *tauhid*[87].

At a time when Japan had expelled *Fir'aun Belanda* (the Dutch Pharaoh) and thus had 'opened the door to, and widened the efforts towards, Islam',[88] the Indonesian *ummah* had to take advantage of the changed circumstances and cooperate with Japan in creating a 'new world'.[89]

84 Helen Hardacre explains the concept of *Hakkō Ichiu* as 'eight corners of the world under one roof'. For Hardacre, the term suggests that '[t]he Japanese were a superior people with a mission to rule the entire world'. Evidently, Indonesians understood this concept in a different way. Helen Hardacre, *Shintō and the state, 1868-1988* (Princeton: Princeton University Press, 1989), p. 40.

85 Words of Muhammad Zain Djambek in M. Slamet, *The holy war 'made in Japan, vol. II, 'Japanese machinations'* (Batavia, 1946), pp. 12-3.

86 Kartosuwiryo, 'Bekal bathin dalam perdjoeangan', SMIAI, 1 March; 'Menoedjoe ke arah dar-oel-Islam dan dar-oes-Salam', SMIAI, 15 March; 'Fardl-oel-'ain dan fardl-oel-kifajah dalam Islam', SMIAI, 1 May; 'Kewadjiban oemmat Islam menghadapi "doenia baroe"', SMIAI, 15 May; 'Baitoel-mal pada zaman pantjaroba dan tarich bait-al-mal zaman Rasoeloellah clm dan choelafa-oer-rasidin r.a.a', SMIAI, 28 June; 'I'tibar madjazy dan ma'any' SMIAI, 15 July; 'Benteng Islam' SMIAI, 1 September 2603 JIY/1943 CE.

87 Kartosuwiryo, 'Bekal bathin dalam perdjoeangan', SMIAI, 1 March.

88 Kartosuwiryo, 'Bekal bathin dalam perdjoeangan', SMIAI, 1 March.

89 Kartosuwiryo, 'Bekal bathin dalam perdjoeangan', SMIAI, 1 March; 'Fardl-oel-'ain dan fardl-oel-kifajah', SMIAI, 1 May.

The apex of Kartosuwiryo's positive attitude toward Japanese rule was reached in May 1943, when he wrote: 'Whether one likes it or not, each individual and group will become a member of the Big Family, the Greater East Asia Family', and each of its parts 'has to feel obliged to work, help, and support it with full conviction and consciousness, in the effort to reach common prosperity'. Cooperation with Japan had become *wajib* (obligatory).[90]

It is on this basis that Kartosuwiryo advocated the unification of all those who had been contributing to building the Greater East Asia sphere into one front. His understanding of Japan's *dunia baru* ('new world') as an embryonic Islamic state became explicit: the front was called *Benteng Islam* (Islamic Front), and the new world represented the bridge to the *dar al-akhirat*, the afterlife.[91] The goal of the *Benteng Islam* was to implement religious precepts and further Islamize Indonesia under Japanese rule. To ensure the success of such a project, the front had to rely on a combination of the *ummah*'s genuine belief, the Islamic leaders' knowledge and the Japanese national government's authority. Kartosuwiryo appeared very confident that Japan would support this idea: 'As the Supreme Government in Tokyo and the military authority located here have already granted the Islamic *ummah* the freedom to follow its religious duties, now all that is left are the lower levels of the National government.'[92]

Even though at this point Kartosuwiryo still seemed pleased with the Japanese attempts to coordinate the nationalist movement, by 1949 he was to describe their rule as a circus in which the animals (Indonesian nationalist leaders) were only free to act within the limited range of movement allowed and orchestrated by their trainer, Japan.[93] Using less picturesque terms, Benda has made a similar point about this tendency of the Japanese regime:

> Until almost the end of the occupation [...] it was they who held the keys to all power, and it was they who rigorously maintained the limits within which urban elites, especially, were allowed to move. Whether nominally exercising the authority of 'independent' governments or whether playing less elevated roles as leaders of as-yet dependent peoples, the scope of nationalist elites was pitifully restricted, their activities narrowly circumscribed, and their bargaining power vis-à-vis the occupying power virtually non-existent.[94]

90 Kartosuwiryo, 'Kewadjiban oemmat Islam menghadapi "doenia baroe"', SMIAI, 15 May and 'Benteng Islam', SMIAI, 1 September.

91 Kartosuwiryo, 'Kewadjiban oemmat Islam menghadapi "doenia baroe"', SMIAI, 15 May.

92 Kartosuwiryo, 'Benteng Islam', SMIAI, 1 September.

93 Kartosuwiryo, 'ad-Daulatul Islamiyah', March 1949, in Al Chaidar, *Pemikiran politik*, pp. 815-20.

94 Benda, 'The structure of Southeast Asian history', p. 135.

Yet Kartosuwiryo's support of Japan's rule had apparently paid off. In May 1943 he was reported to be mayor of Bandung,[95] and by June he succeeded in setting up a treasury for the Islamic community – the *bait al-mal* – under MIAI's sponsorship.[96] As it was explained in a series of articles published in *Soeara MIAI*, the function of the *bait al-mal* was socio-economic. In this transitional period when the *ummah* was 'striving for the realization of the Co-Prosperity Sphere', the *bait al-mal*'s finances were to be used to support the war. During times of peace, this treasury would have also collected wealth from unclaimed inheritance, *dhimmi*'s (tax-paying non-Muslim monotheist) taxes and war spoils, taking up all the functions of a treasury.[97] The *majelis bait al-mal* was operated at a regional level in the Bandung area by Wondoamiseno and Wiranatakoesoema. Kartosuwiryo's plan to extend it to every province in Java soon encountered Japanese opposition.

As MIAI gained socio-political success, Japanese administrators began to fear that the anti-Dutch sentiments predominant in pre-invasion Islamic circles would be translated into anti-Japanese sentiments. Furthermore, Benda has suggested that it was the creation of the *bait al-mal* as a monetary institution that tipped the balance and brought Japan to the decision to disband MIAI entirely.[98] Within two weeks of the dissolution of MIAI, the Majelis Sjoero Muslimin Indonesia (Masjoemi or, in current usage, Masyumi) was established in its place.[99] Masyumi's leadership was entrusted to Muhammadiyah and Nahdatul Ulama, whom the Japanese saw as less politicized, thus leaving PSII and the other former political parties with no role to play.

THE RISE OF SECULAR NATIONALISM

At the end of 1943, Putera was also dissolved, and replaced with the Jawa Hōkōkai, by far the most successful of all the Japanese attempts to mobilize the Javanese population. This group retained

95 'Ketoea Dewan MIAI mengoetjapkan terima kasih', *Asia Raya*, 18 May 1943.

96 The *bait al-mal* is a Qur'anic institution representing a communal treasury in which Qur'anic taxes are deposited, and through which the community could support those in need of financial help, such as widows, orphans and the poor. 'Gambar soesoenan baital-mal M.I.A.I.', SMIAI, 1 July 1943; Kartosuwiryo was appointed secretary.

97 Kartosuwiryo, 'Baitoel-mal pada zaman pantjaroba', SMIAI, 28 June 1943.

98 Benda, *The crescent and the rising sun*, p. 145-6; for further details on the Japanese era *bait al-mal*, see pp. 144-7.

99 'Pemboebaran MIAI', *Asia Raya*, 2 November 1943, and 'Majelis Sjoera Moeslimin Indonesia', *Asia Raya*, 23 November 1943.

Soekarno as its leader, and throughout the year it enjoyed increased freedoms and support from the Japanese – including the creation of a military wing, the Barisan Pelopor (Pioneer Corps) – tipping the balance in favour of the secular nationalists. As Japan was the ultimate gate-keeper of the political sphere, the rising prominence of the secular nationalists had wide-ranging effects. By the time the government declared, in early September, that Indonesia would obtain independence 'in the near future',[100] the tables had turned and Islamic groups' dominance was limited to the social sphere.

It was not until late December, when Japan was increasingly losing ground on the international scene, that local authorities once again embraced Islam as a key element of their anti-Western propaganda. In an attempt to identify their defence as a holy war, they added a religious flavour to the Pembela Tanah Air, (Peta, Army for the Defence of the Fatherland) by placing the Muslim crescent on its flag. They also allowed Masyumi to have its own armed wing.

Hizboellah was placed under the direction of Wahid Hasyim and was open to Indonesian Muslims between 17 and 25 years of age. Trainees came from all over the archipelago, and in February 1945 the first group of 500 started military and ideological training in Cibarusa, West Java, under the leadership of K.H. Zainul Arifin. Among the several *ulama* providing spiritual training was K.H. Moestafa Kamil from Singaparna, the above-mentioned Sarekat Islam leader.[101] In April 1945 Kartosuwiryo became a trainer for the Banten branch of the Barisan Pelopor; he was never a member of the Hizboellah.[102] It should not be a surprise that a leader of the Islamic nationalist move-

100 Benda, *The crescent and the rising sun*, p. 173.

101 K.H.M. Hasyim Latief, *Laskar Hisbullah* (Surabaya: Lajnah Ta'lif wan Nasyr PBNU, 1995), pp. 11-22.

102 'Nama-nama kepala rombongan jang akan dikirimkan keloeroeh Syuu oentoek Hooshi-II', *Indonesia Merdeka*, 25 April 1945, p. 6. Several scholars have argued that Kartosuwiryo was a Hizboellah leader in West Java (ranging from Pinardi, *Sekarmadji Maridjan*, p. 29 to Merle C. Ricklefs, *A history of modern Indonesia since c.1200*, 3rd ed [Basingstoke: Palgrave, 2001], p. 227), but I was unable to find any primary source supporting this statement. Hizboellah leaders in Bandung were Aminuddin Hamzah, Kamran, Hoeseinsyah, Utarya, Gofur Ismail, Arustandi, Ahim, Samsudin Hamid, Mokhtar, H. Junaedi, Kadar Solihat, Zainal Abidin and Syahbandar; the Cimahi area was led by Umar Damiri and H Naswari; Kamran and Husainsyah coordinated Hizboellah across West Java. The West Java branch of the Sabilillah armed wing - a sister organization of Hizboellah - were instead established in February 1946, and among its leaders figured Isa Ansyari, Ismail Napu, KH Joesoef Taoeziri, H Jaenuddin, Ajengan Toha and A. Mokhtar. Usman Jauhari, 'Peranan Hizboellah-Sabilillah dalam perlawanan bersenjata terhadap Belanda di Jawa Barat pada masa revolusi fisik (1945-1959)' (thesis, Universitas Padjajaran, Bandung, 1987), pp. 34-5. The first group of Hizboellah fighters in West Java completed their training on 20 May 1945 under the leadership of Kahar Mudhakkar, the future DI leader in South Sulawesi; 'Toendjoekkanlah kepada doenia, bahwa bangsa Indonesia adalah bangsa jang masih hidoep!', *Asia Raya*, 22 May 1945, in Benda, *The crescent and the rising sun*, p. 140.

ment became part of the cadre of the secular Pioneer Corps instead of joining Masyumi's military wing. As mentioned, former PSII members had been effectively expelled from – or, perhaps more accurately, had never been included in – Masyumi, to the extent that politicized Islamic nationalists had infiltrated the Jawa Hōkōkai, gaining particular influence in Bandung and the Priangan area.[103]

Despite their mixed constituencies, their joint effort in preparing post-occupation institutions, their common goal of independence and their agreement over the need to protect Japan against the Allies, Masyumi appeared uninterested in Jawa Hōkōkai's proposal to merge the two organizations. The Muslim party was aware that it would have meant the loss of its autonomy as well as of its leverage in securing a role for Islam in the future state of Indonesia.

CONCLUDING REMARKS

Between 1929 and 1936 Kartosuwiryo was propelled towards the leadership of Sarekat Islam, and they coordinated a radicalization of Islamist politics and non-cooperation. In the aftermath of Tjokroaminoto's death, the *hijrah* policy became a dominant feature of the party's policies, especially as secular nationalists retreated towards cooperation with the Dutch to achieve self-governance. As De Jonge's repressive policies cornered Sarekat Islam and Kartosuwiryo, several long-standing members withdrew their support from the party, eventually leading to Kartosuwiryo's expulsion.

At the time of the Japanese landing in 1942, Indonesia and the Netherlands had already been rapidly drifting apart. Dai Nippon succeeded in finding its niche in the hearts of most Indonesians, harvesting support in rural and urban areas by co-opting political and administrative agents. The religious movement grew stronger under Japanese rule, as it became more coordinated, created a stronger structure and, most importantly, was provided with an armed wing: in 1948 this would become the core foundation for Kartosuwiryo's Darul Islam.

While the Allied forces were making progress against the Axis powers, Japan agreed to prepare Indonesia for independence. Japan first supported political Islam as an instrument for deepening its hold on the country's population, but when the secular nationalist elite was deemed more suitable for the task of laying the foundations of the new state, the Japanese shifted their support accordingly.

103 Benda, *The crescent and the rising sun*, p. 266.

3

Religious resistance and secular politics
Laying the foundations of the Indonesian state (1945-1947)

> *We didn't want to leave West Java behind, we didn't want to see the* ummah *and the Indonesian people in West Java become slaves of the evil Dutch, we didn't have the heart to listen to the moans of the Republicans who wished to retreat to Yogya[karta]. [...] for whom were we withdrawing to Yogya? And what would we do, then, if the Dutch took Yogya as well? What would be the fate of the people left behind? Wasn't that a betrayal? [...] Eventually, with resolute hearts, we decided not to join the withdrawal to Yogya and to continue instead the resistance against the occupying Dutch soldiers, joining the Sabilillah group in West Java.*[1]

Japan had made new concessions to Islamic groups in the social and religious fields, but it quickly stepped back when it came to determining the position of Islam in the new state, fully delegating the definition of such relation to local leaders. In late April 1945 Japan formed the Komite Nasional Indonesia Pusat (KNIP, Preparatory Committee for Independence), with the intention of initiating a debate about the ideological foundations of the future Indonesian state. On an increasingly dynamic political stage, the inexperienced leaders of Muhammadiyah, Nahdatul Ulama and Masyumi were quickly sidelined by the nationalist elite. When in May the debate became polarized around the question of whether Indonesia should be an Islamic or a secular state, Soekarno's camp emerged as the winner.[2]

The conclusive speech, delivered by Soekarno on 1 June, ignored the controversy that had dominated the committee's sessions and proclaimed, in the name of national interest, unity and harmony, that Indonesia was to be built on the Pancasila, or the five

1 Confession of Sjarif Hidajat, Darul Islam member, arrested on 2 July 1961. 'Confession letter of Sjarif Hidajat, former member of Kartosuwiryo's group', 10 September 1961, Penumpasan DI-JaBar, [folii], Arsip Angkatan Bersenjata Republik Indonesia [hereafter AABRI DI], Jakarta.
2 Benda, *The crescent and the rising sun*, pp. 169-94 and pp. 179 onwards.

principles of *kebangsaan* (nationalism), *perkemanusiaan* (humanitarianism), *permusyawaratan-perwakilan* (deliberation among representatives), *kesejahteraan* (social welfare) and *ketuhanan* (belief in One God).[3]

A smaller committee was arranged to address the complaints coming from the Islamic faction and to ease emerging frictions. On 22 June the participants reached a common declaration meant to serve as the new constitution's preamble. While it did not recognize the idea of an Islamic state, this version of the constitution accepted sharia law by affirming 'the obligation for adherents of Islam to practise Islamic law'.[4]

This clear reference to Islam in the constitutional preamble prompted a reaction from the Christian representatives, and that sentence – later to become known as the Piagam Jakarta (Jakarta Charter) – disappeared from the final draft presented on 13 July, being replaced instead with a declaration of freedom of religion. The members of the Islamic faction had intended to further debate these changes, but as Japan was losing ground in the Pacific and would soon capitulate, Indonesian politicians felt compelled to accelerate their preparations for independence and to work with what they had. By 7 August the committee had been cleansed of all Japanese members, and on the 11th, in the aftermath of the explosion of the atomic bombs in Hiroshima and Nagasaki, Japan reassured Soekarno and Hatta that independence would be granted on the 24th of that month.

This chapter analyses the end of Japanese rule in Indonesia, the return of the Dutch and the dynamics surrounding Soekarno's establishment of the Indonesian Republic. I focus in particular on Masyumi's reaction to Soekarno's decision to declare Indonesia a non-confessional state and on his readiness to re-engage in diplomatic talks with the Dutch. Kartosuwiryo had been sidelined in 1944, but we see him now returning to the political scene, first as Masyumi's executive committee secretary (in 1945), and then as a party representative at the KNIP (1946 and 1947) and a candidate for the post of junior Minister of Defence (July 1947).

3 Boland, *The struggle of Islam*, pp. 15-23; Herbert Feith and Lance Castles (eds), *Indonesian political thinking, 1945-1965* (Ithaca: Cornell University Press, 1970), pp. 40-9.

4 '*dengan kewadjiban mendjalankan Sjari'at Islam bagi pemeluk-pemeluknja*'; see Soekarno, Hatta et. al., 'Piagam Jakarta: Preamble to Undang-Undang Dasar Republik Indonesia 1945', in Greg Fealy and Virginia Hooker (eds), *Voices of Islam in Southeast Asia* (Singapore: ISEAS, 2006), pp. 209-10. The members of the committee were Soekarno, Hatta, A.A. Maramis, Abikoesno Tjokrosoejoso, Abdoelkahar Moedhakkir, H. Agoes Salim, Achmad Soebardjo, Wahid Hasjim and Moehammad Jamin.

Kartosuwiryo's base was still the Priangan, and when the Dutch launched their invasion of West Java in July 1947, he rejected any further involvement in national politics in favour of organizing the defence of his region. It was in the midst of this invasion that Kartosuwiryo transformed the West Java branch of Masyumi into the Darul Islam group, setting aside his commitment to the parliamentary struggle, an effort that he had renewed as recently as August 1946.

At the national level, in the years following the Japanese capitulation, Masyumi would become more insistent in its demands for an Islamic state, also calling it a *darul Islam.* In 1945 the Party proclaimed armed resistance to the Dutch a *jihad,* and occasionally Masyumi took an aggressive stand against the Republican administration. Political clashes soon had their counterpart on the battle ground, as Republican troops and Islamic militias tended to keep separate. The Dutch invasion and the ensuing treaty (the Linggadjati Agreement) further heightened tensions, as West Java was declared *de facto* Dutch territory, thus establishing the end of Republican authority over the region.

SHIFTING CENTRES OF POWER: TOKYO, JAKARTA, LONDON, THE HAGUE

Japan's plan to transfer sovereignty to Indonesian leaders was halted by its defeat in World War II. Japan surrendered on 15 August, and the Allied forces, on behalf of the South East Asia Command (SEAC), took control of the Pacific front immediately thereafter. Yet as the British were unable to land until late September, Java was left to its own fate as a contested space between the retreating Japanese, the Indonesian nationalists and the re-invading Dutch troops.[5] The enthusiasm that had swept across the archipelago at the Japanese landing was experienced by neither the SEAC nor the Dutch troops.

The news of Japan's surrender took weeks to seep through and out of Jakarta, fomenting unrest and chaos between diplomacy-oriented politicians and revolution-minded *pemuda* (youth). The first and perhaps most significant of such incidents was the kidnapping of Soekarno and Hatta by a group of radical nationalists who wanted independence declared before Japan transferred authority to the Allies.

5 For a detailed account of the British occupation, see Richard Mcmillan's, *The British occupation of Indonesia, 1945-1946* (London: RoutledgeCurzon, 2005) and 'British military intelligence in Java and Sumatra, 1945-46', *Indonesia and the Malay World* 37-107 (2009).

Soekarno proclaimed independence on 17 August without the support of Soetan Sjahrir, who was head of the underground anti-Japanese movement, or that of the Islamic wing, which demanded a more prominent role for religion. Hatta chaired a final informal meeting of the preparatory committee on 18 August and concluded that Indonesia only had a chance as an independent nation if no mention of Islam was made in the constitution.

The Jakarta Charter was excluded from the final version of the Indonesian constitution, and to placate the Islamic nationalists, Soekarno specified that this constitution was 'temporary', 'quick' and only applicable to the revolution (*sementara, kilat, revolutiegrondwet*). Soekarno also promised that 'later in the future [...] if we live in a safe and orderly state, we will gather once again the elected representatives of the people, who will enable us to make a more complete and perfect constitution'.[6] Soekarno's failure to follow up on the 'temporary' aspect of the constitution deeply informed Kartosuwiryo's decision to proclaim the Negara Islam Indonesia in 1949.

In the weeks following their surrender, the Japanese were still in charge. The British commander requested, albeit unsuccessfully, that all internees remain in the camps, so as to avoid the spread of vengeful violence. Lawlessness was rampant in the towns and the countryside, with the Japanese, Europeans and Chinese becoming the favourite targets of local gangs. Jakarta was the centre of a struggle for power among the Dutch, Japanese and Indonesians, in the midst of which British troops quietly mediated to re-establish law and order. On the political front, Soekarno and Hatta acted as if the proclamation had been forced upon them. They did very little to establish government structures, instead focusing on diplomacy and leaving most of the action to the so-called *laskar* (militia), both in Jakarta as well as in the neighbouring areas. The apex of this conflict in strategy was reached in mid September, when Soekarno interrupted a mass rally in the capital with calls for peace and order instead of showing his support for the revolutionary intent of the demonstrators.

By the end of the month, the Japanese mayor had indirectly handed over control of the city to his Indonesian counterpart, Suwiryo, and Dutch attempts to regain it were stonewalled by the

6 Endang Saifuddin Anshari, *Piagam Jakarta 22 Juni 1945: Sebuah konsensus nasional tentang dasar negara Republik Indonesia 1945-1959*, 3rd ed. (Jakarta: Gema Insani Press, 1997), p. 48. A recent discussion of the Jakarta Charter and its current impact on Indonesian politics can be found in Nadirsyah Hosen, *Shari'a and constitutional reform*, pp. 59-69.

Allies, who insisted that the Dutch not re-take political control. An official Dutch municipal administration was not constituted until February 1946. In the latter part of 1945 Jakarta functioned as the formal capital of both the Indonesian Republic and the Netherlands Indies, its *de facto* control being a crucial step on the road towards *de jure* authority over all of Java, if not over the entire former East Indies' territory. But when British troops succeeded in bringing the city under total control in December, most *laskar* fled the town, and the Republican government gradually withdrew to Central Java, leaving Jakarta in the hands of the Europeans.[7]

Within weeks of the Japanese surrender, before the British assumed control of Jakarta, Soekarno had already formed the first Republican cabinet. Having transformed the KNIP into a legislative body, Soekarno called on Indonesians to form political parties and to begin preparations for parliamentary elections, scheduled for the following year in January. The nationalist front was far from united, and in October the socialist Soetan Sjahrir released his *Perjuangan kita* (Our struggle) pamphlet, indirectly accusing Soekarno of cooperation with the Japanese and of displaying sympathies for Tan Malaka. Tan Malaka was the leader of the communist group, who, it had emerged, had in October and November been preparing for a coup. To avoid the potentially destabilizing alliance of Sjahrir with Tan Malaka, in mid November Soekarno offered Sjahrir the opportunity to form the cabinet.

The post-World War II reorientation of the nationalist movement was evident to Van Mook as soon as he landed on Java in October 1945. The Lieutenant Governor-General realized that the Japanese occupation had strengthened the nationalists to the point that their struggle for independence had gained too much momentum to be restrained by military force. Restraining the movement was even less tenable because the Netherlands would have had to rely on British troops, which had neither an interest nor a stake in reinstating Dutch colonial rule. Further widening the existing rift between Jakarta and The Hague, Van Mook initiated talks with the nationalist leadership, as he saw a viable solution only in diplomacy. More importantly, he saw the solution in recognizing the different status of Java *vis-à-vis* the rest of the archipelago, as the Netherlands had indeed succeeded in restoring pre-war order in the eastern islands.[8]

7 Robert Cribb, 'Administrative competition in the Indonesian revolution: The dual government of Jakarta, 1945-1947' in *The Indonesian revolution*, pp. 129-46.
8 J.J.P. de Jong, 'Winds of change: Van Mook, Dutch policy and the realities of November 1945', in *The Indonesian revolution*, pp. 163-82.

The Allies had been quite explicit in their unwillingness to negotiate with a former collaborator of the Japanese (meaning Soekarno), and so it was that the recognition of Sjahrir's cabinet as representative of one portion of the Indonesian archipelago and his voluntary agreement to a federation with tight connections to the Netherlands made it possible, in late 1946, the signing of the Linggadjati Agreement.

In the window between the Japanese defeat and the Dutch return, the political scene changed dramatically. The largest party during this time was the new Partai Nasional Indonesia (PNI), which, its name notwithstanding, had nothing to do with Soekarno's party, as it represented professionals and civil servants. However, the party with the widest and deepest support in late 1945 – and until the end of the decade – was Masyumi, which had reorganized itself in November. The next party to form was the Partai Sosialis (Socialist Party), which was established in December and included both Amir Sjarifuddin's and Soetan Sjahrir's constituencies. Several other parties were founded in 1946, yet only these three played significant roles during the revolution and in the early years of the Republic.

In the months following the Indonesian proclamation of independence, Kartosuwiryo regained his position as secretary of Masyumi's executive committee, and he was also chosen as party representative for the KNIP general assemblies in 1946 and 1947, and for its Working Committee (Badan Pekerja) in 1947.[9]

At the November 1945 congress, former Sarekat Islam and Partai Islam Indonesia (PII) members dominated the central board, whilst NU and Muhammadiyah leaders were only found in the Majelis Sjoero (consultative assembly). The boards of the two departments were a bit of a potpourri, with Agoes Salim and Mohammad Roem from the Awareness Committee sitting next to Kartosuwiryo, Muhammad Natsir, K.H.A. Sanoesi, and K.H. Abdoelwahab.[10] In the meantime Muhammad Natsir acted as vice-president of the KNIP working committee.[11] This fragmentation of the membership of the core bodies of the party created the conditions for Masyumi's political incoherence in the 1950s. As

9 D. Noer and Akbarsyah, *K.N.I.P.: Komite Nasional Indonesia Pusat. Parlemen Indonesia 1945-1959* (Jakarta: Yayasan Risalah, 2005).

10 Deliar Noer, *Masjumi: its organization, ideology and political role in Indonesia* (master's thesis, Cornell University, Ithaca, 1960).

11 'Overzichten van berichten betreffende het republikeinse leger in de Maleise pers van West-Java 1945 Oktober-1946 April', p. 59, AMK: Supplement (1664) 1826-1952 [hereafter Supp] no. 78, NA.

old fractures had not yet healed, it is not surprising that Masyumi failed to bring about a defined platform for Indonesia's independence in Islamic terms. Within a year, the leadership would change dramatically.[12]

In the period following the SEAC occupation of Java, three dynamics - Soekarno's neglect of Islam, the Republic's weakness in asserting its sovereignty against Dutch claims, and Masyumi's lack of a political strategy to gain a more dominant position in national politics (despite its large following) - led to the Islamization of the ideological struggle as well as the polarization of Republican and Islamic troops on the territory of West Java.

MASYUMI'S ISLAMIZATION OF THE IDEOLOGICAL STRUGGLE

In early October 1945 the Poentjak Pimpinan Masjoemi Batavia (Masyumi Jakarta Leadership Summit) declared a *perang sabil* against the Japanese and the Netherlands Indies Civil Administration (NICA). According to a Dutch overview of the Malay press in West Java, Masyumi was calling upon Indonesians to work towards unifying religion and state.[13] This call was not an isolated case.

While Van Mook was informing The Hague that nationalist groups in Java had radicalized, displaying 'hard fanaticism', Kiyai Haji Hasjim Asj'ari, founder and chairman of Nahdatul Ulama and now chairman of Masyumi's Majelis Sjoero, issued a declaration of holy war against the Dutch. Published on 20 November 1945 in *Kedaulatan Rakyat*,[14] this declaration called upon all Muslims to defend the newly independent Indonesia from the 'infidels who obstruct our independence' and the NICA. Such a defence was declared an individual duty (*fard al-'ain*), and whoever died in the

12 Dewan Partij: Soekiman, from its PSII splinter Partai Islam Indonesia, was the chairman, with Abikoesno (PSII) and Wali al-Fatah (PII) as his vices; Harsono Tjokroaminoto (PSII) and Prawoto Mangkoesasmito (SIS) were the secretaries. Majelis Sjoero: KH Hasjim Asj'ari as chairman, Ki Bagoes Hadikoesoemo, K. Wahid Hasjim and Kasman Singodimedjo as vice-chairmen. Masjoemi, *Partai Politik Islam Indonesia* (Bukit Tinggi: Dewan Pemimpin Daerah Masjoemi Soematra Barat). This pamphlet was most probably printed on the occasion of the 22 April 1946 congress.

13 'Overzichten van berichten betreffende het republikeinse leger in de Maleise pers van West-Java 1945 Oktober-1946 April', p. 34, AMK: Supp no. 78, NA.

14 *Kedaulatan Rakyat* [hereafter KR], 20 November 1945 in Amiq, 'Two fatwas on jihad against the Dutch colonisation in Indonesia: A prosopographical approach to the study of fatwa', *Studia Islamika* 5-3 (1998), p. 86.

fighting was to be a martyr.[15] At the Nahdatul Ulama congress, held in March 1946, it was decided that all Muslims – men and women, adults and children, armed and unarmed – living within a 94 km radius from occupied areas had the individual religious duty to fight the Dutch. For those living outside the given distance, theirs was instead a collective duty (*fard al-kifaya*).[16] The legal grounds for this resolution were found in the fact that Indonesia had been declared 'land of Islam', *dar al-Islam*, in 1936, making the defence of its territory and population against infidel invasions *wajib*.[17]

Asj'ari's *fatwa* also announced that 'whoever divides our unity is liable to be killed'. The view that 'splitters' should be equated with apostates was derived from the idea that whoever undermined a united front was 'a Dutch agent'. It is not far-fetched to suggest that this was a veiled accusation of the nationalists' readiness to cooperate with Dutch colonial authorities.[18]

The modernist wing, in charge of Masyumi's central board, was reluctant to endorse Asj'ari's *fatwa*, declaring a *jihad* against the Dutch, and to call the whole community to such a duty. The central congress had already rejected a motion proposed by the Kaoem Moeslimin Indonesia Angkatan Sendjata (Indonesian Muslims Armed Group) to declare 'war on the way of God' (*jihad fi-sabilillah*) a collective religious duty.[19] However, it felt compelled to endorse the pressures advanced from several quarters[20] and supported the plan to prepare the Islamic community for such a *jihad*.[21] To show

15 Islamic *fiqh* categorizes actions in five groups: *haram* (prohibited), *makruh* (contemptible), *mubah* (permitted), *mustahabb* or *sunnah* (recommended). The *wajib/fard* (obligatory) actions are further distinguished between those that pertain to the individual (*fard al-'ayn*) or those that fall upon the entire community (*fard al-kifaya*).
Nahdatul Ulama literature refers to the '*jihad* resolution' as being released either at the NU Java and Madura congress held in Surabaya on 22 October 1945, or possibly at the Central Java congress held in Purwokerto from 26 to 29 March 1946. *al-Djihad*, 2 April 1946; Amiq, 'Two fatwas on jihad', pp. 87-9.

16 'Resoloesi tentang djihad', *al-Djihad* no. 30, 2 April 1946.

17 This opinion was given by Shaykh Muhammad Salih al-Ra'is, who is described by Amiq as the *mufti* of the Hadramis, via a *fatwa* that was later sent to Nahdatul Ulama leaders. The *fatwa* was eventually approved by the NU Banjarmasin congress in 1936; Amiq, 'Two fatwas on jihad', pp. 90, 108-9.

18 This approach is explicit in Kartosuwiryo's 1949 *ad-Daulatul Islamiyah* and *Manifesto politik no. 1/7*, in which Republican leaders and supporters are accused of being 'Dutch agents', and thus enemies of war.

19 'Kaoem Moeslimin Indonesia Angkat Sendjata', KR, 15 October 1945.

20 During the *khutba* for Idul Adha (mid November 1945) in Bandung, Kiyai Abdoessalam had called on the large crowd to fight a holy war against the Netherlands; in 'Militaire, politieke en economische gegevens uit de Maleise pers betreffende de residenties Batavia, Buitenzorg, Krawang, Bandung, Surakarta, Djokjakarta, Semarang en Kedu', p. 11, AMK: Supp no. 76, NA.

21 '60 Miljoen kaoem Moeslimin Indonesia siap berdjihad fi Sabilillah', KR, 9 November 1945.

its support of this plan, the congress decided in favour of creating a new armed wing, the Sabilillah (lit. 'on the path of God'), which was a special corps of the Tentara Keamanan Rakyat (TKR, People's Security Army) placed under the direct supervision of Masyumi to support the already active Hizboellah.[22]

These steps confirmed the party's general understanding of *jihad* as a duty to be pursued only by a portion of the population – namely, the armed-youth wings – whilst the rest of the population was to concentrate on 'studying the social sciences' and entering the world of politics. Studying and engaging in politics were crucial as Masyumi leaders believed that change was only possible through political action.[23] As Harun Nasution has argued, the modernists sought to create an Islamic state by first preparing its society, whilst the traditionalists believed it impossible to create an Islamic society without first establishing the appropriate government structures.[24] In the revolutionary context of 1946, this distinction was to become blurred, and Kartosuwiryo's explanation of Masyumi's strategy will show the uncompromising primacy of independence.

Masyumi's dedication to establishing an independent Islamic state was constantly emphasized in the pages of its bulletin *al-Djihad.* Beginning in February 1946, this periodical conducted a propaganda campaign in support of a holy war, the *hijrah* policy and an Islamic state, or *darul Islam.* On 13 February it celebrated the prophetic migration to Medina and Muhammad's defence of the Islamic city-state as models of political action, suggesting that readers should rise in an Islamic revolution as a free and independent *ummah* 'demanding freedom for its religion, people and islands'.[25]

This same month, the party congress unveiled the two pillars of its political agenda: an unshakable dedication to the formation of a *darul Islam,* that is an Islamic state, and a commitment to do so through parliamentary consultation. This approach was reaffirmed

22 'Barisan Sabilillah', KR, 17 November 1945.

23 'Masjoemi, toelang poenggoeng Republik Indonesia', *al-Djihad* no. 26, 28 February 1946. Members of the Masyumi branch in Cicalengka were reportedly shouting – during a party meeting in early January – 'Freedom and paradise'; in: 'Militaire, politieke en economische gegevens uit de Maleise pers betreffende de residenties Batavia, Buitenzorg, Krawang, Bandung, Surakarta, Djokjakarta, Semarang en Kedu', p. 16, AMK: Supp no. 76, NA.

24 Harun Nasution, 'The Islamic state in Indonesia: The rise of the ideology, the movement for its creation and the theory of the MASJUMI' (master's thesis, McGill, Montreal, 1965, pp. 76-7).

25 'Revoloesi Islam', *al-Djihad* 24, 13 February 1946. In addition to several articles published throughout the year 1946 (see, for example, 'Revoloesi Islam', 13 February and 'Peperangan sekarang soedah djadi fardoel 'ain', 20 April) the magazine also published boxes containing advertising slogans such as *SIAP sedia untuk berdjuang fiSabilillah, Djihad Sabil, Daroel Islam itoelah toedjoean kita, Berdjihadlah! FiSabilillah!*

by the party's manifesto in June 1947,[26] and maintained well into 1948,[27] further strengthened by the temporary character of the 1945 constitution and by Soekarno's pledge to establish a representative democracy. Masyumi accepted the Republican constitution as a 'stepping stone' towards the realization of Islamic ideals in the state; it recognized Pancasila's harmony with Islamic principles;[28] and it laid out its domestic and international agendas as a mixture of mild pan-Islamism, democracy and spreading Islamic teachings in Indonesian society through education and *dakwah* (Islamic propaganda).[29]

In this spirit, over the following months *al-Djihad* often suggested that Masyumi was the most prominent agent of Islamization of the Republic, and that an Islamic state was the 'logical' solution for Indonesia.

The magazine articulated its dedication to the formation of an Islamic state as such:

> If 33 years ago Islam was only a final coating, considered as just enough to function as a link between organizations, now it is not like that. This Masyumi has a 100% Islamic soul, the spiritual connection among all Masyumi members is Allah's religion, Masyumi's flag is the crescent and the star on a red and white background, Masyumi's aim is the *darul Islam*, or an Indonesian Republic based on Islam.[30]

Regarding its commitment to parliamentary consultation, it held that:

> Now Indonesia is independent, and the Republic is shaped to be based on the people's authority. Although the Constitution does not fulfill yet the desires of the Islamic community, for the time being this is enough, and we are happy and grateful. But Masyumi is aware that the majority of Indonesians are Muslims, and feels

26 'Rencana dari Masjoemi', 20 June 1947, Arsip Kementrian Pertahanan 1946 [hereafter KemPert], no. 1045, ANRI.

27 'Cursus Masjumi', 27 April 1948, Arsip Kepolisian Negara 1947-1949 [hereafter KepNeg], no. 514, Arsip Nasional Republik Indonesia [hereafter ANRI], Jakarta.

28 As the Pancasila were never modified, this became a common exercise for Muslim intellectuals and scholars in the early 1950s.

29 Noer, 'Masjumi: Its organization', pp. 70-5.

30 'Masjoemi, toelang poenggoeng Republik Indonesia', *al-Djihad* no. 26, 28 February 1946. This was also worryingly reported by Dutch sources; see *ANP-Aneta Bulletin*, 'Kentering in de Masjoemi in Indische [archipel]', Documentatie dienst van ANP-Aneta 10 October-27 December 1946, pp. 423-7.

responsible for their safety and feels obligated to provide them with an Indonesian state based on Islam.[31]

The idea that the 1945 constitution was temporary was also supported by the belief that elections to form a new constitutional assembly (*konstituante*) would be held soon after the Dutch left the country. This new text, then, had to be drafted following 'the desires of the Islamic community'. It is on these foundations that Masyumi intended to re-open the debate with the secular nationalists whilst at the same time giving its support to Soekarno. Masyumi, in fact, endorsed Soekarno's representative-democratic system, and it based its political opposition on the conviction that the party's large base would – given an electoral opportunity – affirm its political standing and bring forward the necessary changes to establish the Islamic state.

Although Kartosuwiryo's Garut speech, *Haloean politik Islam*, delivered in June 1946, affirmed mainstream Masyumi policies, his name did not appear among the party's executives at a meeting held in Yogyakarta on 7 November 1946,[32] perhaps anticipating the fracture with the party board that would ensue later in 1947.

Kartosuwiryo's Haloean politik Islam

The Dutch invasion of Java in July 1947 transformed the Priangan into a theatre for total warfare and would push Kartosuwiryo to abandon formal politics. But in mid 1946 he was still participating in the political process in the rank and file of Masyumi, upholding the party's commitment to parliamentary struggle, cooperation and unity. Kartosuwiryo's continuing dedication to the cause was best expressed in a speech he delivered in July 1946 in Garut, later printed by the Dewan Penerangan Masyumi Daerah Priangan (Priangan regional Masyumi Information Office).[33]

After considering the differences between Western and Islamic politics, the pamphlet then focuses on the strategy the *ummah* should follow to ensure the attainment of God's will on earth (the *dar al-Islam*) and in the afterlife (the *dar al-salam*) in the specific historical context of Indonesia's struggle for independence. Following

31 'Gemeene Be(e)st kita sabil! Masjoemi haroes djadi Chalifah di Indonesia', *al-Djihad* no. 26, 28 February 1946. The congress was held in Solo, on 13 and 14 February 1946.

32 Soekiman, Masjkoer, Zainoel Arifin, Djojomartono, K.H. Abdoel Wahab, Oesman, Mawardi, Soedjono and Dahlan. *al-Djihad*, 09 November 1946, appended in 'Regerings Voorlichtingsdienst, Government Information Service, D.N. 718', [1946], APG no. 997, NA.

33 Kartosuwiryo, *Haloean politik Islam* (Garut: Dewan Penerangan Masjoemi, 1946).

a line of thought he had first set out in the late 1920s, Kartosuwiryo insisted that Islam was equally concerned with worldly and eternal salvation, and that only through the establishment of a *dar al-Islam* could Muslims be guaranteed salvation and admission to the *dar al-salam.*

The political efforts of the Indonesian *ummah* were aimed at the establishment of an Indonesian republic based on Islam, in which the government guaranteed the implementation of sharia law in its widest and most complete formulation. Grounding the government in sharia law would allow Indonesia's Muslims to pursue their obligations and would guarantee all Indonesians their freedom from slavery.

Compared with the ideas contained in Kartosuwiryo's writings through the 1920s-1930s, there is nothing new in his describing active participation in the effort to free Indonesia from foreign imperialists as a 'religious duty'. Surely, though, some change in attitude is detectable, as he now encouraged the formation of a unitary front, and supported the parliamentary avenue towards establishing an Islamic state. Conscious of the fact that so many skilled political parties were angling for primacy in the race to control the national government of the soon-to-be independent state, Kartosuwiryo argued that constructive cooperation was the only defence Indonesia had against civil war. Kartosuwiryo realized that the *ummah* would have much competition in this race, and that it was certainly possible that communism, socialism or nationalism would win. As such, the *ummah* should strive to build a new world in full conformity with the Qur'an – a *dunia Islam* or *dar al-Islam.* He heavily condemned fanaticism, as it 'easily threatens the unity of the nation (*persatuan bangsa*) and the success of the struggle, causing splits and betrayals unwished for at a time when all citizens ought to feel compelled to join in the National Revolution'.

Kartosuwiryo preached the necessity of having 'ideology' to work hand in hand with 'reality'. For Kartosuwiryo, 'ideology' dictated the goals of the effort, while 'reality' determined its means in accordance with the current time and society:

> An ideologically driven fighter never stops in his effort to reach and achieve his ideal, maybe once he will appear as running back, jumping right or left, flying west or east because the conditions and reality of society do not allow for anything else, but [...] in his eyes and heart he never left his ideology.[34]

34 Kartosuwiryo, *Haloean politik Islam*, p. 12.

In this understanding, the national revolution was a struggle that had to begin inside individual persons before it could move to broader communal and societal contexts on the road to national independence; this was true for Kartosuwiryo, whether the revolution were to be pursued by diplomacy or by weapons. No portion of Indonesia's population was relieved from its duty and responsibility to defend the country and build national sovereignty. But the task that rested solely on the Muslims was the social revolution: a struggle aimed at deconstructing colonialism from within society, thereby effecting a change on the *ummah* itself. The broader social revolution, however, could only be carried out by those who had already succeeded in the revolution at the individual level and who had fully conformed their souls to Islam.

To Kartosuwiryo, both the national and social revolutions – now explicitly defined as *al-jihad al-asghar* and *al-jihad al-akbar*, respectively – were necessary to eradicate colonialism by acting on external (state and government) and internal (citizens' souls) objects of foreign domination. As stated above, modernists and traditionalists developed different strategies to achieve an Islamic state, and Kartosuwiryo concluded that in the current context it would be inappropriate to adhere to dogmatic divisions between social and national revolutions. He suggested instead that the revolutions should be pursued at the same time. Because ensuring *de facto* and *de jure* independence was an urgent goal, Kartosuwiryo argued that initially a stronger emphasis was to be placed on the national struggle: the *ummah* would concentrate its efforts on supporting the physical revolution, while delegating the social revolution to the Islamic leadership. Only once the foreign oppressor had left and Indonesia was free would the rest of the population be involved at the social level.

After independence, the establishment of an Indonesian state based on Islam could be achieved in either a top-down or a bottom-up fashion, depending on the *ummah*'s level of representation in, and influence on, national governing bodies. In the first scenario, even though the executive bodies were not dominated by Muslims, those involved in the legislature would have the duty to comply with Islamic regulations, and thus would advance the formalization of an Islamic government. Because of this possible discrepancy between the legislative and the executive bodies, Kartosuwiryo argued in favour of conducting military and political courses for the *ummah* to ensure a high level of awareness and education at the grassroots level. He also invoked unity and cooperation between *ulama* and intellectuals, as the former knew the sharia and the latter the rules of government.

In case this attempt to coordinate *hukum*, *hakim* and *mahkum* (law, judge and sentence) at the national level failed, Kartosuwiryo advanced an alternative strategy: the *ummah*, still responsible for the implementation of Islamic law at the personal level, would create its own *dar al-Islam* (note the similarity with the 1938 MIAI speech). Seen as part and parcel of the individual revolution, the involvement of the *ummah* in legal matters was the first step towards an Islamic social revolution, also called an Islamic people's revolution. It is this social dimension of the *ummah*'s organization and mobilization that Kartosuwiryo had in mind when he established the Darul Islam in 1948.

TROOP POLARIZATION IN WEST JAVA: REPUBLICAN ARMY AND ISLAMIC MILITIAS FROM THE BRITISH LANDING TO THE RENVILLE AGREEMENT

While the leaders of the nationalist movement in Jakarta were busy with diplomatic talks, Bandung and the Priangan were gradually becoming the centres of a power struggle for regional control. In May 1946 the Republican government began integrating and rationalizing irregular troops, with the goal of creating a unified army. In the following paragraphs I lay out the premises of this attempt at integration in West Java and the impact of this political decision on the relations between regular soldiers and the Islamic militias. Most skirmishes resulted from the scarcity of weapons; the Islamic militias' disapproval of Republican soldiers' unwillingness to fight; and the Republican soldiers' grudges against the popular support enjoyed by the Islamic militias.

This delicate balance between Republican and Islamic soldiers was further upset by the Dutch invasion of West Java in July 1947. Republican troops and Islamic militias scattered across the Priangan, and as Masyumi was gaining increased footing in the territory, the military confrontation became politicized, with the Republic accusing Masyumi of attempting to become a substitute government. It is in this context that Republican and Islamic troops clashed in Blubur Limbangan and that Kartosuwiryo began the re-structuring of the provincial branch of Masyumi under the name of Darul Islam.

Seeking a structure

The 3rd Division of the TKR (later to become the Siliwangi Division of Tentara Negara Indonesia, TNI) was initially stationed in

Tasikmalaya under the leadership of Aroedji Kartawinata (a former PSII cadre; see Chapter 1), but in late October 1945 – just before its command was transferred to Nasution – the division was moved to Malangbong for unspecified 'political priorities'.[35] Militias operating in the Bandung area had formed the Markas Dewan Pimpinan Perdjoeangan (MDPP, Resistance Leadership Council Headquarter) under the leadership of Soetoko (from Pesindo) and Kamran (Hizboellah leader and future chief of the Tentara Islam Indonesia, TII) as early as January 1946, with the goal of countering the impact of Nasution's Republican troops.[36]

Having broader authority than any of the militia leaders, Nasution began to disarm the MDPP within a month of its formation. He incorporated its soldiers into the TKR and expanded the authority of his own army division. But Nasution did so without considering that the MDPP had been formed with the specific intention of opposing the influence of Republican troops across the region. By the end of February, Kamran and Soetoko formed another coordinating body that was politically neutral and aimed at the establishment of Indonesia's independence. The Majelis Persatoean Perdjoeangan Priangan or Markas Pimpinan Perdjoeangan Priangan (MPPP, Priangan Fighting Unity Council or Leadership Centre) was stationed in Bale Endah, near Ciparay, the most advanced position Indonesian troops had managed to occupy in their struggle for regional defence.[37]

In the meantime, British troops had begun their operation to bring Java under control on behalf of the SEAC. After a few months of long-distance attacks, on 20 March 1946 the 15th Indian Corps of the British artillery heavily attacked the Bandung headquarters of the Tentara Republik Indonesia (TRI, Army of the Indonesian Republic), a group composed largely of Nasution's Siliwangi

35 Lukman Madewa, *Esa hilang dua terbilang: Album kenangan Kodam 6/Siliwangi 1946-1977* (Bandung: Kodam 6, 1977), p. 24.

36 The MDPP was formed by Pesindo, Hizboellah, Sabilillah, Pemuda Indonesia Maluku, Barisan Banteng and Kebaktian Rakyat Indonesia Sulawesi (Horikoshi, 'The Dar-ul-Islam movement', p. 66) and Barisan Pemberontak Rakyat Indonesia (BPRI), Angkatan Pemuda Indonesia (API), Barisan Merah Putih, Lasjkar Wanita Indonesia (Lasjwi) (Usman Jauhari, 'Peranan Hizboellah-Sabilillah', p. 43. John R.W. Smail, *Bandung in the early revolution 1945-1946: A study in the social history of the Indonesian revolution* (Ithaca, NY: Department of Asian Studies Cornell University, 1964) offers a detailed investigation of the events that occurred in Bandung between 1945 and 1946 based on Indonesian sources, Siliwangi's military publications and the newspaper *Mederka*. Madewa, *Esa hilang dua terbilang*, p. 24. refers to MDPP as Markas Daerah Perjuangan Pertahanan Priangan.

37 Smail, *Bandung in the early revolution*, pp. 129-30, 143-5; Dinas Sedjarah Kodam VI Siliwangi, *Siliwangi dari masa ke masa* (Jakarta: Fakta Mahjuma, 1968), p. 505; the second name, 'Leadership Centre', is used in Jauhari, 'Peranan Hizboellah-Sabilillah', p. 42.

soldiers.[38] Following these attacks, both Siliwangi troops and the MPPP were forced to abandon their positions, allowing the Allies to take control of the city. The MPPP established its new headquarters in East Priangan, which, along with Cirebon, were the only areas controlled by the Republic.

Following a British ultimatum, by the morning of 25 March Nasution had led his TRI division out of Bandung and into Garut. But he added that he 'could not be responsible for extremist elements'.[39] This note is quite significant, as it shows that the level of friction between Nasution and the militias was high, as was his frustration over his inability to control them. The colonel was referring to Hizboellah, Sabilillah and Pesindo militias, which he had unsuccessfully tried to incorporate into his own division for several months. Not only were these militias generally more skilled than the majority of his regular troops, but - and more significantly - Nasution was not confident his troops could successfully face the Dutch by themselves, as suggested by Robert Cribb.[40]

The MDPP, too, had moved to Garut, but it had changed its name to become the Resimen Tentara Perdjoeangan (RTP, Fighting Army Regiment), under the exclusive leadership of Soetoko. Within weeks, the RTP was placed under Nasution's Siliwangi Division's command. Also in May 1946, one of its five battalions, composed only of Hizboellah and Sabilillah soldiers and possibly having its origins under Kamran's command, now came under the Command of Major Hoeseinsjah.[41] This regiment had been able to maintain independence of action for a full year, but by May 1947

38 On 5 October 1945 the president of the Indonesian Republic issued a statement for the formation of the Tentara Keamanan Rakyat; this was transformed once again into the Tentara Keselamatan Rakyat on 7 January 1946 and finally into the Tentara Republik Indonesia on 24 January of the same year. See Jauhari, 'Peranan Hizboellah-Sabilillah', p. 50. Jakarta and Bandung had been occupied by the 7th December Division on 27 August 1946; see MD, AS nos. 2220-2225, NA. For details of British troops movements and the substitution of British troops with Dutch soldiers in Java and Sumatra, see 'The Allied occupation of the Netherlands East Indies, September 1945-November 1946', War Office [hereafter WO] 203/2681; 'War Diaries of the 23rd Indian Division in Java, October 1945 to November 1946', WO 203/6159; 'War Diaries of the 15th Indian Corps January-September 1946', Foreign Office [FO 371/9791]; National Archives of the United Kingdom, Kew [hereafter NAUK].

39 'War Diary, GS Branch, HQ 15 Indian Corps, summary of main events for March 1946', FO 371/9791, NAUK; Madewa, *Esa hilang dua terbilang*, p. 24.

40 Horikoshi, 'The Dar-ul-Islam movement', p. 67; Robert Cribb, *Gangsters and revolutionaries: The Jakarta people's militia and the Indonesian revolution 1945-49*, Southeast Asia Publications Series (Sydney: Allen & Unwin, 1991), pp. 163-6.

41 Jauhari, 'Peranan Hizboellah-Sabilillah', pp. 46, 53. The other battalions were composed of BPRI/*Garuda Hitam* under Major Riva'i, Pesindo/*Taruma Jaya* under Major Sudarman and the Bat. Gabungan under Major Pellupessy.

it was forced to become the 9th Regiment of the 2nd Brigade of Nasution's Siliwangi Division.[42]

Notwithstanding the Republican government's efforts to incorporate irregular militias into the national army, the unification of Siliwangi, Hizboellah and Sabilillah troops was far from happening in reality. The integration and rationalization of irregular militias that began in May 1946 had yet to be achieved by the end of 1947 thanks to widespread tensions and major conflicts.[43] The order for Hizboellah and Sabilillah troops to merge into the TNI National Army was ratified by Soekarno on 2 January 1948 together with the Renville Agreement, but most of the Islamic militias refused to follow these orders and continued to act as separate armies.

A Pasoendan police report, dated October 1948, regarding the arrest of a former Hizboellah soldier, and later TII lieutenant, exemplifies the problems relating to the integration of Islamic militias into the national army: Doendoeng, originally from the Garut area, had been part of the Japanese Peta, and after the capitulation he had chosen to join Hizboellah to comply with what he felt was his religious duty. During the rationalization process, Doendoeng was incorporated in Hoeseinsjah's battalion and deployed in Cibatu. Six months later he became a TRI lieutenant, soon to be transferred to the Imam Bondjol battalion of the TNI. All this happened despite his open refusal to join the secular Republican forces. He eventually deserted the TNI and again joined Hizboellah when the Islamic militias refused to withdraw to Central Java in January 1948, thus becoming a member of the TII.[44]

Besides the tensions related to individual soldiers' allegiances, frequent skirmishes between Islamic and Republican troops were taking place across the whole region, as the troops were becoming increasingly polarized. The root of these clashes was Hizboellah and Sabilillah's frustration at seeing that TNI troops were better armed but unwilling to fight, as they often abandoned the battlefield, leaving Hizboellah and Sabilillah to face the Dutch. As highlighted in a 1946 police report, when faced with advancing NICA troops, the TNI soldiers stationed in Cibeber retreated, even leaving their weapons behind. Since Hizboellah and Sabilillah were in the area, they picked up the carbines and guns that had belonged to Republican troops and then resoundingly defeated the Dutch.

42 Madewa, *Esa hilang dua terbilang*, p. 25.

43 Abdul Haris Nasution, *Sekitar perang kemerdekaan Indonesia*, vol. 6 (Bandung: Angkasa, 1978), p. 474.

44 'Proces-Verbaal Doedoeng alias Soenardja, Kementerian Dalam Negeri Negara Pasoendan Afdeeling Politie', 16 October 1948, AABRI DI.

Yet the compiler notes that, on many occasions, retreating TNI soldiers refused to hand their weapons over to Masyumi troops, preferring instead to destroy them as a precaution, since Islamic militias were being treated as enemies.[45]

These clashes increased in frequency and intensity throughout 1946 and 1947, especially after the Dutch invaded West Java in July 1947, and thus mirrored the political conflict between Masyumi and Soekarno's Republican government (discussed below).

The Linggadjati Agreement and the Dutch invasion: Implications for national politics

The Republicans' readiness to cooperate with the Dutch soon had serious consequences, as several nationalists turned their backs on Soekarno, Sjahrir and their contingencies. The single event that most upset the fragile balance within the anti-colonial movement was the Linggadjati Agreement, signed by Van Mook and the Indonesian Prime Minister, Soetan Sjahrir, in November 1946. Though KNIP eventually ratified it in 1947, the agreement was strongly opposed by Islamic nationalists. The treaty established a ceasefire and called for the formation of a federative United States of Indonesia (with Java, Madura and Sumatra included *de facto* in Soekarno's Republik Indonesia in Yogyakarta). The federation would be part of the Netherlands-Indonesian Union and under the authority of the Dutch Queen.

The pro-independence front was deeply fragmented among the Islamic, socialist and Soekarnoist factions. However, as the Dutch considered Soekarno, Hatta and Sjahrir to be representative of the movement as a whole, Masyumi was granted less political space than might have been expected from its popular support.[46]

At the end of 1946 Masyumi openly called for armed opposition against a Republican government that pursued overtly accommodationist policies. As announced in a letter sent to all Masyumi branches and published in *al-Djihad*, Wahid Hasjim, Soekiman and Zainal Arifin proclaimed their intention to 'bring down the Indonesian government with arms'.[47]

45 'Laporan tentang Masjoemi dengan Tentara, Kepala Bagian Penjelidik Republik Indonesia Kantor Polisi Soekaboemi', 20 August 1946, AAS no. 2746, NA.

46 Kahin, *Nationalism and revolution*, pp. 196 onwards; Ricklefs, *A history*, pp. 224-5. For a complete analysis of the Federal State, see A. Arthur Schiller, *The formation of federal Indonesia, 1945-1949* (The Hague: Van Hoeve, 1955).

47 'Rapat raksasa Banteng R.I. di Malang, Kementrian Pertahanan Oeroesan A.L.R.I. Bag. C Poesat Jogjakarta', 7 January 1947, KemPert no. 188, ANRI.

Under such pressure, Sjahrir was forced to resign and Soekarno, to form a new cabinet. In June and July 1947 Soekiman, who had been included in the four-man team in charge of appointing new ministers, demanded leadership of the cabinet and several key ministries for the Islamic party. Soekarno refused to accommodate these demands, and Masyumi withdrew from the cabinet, causing a stalemate only solved in November with the formation of yet another cabinet.[48]

In the meantime, Kartosuwiryo had been invited to represent PSII in the First Amir Sjarifoeddin Cabinet as junior Vice-Minister of Defence. However, while his name was included on the official lists drafted on 3-4 July, as well as on the list published by the press, he never accepted the position.[49] First, Soekiman, Salim, Kartosuwiryo and Wondoamiseno had not yet completed their attempts to revive the Partai Sarekat Islam Indonesia, thus leaving their relationship with Masyumi undefined. Second, Masyumi was not participating in the cabinet.[50] Third, Sjarifuddin's cabinet was strongly sympathetic to socialist and communist policies, which did not go down well with Kartosuwiryo.[51] Finally, I would like to suggest that because the Dutch invasion of July 1947 had led to the physical and political isolation of West Java, Kartosuwiryo's absence from the cabinet was connected with his difficulties (and lack of interest) in joining the centre of parliamentary power. Announcing that he 'had not yet become involved with the PSII and still felt committed to Masyumi', Kartosuwiryo eventually declined Soekarno's and Sjarifuddin's offer.[52]

Despite the diplomatic achievements and a climate of relative peace –acknowledged also by the British envoy to Java – on 20 July 1947 the Dutch launched their first military campaign on Republican territory, with the intention of occupying West Java, Madura and Sumatra.[53] The invading Dutch forces expanded from Bandung

48 Noer, 'Masjumi: Its organization', pp. 105-7.

49 'Het Republikeinsche Kabinet Sjarifuddin, IV Kabinet, 3 Juli 1947', APG no. 731, NA; 'Kabinet Sjarifuddin Ve Kabinet (4 Juli 1947-23 Jan 1948)', APG no. 731, NA; 'Kabinet – Sjarifuddin Ve Kabinet (na wijziging op 11-11-1947)', APG no. 731, NA; 'Soesoenan kabinet baroe', *Merdeka*, 4 July 1947.

50 'Partai Sarekat Islam Indonesia', 19 Mei 1947, KemPert no. 1054, ANRI.

51 'Proces-verbaal van verhoor van R. Didi b.Uhap al.Tatang Bachtiar, Onderhoofd van het Ministerie van Voorlichting van de Negara Islam Indonesia (NII); Parket van den Procureur-Generaal bij den Pengadilan Tinggi van de Negara Pasundan te Bandoeng', 26 September 1949, AAS no. 2755, NA; and Dinas Sejarah TNI, *Penumpasan pemberontakan D.I./T.I.I.*, p. 59. This report of the arrest of a Darul Islam member in 1948 mentions that Kartosuwiryo had refused to join the Sjarifuddin cabinet because it was communist. As this might represent one aspect of the problem, it should also be noted that some anti-communist politicians, including Haji Agoes Salim, joined this cabinet in an effort to bring Indonesia out of its stalemate and to obtain full independence.

52 'Kartosuwiryo keberatan', *Merdeka*, 8 July 1947.

53 'Bataljion genietroepen oorlogsdagboek nr B149/101.34', MD: AS no. 2231, NA.

across north-eastern West Java in three directions (east, south-east and south-west), pushing Indonesian soldiers and militias south of Purwakarta, Subang, Sumedang and Majalengka.[54]

Regardless of the fact that a United Nations-sponsored cease-fire had been signed in August, the consequences of the invasion were strongly felt in the months to come. On 23 September Netherlands' Prime Minister, Louis Beel, declared that one of the achievements of the *politioneele actie* ('police action'), as the Dutch called it, had been 'the creation of better conditions for the execution of the political plan of reconstruction laid down in the Linggadjati Agreement'. In fact, Indonesian sources reported that consequent to the invasion, 'All the militias ha[d] left [their headquarters] to reach the various areas of West Java to carry out, at their best, an ideological struggle, sabotage and guerrilla actions.' Rather than supporting Beel's rationale,[55] such comments showed the irreparable political damage caused by the aggression.

Consequences for West Java

Dutch troops first arrived in West Java in March 1947 to relieve the British in Cianjur, but connections between the western province and the rest of the island were not severed until early July.[56]

As the Dutch entered Cirebon on 21 July, the Republican police were forced to move south to Ciwaru. When in 1948 the area officially came under Dutch control, the police force was dissolved and its agents offered the opportunity to work for the occupying forces.[57] This offer, however, was hardly an attractive choice, as it was in fact the only alternative to a forced withdrawal to Yogyakarta or final dismissal from the force. Facing two unsatisfactory options, several officers in Cimahi and Indramayu fled to other villages or to the mountains to avoid forced co-optation in the Dutch ranks.[58]

54 'Laporan keadaan Djawa Barat', 28 July 1947, KemPert no. 1290, ANRI.

55 'Laporan keadaan Djawa Barat', 28 July 1947, KemPert no. 1290, ANRI. Beel's comment in 'Political reconstruction in the Netherlands East Indies, Consul-General Shepherd to Mr. Bevin, Batavia, 22 October 1947', p. 79, FO 480/1, NAUK.

56 'Berita atjara tentang pelaporan R.Legino pembentoe Inspectour Polisian I dari Bandung, RS Joedoprawiro Insp.Polisi II', 30 March 1948, KepNeg no. 526, ANRI. The C division of the 7th December Brigade relieved the British W Brigade in Cianjur.

57 'Berita atjara tentang pelaporan R. Legino', 30 March 1948, and 'Berita atjara tentang Djemino A.P. kl.I dari kantor Kepolisian Keresidenan Cirebon, RS Joedoprawiro Insp.Polisi II', 24 March 1948, KepNeg no. 526, ANRI.

58 'Laporan perdjalanan anggauta Polisi Tjimahi A.P. Kl. I Selam CS dari daerah pendudukan kedaerah Republiek, Mohamad Gondosoebroto', 2 March 1948, KepNeg no. 534, ANRI; 'Berita atjara tentang Ngadiran pegawai Polisi Negara dari Indramaju', 14 April 1948, KepNeg no. 526, ANRI.

The Republican police from Bandung, having already been displaced to Ciparay since March 1946, were on 28 July again forced to move, this time to Bongkor (north of Garut), as the Dutch occupied Majalaya and Ciparay. The fall of Leles and Garut in early August caused them to move further to Wanaraja, whilst the Priangan police (usually stationed in Garut) sought refuge in the surrounding mountains, but only after being ordered to destroy all high-rise buildings they encountered en route.[59] As the Dutch advance from Tasikmalaya had compromised their retreat to Cilawu, the Priangan police did not reach Mount Cikurai until late September, where they hid until Dutch troops found them in mid November 1947.[60]

By now military tensions in West Java had become distributed among the invading Dutch troops, regular Republican Siliwangi soldiers, and those splinters of Sabilillah and Hizboellah militias that had refused to merge with the Republican Army. Despite their rapid expansion, the Dutch lacked territorial control beyond the Cirebon residency. The Republicans had equally limited control, as they ruled only over Liangjulang (Kadipaten). It was Masyumi and its militias that controlled most of the region, with strongholds in the Indramayu and Majalengka regions.[61]

In the Priangan, Masyumi was gradually positioning itself as – and assuming the functions of – a local independent government, attracting the attention of the Dutch resident Van der Harst, as well as of Tasikmalaya's chief of police, Said Soerianatanegara.[62] Masyumi implemented a taxation system in the areas around Indihiang, Mount Cupu and Cisayong in order to buy weapons and supplies for its troops. In addition, the Islamic militias were in the habit of bartering food supplies with starving TNI soldiers in exchange for carbines and guns, as shortages of weapons were occurring across the region.[63]

According to Soerianatanegara, Masyumi's army (namely, Sabilillah and Hizboellah) had as a final goal the establishment of a

59 'Berita atjara tentang pelaporan Soekami Commissaris Polisi dari Bandung, RS Joedoprawiro Insp.Polisi II', 27 March 1948, KepNeg no. 526, ANRI; 'Laporan, Effendi Ardipradja', 24 February 1948, KepNeg no. 534, ANRI.

60 'Laporan, Doelkarnaen', 16 February 1948, KepNeg no. 526, ANRI.

61 'Laporan rahasia Kepolisian Keresidenan Tjirebon', 14 November 1947, Arsip Kabinet Presiden 1950-1959 [hereafter KabPres], no. 1926, ANRI.

62 'Perihal politieke situasi, Kantor Polisi Tasikmalaya', 9 December 1947, KepNeg no. 495, ANRI.

63 'Laporan tentang keadaan didaerah Tasikmalaya Utara, Kantor Polisi Tasikmalaya', 23 December 1947, and 'Perihal keadaan di Tasikmalaya, Kantor Polisi Tasikmalaya', 12 December 1947, KepNeg no. 495, ANRI; 'Politiek-Economisch Verslag betreffende de Residentie Priangan over de maand November 1947, AMK: Rapportage Indonesië 1945-1950 [hereafter RI], no. 327, NA.

'New State' (*Negara Baru*) that would be under the patronage of the Islamic party: 'Until the government comes under Masyumi leadership, there will be no order.'[64]

The Limbangan incident and the nature of the antagonism among Islamic, Republican and Dutch troops

Continuing the pattern already established in 1946, between September and December 1947 Islamic militias and regular Siliwangi soldiers clashed often in their quest for weapons[65] and in reaction to the movements of Dutch troops.[66] As the ceasefire agreement did not require them to withdraw from the positions occupied during their invasion, Dutch troops were stationed all along the line connecting Bandung, Sumedang, Majalengka and Linggadjati.

In September, Endang, the Sabilillah leader in Blubur Limbangan (a village near Cicalengka, Sumedang), had organized a propaganda meeting in Cibuleg. During his speech at the meeting, Endang made some negative comments about the Indonesian Republic, arguing that Sabilillah had to channel its forces towards demolishing the Republic, thereby reinforcing Masyumi's statement made in December 1946. Such comments quickly altered the spirits of some TNI soldiers in Sentot's battalion, who also happened to be attending the meeting, and who felt threatened and offended. Endang and eight of his assistants were thus captured, and the Republican officers agreed that Endang and two of his aides had to be killed under the accuse of treason. The villagers witnessing the events became convinced of the gravity of Endang's statements, agreed on the punishment, apologized for participating at the Sabilillah meeting and swore allegiance to the Republic.[67]

At the end of the month, Dutch troops attacked the village of Blubur Limbangan and occupied it. Coincidentally, the Sabilillah group led by Endang's brother was also in the area. To avenge the execution of his brother, Wiganda struck an agreement with the Dutch. Ten days later, several Siliwangi soldiers deployed in the Garut area were summoned to Blubur Limbangan to receive orders. Soon after their arrival, they were made aware that the

64 'Laporan tentang keadaan didaerah Tasikmalaya Utara', 23 December 1947, KepNeg no. 495, ANRI.

65 'Politiek-Economisch Verslag betreffende de Residentie Priangan over de periode 1 tot en met 15 September 1947', AMK: RI, no. 327, NA.

66 'Politiek Economisch Verslag betreffende de Residentie Priangan over de maand October 1947', AMK: RI, no. 327, NA.

67 '[untitled] folio 7 no. 03409', AABRI DI.

Dutch were about to attack, and to limit the damage inflicted on the civilian population, the TNI dispersed. That same night, the weapons of a local Sabilillah battalion were seized, and two men were found dead. As feelings on the Endang case were still heated, the Sabilillah joined forces with the Dutch troops to capture the Siliwangi officer in charge.

By the time the skirmishes were over, around 350 Masyumi/ Sabilillah members had been arrested in the neighbouring village of Baeud, and the Sabilillah soldiers who had managed to escape joined the Dutch troops. A few days later, a Dutch-Sabilillah patrol of 450 men organized a kidnapping operation in Baeud, which ended in the death of all those captured. The victims, however, were not Siliwangi soldiers, but included Socialist Party members, a Banteng member, a man from the regional inspectorate of Limbangan, civil servants and employees of the Ministry of Forestry.

According to TII lieutenant Syarif Hidayat, in the beginning the Hizboellah were fighting against the Dutch 'colonialists' in support of Soekarno's August 1945 Proclamation. On these grounds, they were incorporated in the Imam Bonjol Battalion of the Republic's TNI. However, Syarif Hidayat vividly recollects TNI's attacks against Hizboellah and Sabilillah soldiers in the Garut and Sumedang areas, and in particular how the events surrounding the killing of Endang had diminished the trust of former Islamic militias in the TNI and the other agencies of the Republic. Inevitably, within a couple of months the chain of events and retaliations spiraled out of control, and clashes spread to Leuwingoong, Malangbong, Pagerageung, Gunung Cupu and the area surrounding Sumedang.[68]

The primary aim of Siliwangi, Sabilillah and Hizboellah troops was the annihilation of colonial power in the archipelago. It is undeniable, though, that friction between Republican and Islamic troops, as well as between secular and religious nationalists, played an important role in directing actions and policies for the next two decades. When in 1962 the Siliwangi Division was conducting sweeps in West Java to cleanse the area of DI-TII soldiers, several of those captured would look back at Blubur Limbangan as the event that had initially set off the antagonism between Islamic and Republican troops. As such, this incident helps us understand how much the dynamics on the ground were dictated by opportunity and necessity, rather than ideology – the latter a concern only the leaders could afford.

68 '[untitled] folio 7 no. 03409', AABRI DI.

West Java on the eve of the Renville Agreement

By the end of 1947 the police had singled out Sabilillah troops in Pagerageung and Tasikmalaya as the most fanatic,[69] and had identified Pagerageung as their military headquarters and Sukawening as their propaganda and political hub. This was the same village where Kartosuwiryo was organizing the party's activities, and Oni coordinated the activities of the Sabilillah.[70]

The first step towards Masyumi's 'New State', was undertaken by the proclamation of a 'Sabilillah Safety Zone' (Sabilillah Keamanan Daerah) on 18 December by a Sabilillah unit which had to relocate to Rancabungur (Indihiang) after Dutch attacks on the Sukawening centre had caused the scattering of Islamic militias across the region.[71] This initiative further reinforced the Republican government's impression that in the Priangan the population did not recognize Republican authority and instead supported Masyumi.

In theory the Republican authority and Masyumi should not have been in competition with each other. However, the tensions arising from the Republic's negotiations with the Dutch and Masyumi's commitment to building an Islamic state inevitably resulted in them setting their agendas on separate registers. Soerianatanegara went as far as accusing the Islamic party of challenging the Republic at the political and military levels, as Masyumi had been openly discrediting TNI troops whilst praising the bravery of Hizboellah and Sabilillah. Civilians reportedly trusted the Islamic militias more than TNI troops, as it appears that the latter often ran away from combat situations with Dutch soldiers, leaving the fighting to the Islamic militias. Soerianatanegara's explanation was that as civilians were generally more sympathetic to religious militias, these militias were better fed and better armed than the Republic's.[72]

The rise of Islamic politics in the Priangan can only be understood in the context of the complex nature of religious and political authority at the time, as explored in Chapter 1. But Sarekat Islam's and Masyumi's political activism and commitment to the formation of a politically conscious *ummah* was a key catalyst for

69 'Perihal keadaan di Tasikmalaya', 12 December 1947, KepNeg no. 495, ANRI.

70 'Laporan tentang keadaan didaerah Tasikmalaya Utara', 23 December 1947, KepNeg no. 495, ANRI.

71 'Perihal keadaan di Tasikmalaya', 12 December 1947, KepNeg no. 495, ANRI.

72 'Laporan tentang keadaan didaerah Tasikmalaya Utara', 23 December 1947, KepNeg no. 495, ANRI.

popular support and engagement, besides traditional patterns of authority.[73]

According to a Ministry of Defence survey, in the Priangan only the members of Masyumi had a full understanding of the current political situation – here defined as 'total war' – and clear expectations for the path ahead, as they were awaiting the call for *perang sabil* that would bring Indonesia to independence.[74] It is in this ideological, military, political and social context that Kartosuwiryo carried out the transformation of Masyumi's West Java division into the Darul Islam movement.

IDEOLOGICAL RADICALIZATION: CALLING FOR HOLY WAR

The physical isolation of West Java from Republican territories caused by the Dutch invasion in July 1947 laid the foundations for the region's divergent political path to independence, a phenomenon further strengthened by the Renville Agreement. The increasingly ideological characterization of the antagonism between the Republic in Yogyakarta and West Java's regional politics paralleled the polarization of troops on the ground. In the wake of previous Masyumi calls for holy war against the Dutch, in mid August 1947 Kartosuwiryo yet again invoked *perang sabil* for Muslims in West Java. This call was followed in late September by a national call for *jihad fi-sabilillah* proclaimed by the central branch of Masyumi.

Kartosuwiryo's Perang sabil

Marking a dramatic change from his *Haloean politik Islam* speech, in *Perang sabil* Kartosuwiryo called upon 'the *ummat Islam* that feels it a duty to establish a *dar al-Islam* and fully implement *hukum Islam*' to rise up against all enemies of religion and the state, the Dutch (*Fir'aun Belanda*), its NICA employees and Indonesian spies.

73 The police reported that local Masyumi leaders were trying to strengthen their membership's approval by holding public and closed meetings to reinforce the attendants' knowledge of Islam. See 'Laporan tentang keadaan didaerah Karesidenan Priangan, Kantor Kepolisian Karesidenan Priangan', received on 28 February 1948, KepNeg no. 495, ANRI.

74 'Kementerian Pertahanan bagian Perantara Warta dan Publikasi, Ichtisar Laporan no. 5, Daerah Priangan, so'al Totalitaire Oorlog', November 1947, KemPert no. 1073, ANRI. According to this report, members of Pesindo, PPN, PPI and the teachers' organization had very little consciousness of the current situation, whilst members of the socialist and nationalist (PNI) parties and a number of civil servants were mostly aware of the situation but did not understand its implications and consequences.

Unity and cooperation were no longer under consideration, the secular nationalists were still entertaining diplomatic relations with the aggressive Dutch, and Republican elements were not quite friends and not quite foes. True 'friends of the struggle' were those who shared the goal of a national revolution aimed at establishing an Indonesian state free from colonial domination, regardless of their religious beliefs or political inclinations.

Kartosuwiryo affirmed his hopes that the Indonesian Republic would conform to Islamic ideology in order that it could be part of the *dar al-Islam* (or *dunia Islam*) in the form of an Islamic state implementing Islamic laws among its citizens, and thus ensuring their worldly and eternal salvation. Yet he was still open to the possibility that, following the revolution, national authority could be in the hands of other political groups that were representative of whichever ideology the population supported in larger numbers.[75]

Continuing to draw parallels with Muhammad's struggle, Kartosuwiryo associated the Dutch with the Quraysh, Soekarno with the Banu Bakr tribe, and the Linggadjati Agreement with the treaty of Hudaibiyah (628 CE).[76] In such a framework, the breach of the Hudaibiyah treaty, Muhammad's attack on Mecca and the *ummah*'s subsequent victory over the polytheistic Arab tribes became the key to interpreting the breach of Linggadjati as an opportunity that legitimized the establishment of a fully sovereign and independent Islamic state. This Negara Islam Indonesia would result from the *ummah*'s commitment to taking up arms in a *perang sabil*, as *jihad* represented the *ummah*'s effort to build and defend its state and religion.

Recognizing the mixed origins of the term *perang sabil*, Kartosuwiryo underlined how the Indonesian word *perang* was attached to the Arabic *sabil* 'path, way' as the shortened version of *fi-sabil-illah*, 'on the path of God'. This meant 'a war for the defence of the sovereignty of the state, and the purity of religion, a war to fight any attempt to colonization from any nation in any way'. *Perang sabil* (thus meaning 'war on the path (of God)') or *perang suci* ('holy war', also bearing the connotation of 'cleansing, purifying')

75 'Keterangan ringkas tentang Perang Sabil S.M. Kartosuwiryo', Arsip Jogja Documenten 1946-1948 [hereafter JogjaDoc] no. 243, ANRI.

76 The treaty of Hudaibiyah was signed in 628 CE by Muhammad and the Quraysh tribe, from which Muhammad himself hailed. The treaty gave individuals and tribes the freedom to choose whether to side with the Quraysh or the Muslims, and allowed Muslims to perform the pilgrimage to Mecca in safety. The following year, the Banu Bakr clan, an ally of the Quraysh, attacked members of the Khuza'a tribe, an ally of Muhammad. Following this breach of the treaty, Muhammad gave the Quraysh three options, from which they chose to end the treaty, hence paving the way for Muhammad's attack on Mecca.

were identified as specific cases of *jihad fi-sabilillah*, for which all connected actions were to be pursued with trust in God (*tawakkal Allah*), and purity of heart and belief (*i'tiqad*).[77]

Although it is likely that on this occasion Kartosuwiryo acted on his personal initiative, soon afterwards the central board of Masyumi followed his lead. In late September 1947, former PSII commissar for sharia and *'ibada* Kiyai Taoefiqoerachman declared the independence struggle a *jihad fi-sabilillah* obligatory for all Muslims. He went further, and, mirroring Kartosuwiryo's definition of 'friends of the struggle', the *kiyai* argued that in addition to those future martyrs who were fighting '*fi sabilillah*' to defend Islam, the nation and the territory, there were also those who did not seek the implementation of sharia, but desired to exhibit their bravery, were hot-tempered or simply sought external praise. Making references to Islamic traditions, the text argued that 'whoever fights to enhance Islam fights on the path of God', even if Islam is not their religion. Like Kartosuwiryo, Masyumi supported cooperation between Islamic fighters and unbelievers, as long as the latter did not cause harm to the former.[78]

Kartosuwiryo's 'holy war'

In Kartosuwiryo's writings, the Arabic root *j.h.d.* assumed several meanings. He strongly opposed Western understandings of *jihad* as 'war', and thus of Islam as a religion only spread by warfare. In his 1936 *Sikap hidjrah*, Kartosuwiryo recorded all Qur'anic verses that referred to *jihad*, explaining each specific *asbab al-nuzul* (context of revelation) and the term's multiplicity of meanings. Kartosuwiryo focused on the difference between the lesser and greater *jihad*, arguing for their respective 'negative' and 'positive, constructive' natures. In this context, Sarekat Islam's *Program djihad* was to be understood as a 'Program for the greater *jihad*', an effort based on *iman* and aimed at a successful *hijrah* by pursuing, searching and obtaining God's mercy and blessing (*mengharap, mencari, mendapatkan Rahmat dan Ridhlo*). This strategy was divided between the individual duty for each Muslim to study *tauhid* and the community's efforts, channelled through the party, to achieve political, economic and social improvement. The early spirit of Sarekat Islam was recalled as the basis of this twofold focus:

77 'Keterangan ringkas tentang Perang Sabil S.M. Kartosuwiryo', JogjaDoc no. 243, ANRI.
78 'Pengumuman ke-I Majelis Sjuro Pusat' by Kyai H. Abdul Wahab and Kiyai Taufiqurachman, 27 September 1947, JogjaDoc no. 243, ANRI.

> Since its birth, Partai Sarekat Islam Indonesia (from its origins as Sarekat Dagang Islam to Sarekat Islam until today), has strived to improve the lives and livelihood of the people [...] because a political movement, especially an Islamic political movement, has to take care of, and regulate, economics [...] as these two matters [Islam and economics] must become one.[79]

A decade later, in *Haloean politik Islam*, the *jihad al-asghar* is identified with the national revolution, and it is a *fard al-'ayn*. Here Kartosuwiryo is ambiguous on the means for undertaking this *jihad*. The effort is referred to once as *jihad fisabilillah bi ma'na al qital wa al-ghazwa* ('struggle on the way of God in terms of fighting and raiding'); another time both armed conflict and diplomacy are listed as valid means for achieving independence. Yet, by September 1947 Kartosuwiryo had dramatically reduced *jihad*'s much wider semantic field, only retaining its 'warfare' meaning.

Kartosuwiryo's narrowing of the meaning of the term *jihad* through his writings, from *Sikap hidjrah* to *Haloean politik Islam* and *Perang sabil*, was prompted by the changing context in West Java. As first mentioned in *Haloean politik Islam*, armed *jihad* in response to an attack on the *ummah* was the only way to establish a fully independent *darul Islam* or Negara Islam Indonesia that implemented *hukum Islam*. The Dutch aggression provided the needed political expedient.

Government reception of Masyumi's and Kartosuwiryo's calls for a jihad

The declarations encouraging holy war made by Kartosuwiryo and Taoefiqoerachman caught the attention of the Minister of Defence in Yogyakarta, who, incidentally, occupied the position that had been previously offered to Kartosuwiryo. The calls for *jihad* garnered some positive feedback and indicated that elements of the army and the government were supporting the Islamic struggle, not just as part of the anti-colonial effort but also as a broader ideology. Some support came from Major Kasman Singodimedjo, a former Peta battalion commander, president of the KNIP in Jakarta, Indonesian *Procureur Generaal* in January 1946, current head of the Defence Ministry's office for military justice and future cabinet minister for Masyumi. Singodimedjo argued that the *darul Islam* ideology was a 'straightaway right' of the Indonesian Islamic com-

79 Kartosuwiryo, *Sikap hidjrah PSII*.

munity and an indirect right for the government, which had to follow the will of the people. Political participation was a right for the Islamic parties that fought in Indonesia, but religion was in and of itself a right for the entire Islamic community.

Singodimedjo also commented that since Asj'ari's call for *jihad* in 1945, not only had the Markas Oelama Angkatan Perang Sabil in Yogyakarta followed suit, but several other individuals had also issued calls for a 'holy war'.[80] The collective enthusiasm for holy war raised two major concerns. First, Singodimedjo argued, 'the time for a general call for holy war was close'. And second, it was still unclear who had the authority to proclaim this 'total' *jihad*. According to Singodimedjo, politically speaking, the authority should belong to the president as the leader of the KNIP, even though in a strictly religious context this would have been the duty of the *imam* and his *majelis syuro*. However, the president had not been recognized as *imam*, and Islamic parties were deeply involved in politics; Singodimedjo argued that in this situation a 'total' *perang sabil* seemed unlikely, thus empowering local leaders.

Kartosuwiryo's call for *jihad* was therefore fully acceptable in religious terms. Furthermore, considering Kartosuwiryo's position as a guerrilla leader in an occupied area, the central government could not 'do anything other than thanking Allah, the One and Only God of the Indonesian Republic, because among his sons are some men as brave and courageous as Kartosuwiryo'.[81]

CONCLUDING REMARKS

In the aftermath of the Japanese surrender, Soekarno's vision for creating an Indonesian state sidelined, in the name of urgency and necessity, Islamic and leftist requests to consider alternative approaches. It was within this context that the Pancasila gained political favour against Islam and that the 'Jakarta Charter' was

80 Maj. Singodimedjo only mentions the Markas Ulama Angkatan Perang Sabil and Kartosuwiryo. However, I have counted at least four other official acceptances of Hasyim Asy'ari's call, as noted above: the NU congress in Surabaya (October 1945); the motion proposed by the Kaoem Moeslimin Indonesia Angkatan Senjata at the Masyumi congress of Yogyakarta (November 1945); the Moektamar Islam in Bukittingi (December 1945); and the NU congress in Purwokerto (March 1946). To these I would like to add the *al-Djihad* magazine's propaganda in 1946 and the establishment of the Sabilillah fighting corps (November 1945), both indicators of the surging interest in pursuing an Islamic armed struggle.

81 'Pendapatan saja tentang pernjataan Perang Sabil oleh S.M. Kartosuwiryo', Letter from Gen. Maj. R. Kasman Singodimedjo to Vice-Minister of Defence, Yogyakarta, 22 October 1947, JogjaDoc no. 243, ANRI.

dropped from the constitution's preamble. Yet, as the 1945 text was to be 'temporary', the religious faction was hopeful that things could still be changed.

Whilst political Islam had lost ground at the national level, Masyumi and its armed wings continued to gain considerable support in the Priangan, at both the military and political levels. The Dutch invasion of West Java in July 1947 and the subsequent diplomatic talks further strengthened this trend, pushing West Java towards independent developments and transforming it into a stronghold of the Islamic nationalist movement. Sabilillah and Hizboellah troops controlled the region, challenging the Dutch as much as the Republican soldiers. Both Kartosuwiryo and the national Masyumi leadership proclaimed a holy war and demanded the establishment of an Islamic state.

4

Building the Islamic state
From ideal to reality (1947-1949)

> *After much preparation, during the 20th gathering of the Dewan Imamah in Cimampang, with the attendance of Kartosuwiryo, K.H. Gozali Toesi, Sanoesi Partawidjaja, Raden Oni, and Toha Arsjad, on 7 August 1949 the Negara Islam Indonesia is officially proclaimed with the words: Proclamation of the Establishment of the Islamic State of Indonesia [NII],*
>
> Dengan Nama Allah, Jang Maha Esa dan Jang Maha Asih,
> *we, the Islamic Community of the Indonesian Nation*
> *announce the establishment of the Negara Islam Indonesia.*
> *And the law that governs the NII is Islamic Law.*[1]

The 1947 invasion of West Java pushed Masyumi to proclaim resistance against the Dutch a *jihad* obligatory for all Muslims. Following the discord over the Linggadjati Agreement Sjahrir was forced to resign, then Masyumi refused to join Sjarifuddin's 'socialist' cabinet, and by late September tensions could no longer be confined to the political field, as they spilled out among the population and onto the battlefield. The violence that had dotted West Java throughout 1946-47 further escalated, even as the Indonesian Republic in Yogyakarta and the Dutch embarked on another round of diplomatic talks.

The Renville Agreement, signed by Van Mook and Sjarifuddin on 17 January 1948, was the outcome of heavy pressure from the United States and the United Nations. The international community had been lobbying to find a diplomatic end to the impasse caused by the military invasion on Java and Sumatra and to establish a roadmap for Indonesia's self-government. The agreement established that West Java (with the exception of the Banten area) and the easternmost part of Java (including Surabaya and Malang) would be officially controlled by the Dutch, whilst the rest of the island would constitute the territory of the Indonesian Republic.[2]

1 *Qanun asasy Negara Islam Indonesia*, AABRI DI no. 9.

2 'Situation in Indonesia truce agreement and "Renville" principles, Consul-General Shepherd to Mr. Bevin', in Correspondence part 2 January to December 1948, p. 3 onwards, FO 480/2, NAUK.

The separation of West Java from the Republican territory and the presence of Hizboellah and Sabilillah troops beyond the Van Mook demarcation line were crucial to the further shaping of the Darul Islam and Tentara Islam Indonesia in the early months of 1948. West Java was coming under Masyumi's control, and the Republican police (Kepolisian Negara)accused the Islamic party of challenging the Republic on the political and military levels.

These accusations were formulated at the same time as the West Java branch of the Islamic party was gradually being transformed into the Darul Islam organization.[3] Kartosuwiryo's decision to pursue this transformation resulted from a combination of factors: the Dutch increase in activity in the Priangan between the end of December 1947 and mid January 1948;[4] the withdrawal of TNI Siliwangi soldiers from West Java to Yogyakarta to be completed by March 1948; the Islamic militias' refusal to evacuate the region and their merger into one umbrella organization; the tensions between the TNI and the militias in the weeks leading up to the withdrawal; the scarcity of available weaponry; and the broad popular support for the Islamic militias. These factors strongly contributed to the shaping of the anti-Dutch resistance in West Java as an Islamic movement under Kartosuwiryo's leadership.

This chapter follows the formation of the Islamic State of Indonesia, from its initial conception in late 1947 to the proclamation of its establishment in August 1949, paying a great deal of attention to the interaction between the Darul Islam and Soekarno's Republic. The material is thus arranged chronologically, identifying four phases in this process. The first phase stretched from November 1947 until May 1948, when Kartosuwiryo, Oni and Kamran unified Hizboellah and Sabilillah into one Islamic Army, giving initial shape to the Darul Islam organization as a defence movement that sought the cooperation of the Republican Army (until its withdrawal from West Java), and led the expansion of Darul Islam control over the Priangan.

The next phase covers the second half of 1948, when the Darul Islam formed a ministerial cabinet, marking the transformation

3 As early as December 1947, Said Soerianatanegara (vice-chief of police in North Tasik) pointed out that Masyumi was increasingly resembling an independent state in the Priangan, undermining the authority of the Republic; see 'Perihal: Politieke situasi', 9 December 1947, KepNeg no. 495, ANRI.

4 In their effort to bring the region under control, the Royal Netherlands Indies Army had targeted several villages around Kuningan and Tasikmalaya. A detailed description of the attacks can be found in 'Laporan tentang keadaan didaerah Karesidenan Priangan, Kantor Kepolisian Karesidenan Priangan', 28 February 1948, KepNeg no. 495, ANRI. For reports of how the Dutch ransacked civilians' houses, stole livestock and bombarded villages, see 'Politiek-Economisch Verslag betreffende de Residentie Priangan over de maand December 1947', 2 February 1948, AMK:RI no. 328, NA. Sabilillah also took revenge on those who did not support Masyumi; see 'Laporan tentang keadaan didaerah Karesidenan Priangan, Kantor Kepolisian Karesidenan Priangan', 28 February 1948, KepNeg no. 495, ANRI.

of the Majelis Oemmat Islam from a socio-political movement to a government body. During this time, Kartosuwiryo released the Constitution of the NII. With Muhammad and Medina as his models, Kartosuwiryo chartered a country – the Negara Islam Indonesia – built around the authority of a leader who embraced the spiritual, political and military legacy of the Prophet. It ought to be noted that at this point the NII still sought to collaborate with the Yogyakarta Republic, sharing the common goal of national independence. It was not until the third phase, from the second Dutch invasion in December 1948 to the Roem-Van Royen Agreement in May 1949 that frictions emerged, eventually leading to the antagonism between the Islamic Army and Siliwangi soldiers and to their ultimate parting of ways.

The last phase analysed here covers the August 1949 proclamation of the Islamic State of Indonesia as a political entity independent from Soekarno's Republic. This phase thus also takes a look at the first attempts of the Masyumi-led cabinet to negotiate with Kartosuwiryo. In fact, despite the continued antagonism on the battlefield, Natsir and some TNI commanders showed sympathy for the Darul Islam, and throughout 1949 the Masyumi-led cabinet strongly supported a political solution to the 'Darul Islam problem'.

GROUNDWORK (NOVEMBER 1947-MAY 1948)

Imagining the Islamic state (November 1947-January 1948)

The first step in the formation of an Islamic resistance organization and an Islamic army in West Java – later to be known as Darul Islam, Tentara Islam Indonesia and Negara Islam Indonesia – was probably taken in late 1947, when Kartosuwiryo, as vice-president of Masyumi for West Java, called for a conference to re-organize the party's constituency.[5] Masyumi's membership in the province

5 According to 'Negara Islam', Territoriaal Troepencommandant West Java, 12 June 1948, APG no. 997, NA, this meeting took place in September 1947; according to 'Majelis Oemat Islam', 'C' Divisie '7 December', 12 August 1948, APG no. 997 NA, and Centrale Militaire Inlichtingendienst [hereafter CMI] Publication no. 91, 29 September 1948, AAS no. 3977, NA, this meeting instead took place in November 1947.
The Islamic community of West Java was also being organized within the context of the creation of the state of Pasoendan (itself part of the scheme for a Republik Indonesia Serikat (RIS, Federal Republic of Indonesia), as in mid October the Islam Conference established the *dewan agama* (religious council) and *dewan al-Islam* (Islamic council), which included a *mahkama Islam, penghulu hakim, hakim nikah* (Islamic court, Islamic judge. and marriage officer, respectively), and an educational division, thus covering all needs of the *ummah*. 'Islamic conference of West Java', 26-29 November 1947, AAS no. 3405, NA; this was followed by a similar initiative in East Java.

was divided into five regional branches – Priangan, Banten, Jakarta, Bogor and Cirebon –, each sub-divided into provincial and village-level branches (*cabang* and *anak cabang*, respectively). The *cabang*-Garut was at the centre of the party's initial transformation in the region, a fact made clear when it changed its name into Majelis (or Dewan) Pertahanan Oemmat Islam (MPOI/DPOI, or Islamic Community's Defence Council).

In order to integrate different constituents into a single body, the party's multiple armed wings, including Sabilillah, Hizboellah, Gerakan Pemoeda Islam Indonesia (GPII, Indonesia's Muslim Youth Movement) and other youth groups, were merged into a single army, the Tentara Islam Indonesia.[6] Around the same time, Kartosuwiryo and his aides added a new article to the party's programme to further stress the adjustments necessary under their current state of war and struggle, namely, that they had the duty to 'defend [the territory] from the attacks of the Royal Army'.[7] Though the TII had become a reality both on paper and as a military body for Kartosuwiryo and his lieutenants, soldiers themselves had not yet been organized around a comprehensive strategy.

In accordance with the Renville Agreement, TNI troops were ordered to evacuate West Java by the end of February 1948. In the weeks between the signing of the agreement and the beginning of the withdrawal, Republican and Islamic soldiers often clashed. Tensions were inflamed by a number of factors, including the troops' different attitudes to combat and their scarcity of weapons, as already discussed. Islamic soldiers accused TNI soldiers of 'sitting around', waiting to withdraw without engaging in battle, and of not making good use of their rifles, whilst the Sabilillah and Hizboellah militias were exposing themselves to harm even without the appropriate equipment.[8]

Feeling the need to optimize their efforts and limit the clashes within the anti-Dutch front, Hizboellah, Sabilillah, Masyumi and TNI chiefs agreed to a meeting that would be mediated by local

6 As it will become evident below, other sources claimed that the Tentara Islam Indonesia was created in February 1948. However, it is possible that already by late 1947 the coordination efforts among Islamic militias in West Java had led to the formation of a unified army.

7 'Majelis Oemat Islam', 'C' Divisie '7 December', 12 August 1948, APG no. 997 NA. Probably it referred to the KNIL, but the report only talks of 'Nederlandse Leger' and 'Tentara Keradjaan'.

8 One such clash, for example, occurred in Sukasari (Maja); here two Hizboellah battalions that had arrived from Gegesik (Indramayu) in January were attacked by the TNI after they had been caught stealing weapons. 'Perlutjutan sendjata terhadap TNI oleh Hizboellah, Kantor Polisi Kabupaten Madjalengka', 19 January 1948, KepNeg no. 565, ANRI.

civilian authorities in Majalengka, which in early 1948 was the hub of military activities in the Priangan. The meeting did not achieve the intended goal of creating a unified army, but the participants at least recognized the need for coordinated action.

On the one hand, Islamic militias formally complained about the inertia of Republican soldiers and requested that other irregular militia groups be incorporated into their own ranks, rather than into the TNI's. On the other hand, TNI commanders diplomatically suggested that their units should simply withdraw to Yogyakarta and surrender the defence of Majalengka to Hizboellah, as having 'two armies in one state' only created friction. Eventually, the parties agreed to arrange another meeting, in which higher officials would participate. TNI was to be represented by Lt. Col. Abimandju and Col. Hidayat (second-in-command of the Siliwangi Division), Masyumi by Kartosuwiryo, and the militias by Kamran (chief of West Java Sabilillah troops stationed in Bantarujeg, south of Majalengka).[9] The prominent place given to them in this meeting confirms Kartosuwiryo's and Kamran's leading roles in the province.

It is interesting to note that the source refers to Masyumi and Sabilillah instead of MOI or TII, suggesting the possibility that until February-March 1948 Sabilillah and Hizboellah may have been coordinating their activities under the command of the MPOI/DPOI, and that the Darul Islam/Tentara Islam Indonesia 'proper' was only established in March 1948.

Even though sources on the second meeting are scattered, evidence suggests that it was held in Cinta, a village under Mount Talagabodas (Sukawening), just before the Siliwangi soldiers' withdrawal in late January 1948. This meeting saw the participation of Col. Hidayat, Major Utaryo, Kartosuwiryo and several civil servants from West Java. On this occasion, Kartosuwiryo expressed his opposition to the TNI's retreat and suggested that they all wage a holy war against the Dutch. What is more, he requested that Siliwangi soldiers leave their weapons behind to be used by those who were ready to fight the Dutch, meaning the Islamic troops.[10]

9 The mediating civilian figures were the mayor of Majalengka, the people's representative and the local chief of police. 'Perlutjutan sendjata terhadap TNI oleh Hizboellah, Kantor Polisi Kabupaten Madjalengka', 19 January 1948, KepNeg no. 565, ANRI.

10 Edi S. Ekadjati, *Sejarah kebangkitan nasional daerah Jawa Barat* (Jakarta: Proyek Penelitian dan Pencatatan Kebudayaan Daerah Jawa Barat, Pusat Penelitian Sejarah & Budaya, Departemen Pendidikan dan Kebudayaan, 1979), p. 207. The two requests mentioned above are also said to having been put forward by Oni and Kartosuwiryo in January 1948; see 'Tanggal2 bersedjarah bagi gerombolan D.I'. [1952?], AABRI DI no. 14.

These demands were rejected by the TNI, and by the beginning of February 1948, roughly 22,000 men – and their weapons – were already on their way to Yogyakarta under the command of Colonel Nasution.[11] Though Indonesian forces outnumbered them, the militias had by now made it clear that they did not intend to leave. Several thousand Hizboellah and Sabilillah militiamen remained in West Java, swelling the numbers of Kartosuwiryo's DI-TII.[12]

During the first week of February 1948, officials of the state of Pasoendan (Negara Jawa Barat) took steps to convince regional Masyumi leaders to surrender their weapons and join the state. The list included several popular and military leaders from Tasikmalaya, Garut and Ciamis, amongst whom were Kamran, Toha Arsjad, Joesoef Taoeziri and Junaidi, but not Kartosuwiryo.[13]

Laying the foundations of the Islamic state (february-march 1948)

According to a 1953 RI government publication, Kartosuwiryo received very little support in his endeavour to create an Islamic state. It is there argued that the majority of those present at the initial gatherings rejected the project of creating an Islamic state in West Java on the grounds that doing so would 'create a *dubbelstaat*, a state within the state.'[14] However, archival sources paint a different picture.

As the Siliwangi soldiers prepared to withdraw, Kartosuwiryo and other Masyumi and Sabilillah officers followed up on their earlier attempts to coordinate Islamic resistance to the Dutch by organizing a conference in Pangwedusan, Cisayong.[15] On 10-11 February 1948, some five hundred delegates and members of five Masyumi branches from across West Java (Tasikmalaya, Garut, Kuningan,

11 Abdul Haris Nasution, *Tentara Nasional Indonesia* (Jakarta: Seruling Masa, 1968); Ricklefs, *A history*, p. 227.

12 By the end of the year more than 50,000 men were in the rank and file of the TII. 'CMI Doc. No. 5176, Documenten betreffende de "Daroel Islam"-beweging', 21 December 1948, AAS no. 2752, NA. Among them were Zainal Abidin's group in Blubur Limbangan, Koernia's in Cicalengka, Enoks's in Wanaraja (Garut), Oni's in Mount Cupu, and Kamran's on the border between Majalengka and Tasikmalaya (Pagerageung area). Nasution, *Tentara Nasional Indonesia*, p. 125; Tanu Suherly, 'Kekuatan gerilya di daerah Priangan pada waktu divisi Siliwangi hijrah tahun 1948'. Paper, Seminar Sejarah Nasional ke-3, Jakarta, 10-14 November 1981, p. 4. This second source provides a detailed list of the various groups on pp. 4-10.

13 'Onderhandelingen met Masjoemi', 9 February 1948, AAS no. 2746.

14 Kementerian Penerangan, *Republik Indonesia: Propinsi Djawa Barat* (Jakarta: Kementerian Penerangan, 1953), p. 215.

15 Dinas Sejarah TNI, *Penumpasan pemberontakan D.I./T.I.I.*, pp. 59-65.

Majalengka and Ciamis), as well as representatives of Persis, Nahdatul Ulama and Muhammadiyah attended the conference, the explicit aim of which was to establish an Islamic state and army.[16]

These party leaders suspended the activities of the West Java branch of Masyumi and agreed on a plan to draft a clearly defined Islamic policy, create an army and elect a leader. Kartosuwiryo was nominated *imam* of the Islamic community in West Java, and Oni chief of the Indonesian Islamic Army in the Priangan. Although most of these actions were not initiated until after the March conference (see below), this meeting had already stated the intention of establishing an Islamic state that would implement Islamic laws in the *daerah istimewa* (special region) between Pagerageung, Cikoneng and Mount Sawal. It also declared a holy war and transformed the Sabilillah into the Tentara Islam Indonesia.[17]

The February meeting was followed by another conference, held on 1 March in Cirebon. Between January and mid March the press recorded a rapid increase in Islamic militias in the Priangan. Until January the town of Maja had been hosting an average of around 300-600 Hizboellah soldiers, but in late February more than 2,000 Hizboellah soldiers, who had been stationed in the area, attacked Bandung, Maja, Majalenka, Sukahaji and Kadipaten. In mid March the Dutch 'W' Brigade noted a 'large concentration' of Tentara Islam, and by April around 3,000 Hizboellah soldiers under the command of Oni and Lubis were in the area.[18]

At the Cirebon conference, Imam Kartosuwiryo, together with Kamran and Raden Oni (heads of the military section), Sanusi Partawidjaja and Toha Arsjad (leaders of the political section) and Kiyai Abdul Halim and Kiyai Haji Gozali Toesi (of the religious section), created the political and military structures needed to confront the Dutch.[19] First, they announced the dissolution of Masyumi and the suspension of its activities in West Java. In July 1948 the Yogyakarta chief of police speculated that behind Kartosuwiryo's dissolution of Masyumi was antagonism regarding Soekiman's 'not

16 Dani Wahdani, 'Politik militer Angkatan Perang Negara Islam Indonesia (A.P.N.I.I.) di Jawa Barat pimpinan Imam S.M. Kartosoewirjo' (thesis, Universitas Padjadjaran, Bandung, Jatinangor, 2003) p. 59, quoting from *Sedjarah Goenoeng Tjoepoe.*

17 'Overzicht en ontwikkeling van de toestand 8 April 1800 uur tot 15 April 1800 uur', Territorial ts. Troepencommandant West Java [1948], MD: AS no. 2224, NA.

18 'Sabilillah liar bergerak di sekitar Tjamis', *Sin Po*, 1 March 1948, and 'Hizbullah moendoer ke Goenoeng Tjiremei', *Keng Po*, 1 April 1948. See also MD:AS nos 2275 and 2288, NA.

19 Dinas Sejarah TNI, *Penumpasan pemberontakan D.I./T.I.I*, p. 63. Some degree of influence was also in the hands of Dahlan Lukman (GPII-Priangan leader), Siti Murtayi'ah (GPII-Putri Priangan leader), Abdullah Ridwan (Hizboellah-Priangan leader) and five other *cabang*-level leaders from Garut, including Saefullah (*cabang* vice-president), who was subsequently arrested and on whose confessions the first Dutch report on the Darul Islam was based.

radical enough' leadership of the party.[20] However, the Masyumi leaders who were gathered in Cirebon declared that it was time for Masyumi to terminate its operations in West Java because of the 'general situation in the region':

> Especially as the political negotiations between the Republican government and the Netherlands are not concluded yet, all Masyumi's subgroups [...] and all the organization's branches are to suspend their activities in the western part of Java beginning 1 March 1948 at 14.00.

The announcement also specified that anyone who had previously held representative roles would no longer have the right to speak for Masyumi, nor for any of its sections.[21]

The various militias were merged to form a unified and structured army – the Tentara Islam Indonesia – which would operate under the command of Kamran on the western side of the Van Mook line.[22] This army was instructed to 'come to power in a tactful way, succeed in taking control of the Republic, and include it[s territory] within the Islamic state'.[23] The political agenda of this new organization was focused on the preparations for a new state, a *Negara Baru.* This 'New State' would be a democratic Islamic state, the existence of which was seen by its founders as an alternative solution to a national state in case the Republican government were dissolved, or a Dutch-promoted state of West Java created.[24]

All matters related to combat were to be determined by the Islamic government in accordance with 'Islamic laws',[25] but no further details are provided. The participants at the March meeting agreed on a list of actions to be pursued in the immediate future to oppose Dutch domination and to strengthen Islamic piety in the area.[26] The last concern addressed at the meeting was the West Java Islamic community's need for a unified leadership, a problem solved by the election of Kartosuwiryo as sole commander of the *ummah* in the region and his confirmation as *imam.*[27]

20 'Darul Islam di Djawa Barat', Djawatan Kepolisian Negara Bagian PAM Yogyakarta, 23 July 1948, JogjaDoc no. 203, ANRI.

21 'Dunia Masyumi menghentikan usahanya', 1 March 1948 in 'Pelaporan No. 14/7/48 Perihal Darul Islam', Jawatan Kepolisian Negara Bagian PAM Yogyakarta, 17 July 1948, JogjaDoc no. 218h, ANRI.

22 'Rencana ketentaraan oemmat Islam', in JogjaDoc no. 218h, ANRI.

23 'Dunia Masyumi', in JogjaDoc no. 218h, ANRI.

24 'Program politik ummat Islam', in JogjaDoc no. 218h, ANRI.

25 'Rencana ketentaraan oemmat Islam', in JogjaDoc no. 218h, ANRI.

26 'Daftar usaha cepat', in JogjaDoc no. 218h, ANRI.

27 'Kesatuan pimpinan', in JogjaDoc no. 218h, ANRI.

Early reactions (March-May 1948)

Possibly because of the increasing presence of Islamic militias in the Priangan area, or possibly because of the geographic spread and high profile of its participants, the Cirebon gathering attracted the attention of the Dutch authority and the Republican police alike. As early as April, the Republican police and the Dutch reported on Masyumi's new military configuration in the Ciamis, Mount Sawal and Mount Cupu areas and its relation to the Darul Islam/Tentara Islam Indonesia,[28] describing this new group as a puritan Islamic movement aimed at the establishment of an Islamic state.[29]

Reportedly, the March gathering was attended by branch leaders from Bandung, Sumedang, Tasikmalaya and Ciamis. The Cirebon regional branch of Masyumi decided to adhere to Kartosuwiryo's transformation; Banten and Jakarta refused the offer, at least for the time being, while Bogor made it clear that it wanted to wait for the result of the Renville plebiscite.[30] The Plebiscite Movement demanded a popular consultation to determine whether Java, Madura and Sumatra would be part of the Yogyakarta Republic or would instead create their own states within the federal structure.

Even though they initially appeared to have lukewarm feelings about the idea, in May 1948 the Banten branch (which included some government representatives) issued intense public propaganda in support of the Darul Islam and against the Republican government,[31] and in August the head of the Majelis Islam in Bogor, Raden Mohammad Sapri, was arrested for forming a TII branch.[32]

In March the established 'Islamic government' was called Majelis Oemmat Islam, a variation on the Garut Islamic Community's Defence Council, MPOI. In the previous months the MOI had been replicated across the region, forming a network of local 'Islamic councils' through which Islamic leaders coordinated the defence of West Java and formed an Islamic mass movement

28 'Beknopt Politiek-Politioneel Verslag van de regentschappen Bandoeng, Garoet, Tasikmalaja, Tjiamis, Soemedang, Cheribon, Koeningan, Indramajoe, Madjalengka, Poerwakarta, Soekaboemi, Tjiandjoer en Buitenzorg, over de maand Maart 1948'; and 'Politiek-Economisch Verslag betreffende de Residentie Priangan over de maand Maart 1948', 28 April 1948; both in AMK:RI no. 283, NA.

29 'Politiek-Economisch Verslag', 28 April 1948; and 'Beknopt Politiek-Politioneel Verslag van de regentschappen Bandoeng, Garoet, Tasikmalaja, Tjiamis, Soemedang, Cheribon, Koeningan, Indramajoe, Madjalengka, Poerwakarta, Soekaboemi, Tjiandjoer en Buitenzorg, over de maand April 1948; both in AMK:RI no. 283, NA.

30 'Majelis Oemat Islam', 'C' Divisie '7 December', 12 August 1948, APG no. 997 NA.

31 'Extract uit D.O.B.I. n.631 dd 10/05/48 Nefis IV dd 9-5-48 Eval A.Z.', APG no. 1000, NA.

32 'Tentara Islam Indonesia', 17 August 1948, APG no. 1002, NA.

dedicated to creating an Islamic state.[33] Between early 1948 and the official proclamation of the Negara Islam Indonesia in August 1949, the MOIs functioned as party branches representing local headquarters of the Darul Islam and coordinating the activities of Masyumi, Sabilillah, Hizboellah and GPII across the island (mostly between West and Central Java).[34] Notably, in September 1948 the Republican police in Yogyakarta still considered these MOIs to be pro-Republican.[35]

Even though the MOI structure was not gathering much institutional support from Masyumi, the more general goal of creating an Islamic state was shared by a number of party leaders, who were also influenced by international events. When Israel, for example, was recognized as a state in Palestinian territory in May 1948, the Dutch government became concerned that the Palestinian question would become yet another piece of the Islamist puzzle in Indonesia, pushing Masyumi leaders towards further action. It is worth noting that the report explicitly singled out Soekiman, Kasman Singodimedjo, Abikoesno, Wondoamiseno, Agoes Salim, Aroedji Kartawinata, K. Ahmad Sanoesi and Kartosuwiryo as politicians who would be particularly sensitive to developments in the Middle East.[36] Indeed these events stirred much interest in Masyumi and Darul Islam circles.

At the 1948 Masyumi congress, held on 28 March in Madiun, Wali Alfatah (who would, in November, become vice-chairman of the Central Board) and Kiyai Ahmad Sanoesi (member of the National Majelis Sjoero) issued a joint declaration in favour of the creation of a *dar-ul-Islam* 'as soon as possible' in order to end the armed national revolution. The congress had gathered after the formation of the DI-TII, and the head of the NII's information office in Tasikmalaya, Abdoelhadi Ibrahim, was present at the congress as Darul Islam's representative. However, neither Wali Alfatah nor Kiyai Ahmad Sanoesi made any reference to Kartosuwiryo.[37]

33 *Qanun asasy Negara Islam Indonesia*, AABRI DI no. 9.

34 'Ontstaan en ontwikkeling der 'Majelis Islam', bezien uit militair standpunt', Territoriaal Troepencommandant West Java, 19 March 1949, APG no. 1002, NA.

35 'Surat dari Jawatan Kepolisian Negara bagian PAM tentang skema dari partai-partai yang dalam perjuanganya menentukan sikap pro dan anti-pemerintah', 9 September 1948, JogjaDoc no. 233, ANRI.

36 'Hr.TOL' (untitled), 21 May 1948, APG no. 1005, NA.

37 'Darul Islam di Djawa Barat', Djawatan Kepolisian Negara Bagian PAM Yogyakarta, 23 July 1948, JogjaDoc no. 203, ANRI, states that 'the characteristics of the Darul Islam survive also amongst Masyumi circles in the Republican territory, as evidenced in the speeches of Wali Alfatah and Kjai A. Sanusi'. This is the first instance in which the DI-TII is ignored as a model by other Islamic leaders advocating for an Islamic state; the reasons for and consequences of this attitude are further discussed in Chapter 6.

Although they both argued in favour of an Islamic state, the speeches reflect the well-established difference between modernists' and traditionalists' strategic approaches to the creation of an Islamic state, as one focused on society and the other on institutions as primary engines of the transformation.

Sanoesi doubted that a *dar-ul-Islam* could be established in Indonesia because of the limited support enjoyed by Masyumi among peasants and labourers. Openly challenging Soekarno's Pancasila philosophy, Sanoesi stated that Masyumi's aim could only be achieved if the three fundamental elements of the state – the people, the government and the laws – were Islamic. On the other hand, Wali Alfatah expressed a more optimistic view of the future position of Islam in Indonesian politics, as he trusted that Soekiman, as Minister of the Interior, would exert pressure on the civil servants to return to the occupied areas of the Republic and proclaim an Islamic state.[38] It is perhaps on these grounds that in April the Dutch suggested that Soekiman was the leader of the Darul Islam.[39]

The Pasoendan State, as noted above, had been trying to co-opt regional Masyumi leaders into their Negara Jawa Barat project, in February 1948. The president of this state, R.A.A. Wiranatakoesoema, had demonstrated an interest in realizing an Islamic political option for independent Indonesia as early as March 1947, and in April 1948 he participated in the formation of the MPOI in Bandung, for which he had shown open support. As the Islamic national movement in West Java assumed structural shape and increased its territorial control (see below), Kartosuwiryo decided to approach Wiranatakoesoema to suggest that they engage in a common struggle to ensure that West Java's independence would be established in Islamic terms. When directly contacted by Kartosuwiryo in August 1948 and by the Tentara Islam Indonesia in late February 1949, however, Wiranatakoesoema appeared reluctant to cooperate.[40]

Aside from these political reactions to the re-structuring of Masyumi, another key player in the success of the Darul Islam

38 'Kutipan Pidato2 pada tgl 28/3-'48 (Kongres Masjumi di Madiun) dari 1. Wali Alfatah 2. KA Sanoesi', JogjaDoc no. 243, ANRI.

39 'Daroel Islam', 5 June 1948, APG no. 1002, NA.

40 'CMI Signalement: de verhouding tussen Wali Negara van Pasoendan Wiranatakoesoema en de Daroel-Islam', March 1949, AAS no. 3979, NA. Interestingly, an earlier Dutch document argued that Darul Islam troops were actively opposing the Negara Pasoendan project in favour of a state truly independent of Dutch influences; see 'Beknopt Politiek-Politioneel Verslag van de regentschappen Bandoeng, Garoet, Tasikmalaja, Tjiamis, Soemedang, Cheribon, Koeningan, Indramajoe, Madjalengka, Poerwakarta, Soekaboemi, Tjiandjoer en Buitenzorg, over de maand April 1948', AMK:RI no. 283, NA.

was the local population. Local villagers in the Priangan openly endorsed Islamic militias' activities and supported them in their struggle, to the point that TNI soldiers often complained about this favouritism.[41]

Initial expansion (March-May 1948)

As mentioned above, the numbers of Islamic militias in the Priangan swelled from a few hundred to a few thousand in the short span between the beginning of the Siliwangi withdrawal until the end of March. This increase in number soon had consequences, especially as Hizboellah and Sabilillah were not the only irregular troops in the area, and the regular TNI had not completely evacuated the region.

In addition to clashing with TNI soldiers over weapons and supplies, throughout 1948 the troops of the Islamic Army also became engaged in a struggle to expand the territorial scope of the MOI-controlled areas at the expense of other guerrilla groups and the Dutch.

As territorial expansion had become a strategic priority, Kartosuwiryo and his military aides had divided West Java in three areas, depending on the degree of control that the Majelis held. The *Daerah Satu* (shortened in the original documents as D.I and meaning Region One) included villages controlled by the Darul Islam and implementing Islamic law. The *Daerah Dua* (D.II, Region Two) included the areas where the Darul Islam, the MOI or the TII had freedom of movement and strong influence. Lastly, the *Daerah Tiga* (D.III, Region Three) included those areas where the Darul Islam only had a limited degree of influence.[42] According to this organizational scheme, in May 'Region One' included the area enclosed within Tasikmalaya, Ciawi, Panumbangan and Mount Sawal; the D.II encompassed the area between Cileungjji (Ciamis), Cisayong (Tasikmalaya), Nagrek, Darmarata, Talaga and Mount Sawal; and the D.III stretched eastward to Majalengka and Cikijing, and southeast to Lakbok, Parigi, Cikatomas and Tasikmalaya.[43]

The Dutch attempt to cleanse Mount Sawal's surroundings of Islamic fighters created considerable difficulty for the militias' operations, but at the same time it provided the fighters with renewed

41 'Tindjauan singkat tentang keadaan daerah Keresidenan Prijangan', 31 March 1948, KepNeg no. 495, ANRI.

42 *Qanun asasy Negara Islam Indonesia*, AABRI DI no. 9; 'Majelis Oemat Islam', 12 August 1948, APG no. 997, NA, pp. 6-7; CMI Publication No. 91, 29 September 1948, AAS no. 3977, NA, pp. 8, 13.

43 CMI Publication No. 91, 29 September 1948, AAS no. 3977, NA.

strength and motivation. In retrospect, Dutch efforts to purge the Darul Islam from the Priangan were highly ineffective and mostly counterproductive. The Dutch Army had dispersed Islamic troops in Cikatomas, but this only resulted in the splitting of the militias between Cikalong (to the south) and Leuwisari (to the north). Similar attacks on the Mount Cupu area had spread Darul Islam soldiers to Cisayong, Ciawi, Indihiang and the southern districts. Further, Darul Islam troops had re-emerged in Pangerageung and Cineam, where they shared control of the territory with the communist Bamboe Roentjing militias.[44]

As a result of the successful political guidance of Kartosuwiryo and the able military leadership of Kamran and Nur Lubis, the Darul Islam expanded widely. By May 1948 the Majelis Oemmat Islam-Darul Islam had established its territorial presence across the Priangan, while at the same time strengthening its political structure.

A STEP CLOSER TO ESTABLISHING THE ISLAMIC STATE (MAY-DECEMBER 1948)

Institutional and territorial consolidation

In the second half of 1948, the Darul Islam's efforts were channelled into consolidating the movement's control over West Java and opposing the Dutch in both military and political capacities. In early May 1948 Kartosuwiryo, Sanoesi Partawidjaja, Kamran, Toha Arsjad, and Kiyai Gozali Toesi led a conference in the vicinity of Bantarujeg (Majalengka) to establish the *majelis imamah* or *kabinet* (guiding assembly, or cabinet), an act that marked the transformation of the MOI from a socio-political mass movement into a government body.[45]

On 27 August Kartosuwiryo released the Constitution of the Islamic state, and in the following months he continued to structure and give a clearer shape to this political entity. The Negara Islam Indonesia was to be a republic, led by an *imam* and based on sharia law. The *imam* had to be elected, his actions would be pursued only in the interest of the public and his authority would be submitted only to the sharia. He was entrusted with law-making, a process whose principle aim would be the formulation of laws

44 'Tjatatan ringkas dari laporan2 jang ketrima antara tanggal 22 sampai 31 Agoestus 1948 tentang kedjadian2 dalam kaboepaten Tasikmalaja', 1 September 1948, APG no. 1080, NA.
45 Dinas Sejarah TNI, *Penumpasan pemberontakan D.I./T.I.I.*, p. 64.

inspired by sharia principles and, at the same time, able to deal with the needs of a modern Islamic society.

Similar paradigms of government were suggested by other groups across the archipelago, especially in Aceh and South Sulawesi, as mentioned in the preface to this book. Yet, despite having a vision starkly different from Soekarno's, the Darul Islam was still far from positioning itself in opposition to the Republic, keeping its focus instead on regional anti-Dutch activities. For the Darul Islam, the Islamic state was in a state of war, or *jihad*, with the Dutch forces, and every member of the Islamic *ummah* had the religious duty to fight *fi Sabilillah.*[46]

July and August, which that year corresponded to the fasting month of *Ramadhan*, had been quieter than the rest of the year. Yet even amidst reduced clashes and increased arrests, the Darul Islam had nonetheless succeeded in consolidating its presence in the region.[47] By the end of September 1948, the D.I area included the territory that had been under D.III in May. The D.II stretched southwest to Pameungpeuk and Mount Cupu, northwest to Tanjungsari and Tanjungkerta (Sumedang), north to the railway in Sukamelang, east to Cirebon, and then curving back in to Cikijing and Mount Sawal. The D.III had expanded further into the Garut regency in Bungbulang, towards Bandung, Indramayu and Cirebon in the north, and east into Central Java, with Salem under Darul Islam influence.[48]

The expansion towards the east was led by Amir Fatah, commander of the mobile division of the TII. Through October and December he would push into the neighbouring province and become head of the Central Java division of the Darul Islam.[49] Here the Darul Islam won the support of smaller Islamic groups, including the *Moedjahidin* of Pekalongan, Tegal and Brebes, which then became the core of the local Darul Islam.[50] In the west, the TII had regiments in Bogor, Jakarta and Banten as early as June 1948.[51]

46 'Maklumat Negara Islam Indonesia no. 1, 25 August 1948, JogjaDoc no. 218e, ANRI.

47 'Beknopt Politiek Politioneel Verslag van de regentschappen Bandoeng, Garoet, Tasikmalaja, Tjiamis, Soemedang, Cheribon, Koeningan, Indramajoe, Madjalengka, Poerwakarta, Soekaboemi, Tjiandjoer en Buitenzorg' for the months of July and August 1948, AMK:RI no. 284, NA.

48 CMI Publication no. 91, 29 September 1948, AAS no. 3977, NA.

49 'CMI Doc. No. 5176, Documenten betreffende de "Daroel Islam"-beweging', 21 December 1948, AAS no. 2752, NA.

50 CMI Publication No. 97, 18 November 1948, AAS no. 3977, NA.

51 'Rapport van Bk. Bandoeng inzake Islamitische stromingen in de residenties Priangan en Cheribon', Archief van de Marine en Leger Inlichtingendienst, Netherlands Forces Intelligence Service en Centrale Militaire Inlichtingendienst in Nederlands-Indië [hereafter AIntel] no. 1705, NA.

Structuring the Islamic State

According to a 1950 document drafted by the Ministry of the Interiors of the Indonesian Republic, on 13 October 1948 the leaders of Islamic organizations (including Anwar Tjokroaminoto and Abikoesno Tjokrosoejoso), national leaders (including Muhammad Natsir, Kasman Singodimedjo and Soekarno), and military commanders (including General Sudirman) were given copies of the *Qanun asasy Negara Islam Indonesia*, the Constitution of the NII. The compiler of the 1950 document mentions that these leaders had also received a request to provide moral and material support to the NII's struggle, but 'They were all warned by the events of Madiun and kept that as a learnt lesson', and thus refused to get involved with the Darul Islam.[52] In the aftermath to the Siliwangi withdrawal to the Solo area, this TNI division clashed with anti-government communist troops whose stronghold was in Central Java. In mid September, as political tensions escalated, PKI and Pesindo troops gathered in Madiun and took control of the city, proclaiming a National Front government (this is further discussed on p. 173).

The Constitution of the Negara Islam Indonesia is composed of fifteen chapters comprising a total of thirty-four articles. It deals with several aspects of creating and maintaining a state, paying particular attention to the structures of Islamic political authority. The constitution provides for the establishment of a parliament (*majelis syuro*), an executive committee (*dewan syuro*) and an advisory council (*dewan fatwa*). It considered matters regarding the powers of the national government, regional divisions, finance, the judiciary, rules of citizenship, matters of national defence, education, economy, flag and language, and procedures to amend the constitution.[53]

Such structure closely resembles that of the Indonesian Republic's Constitution, and some of the more general matters regarding the state also seem to have been inspired by it. However, considering the historical understanding of *qanun* as a set of religious laws in accordance with the current time, it would not be fair to belittle the importance of this constitution as an Islamic text simply because of its concern with mundane aspects of politics and its parallels with a secular constitution. After all, Islamist ideologies 'are not con-

52 'Ichtisar gerakan DI/Kartosuwiryo', Kementerian Dalam Negeri Yogyakarta, 24 July 1950, KabPerd no. 150, ANRI.

53 I have here used the text as it appeared in 'De grondwet van de Daroel-Islam', Ministerie van Binnenlandsche Zaken Negara Pasoendan, 26 October 1948, AAS no. 2752, NA.

tinuous with historical Islam, but rather are modern constructions influenced by current conjunctions', as Sami Zubaida has argued in the case of the Islamic Republic of Iran.[54]

Together with the 1949 criminal code, this text remains one of very few attempts to formally structure an Islamic state in the Sunni Muslim world in the twentieth century, possibly only equalled by Nabhani's *Niẓām al-Islām,* which was published in 1952 and is still today the blueprint for creating an Islamic state for the global Hizb ut-Tahrir movement.

Kartosuwiryo's Constitution opens with a preamble explaining the historical circumstances in which the Islamic state had come into being. The Renville Agreement is described as a blessing in disguise, as from then on the *ummah* of West Java, under the leadership of Masyumi, would lead a 'second revolution' of resistance in name of Islam – a *jihad.* Kartosuwiryo regarded the NII as a 'gift of God' (*Kurnia Allah*) to the Indonesian people. Formally a republic (in the text defined as *jumhuriyyah* and *republik*), this Islamic state saw the Qur'an and *hadith sahih* as the highest laws and believed it had the duty to enforce Islamic law on its community whilst ensuring freedom of religious belief and practice to all its citizens. The *majelis syuro* was entrusted with both the duty to elect the *imam* and the power to make laws, although in a state of emergency the *imam* and the *dewan imamah* (whose members were appointed and discharged at the *imam*'s discretion) could take over. The *imam*'s oath was to be given before parliament, acknowledging the paramount importance of acting for the benefit of Islam and the state. The *imam* was allowed to stay in office as long as he acted according to the sharia, fulfilled his oath, and governed in accordance with the teachings of Islam.

Kartosuwiryo insists on the figure of the *imam.* This *Qanun* gives the *imam* almost unlimited powers and authority, with the only limit being parliamentary approval in the law-making process. He would also have an advisory council, the *dewan fatwa,* composed of up to seven *mufti* and headed by one Great Mufti to guide him in his decisions. The *imam* had the rights to declare siege and war and to rule by decree. He was head of the armed forces; appointed and received ambassadors and consuls; decided on matters of amnesty, abolition of punishment, clemency and re-education; and conferred titles, decorations and honours.

54 Sami Zubaida, 'Is Iran an Islamic State?', in Joel Beinin and Joe Stork (eds), *Political Islam: Essays from* Middle East Report (Berkeley: University of California Press, 1997), p. 104. Sami Zubaida has argued as much for the case of post-revolution Iran, and the same holds true for the Negara Islam Indonesia.

In a socialist vein, the *Qanun* sanctioned the right for all citizens to work and to maintain appropriate standards of living. It also established the principle of mutual aid for matters pertaining to the life and livelihood of the people, and the right-duty to pursue an education, which would be facilitated by the government's establishment of a system of Islamic schooling. The state would control 'the branches of production of major importance to the nation and its people', as well as soil, water and natural resources in order to ensure maximum benefit for the people.

Reaching out: Promoting the common goal

With the TNI officially evacuated from West Java, the Islamic Army supplied the only organized anti-Dutch troops. Although they were not the only 'irregulars' operating in the province, the NII was establishing itself as a regional political institution with links to the centre, whilst the various *laskar* did not have a central leadership. In October 1948 the Dutch Army labelled Kasman Singodimedjo, Sangadji and Anwar Tjokroaminoto as the Jakarta supporters of the Tasikmalaya-based Darul Islam,[55] and in December of that year Kartosuwiryo himself announced that Abikoesno and Anwar Tjokroaminoto were 'representatives of the NII in the Republican territories'.[56]

As the DI-TII affirmed its position in the Priangan as a military and civilian institution, Kartosuwiryo and his aides saw an opportunity to reach out to the Republican government to ask for recognition of their successes against the Dutch and for support in continuing the struggle.

On 3 October 1948, K.H. Zainal Hasan Thoha (political chief of MOI in Ciamis) and Nur Lubis (the Batak commander of TII's 3rd Battalion in Tasikmalaya and Ciamis) sent letters to Muhammad Natsir (at that time Minister of Information), the chief of the Republican delegation in Yogyakarta, Mohammad Roem, and the vice-president, Mohammad Hatta.[57] These three letters appealed for material help – namely, weapons – from the Republic, expressing the 'hope' that the Republic would be interested in West Java's struggle against the occupying forces.

55 'Beknopt Politiek-Politioneel Verslag der vreemdelingen- en inlichtingen Dienst (VID), no. 10/1948', APG no. 1068, NA.

56 'Maklumat Negara Islam Indonesia no. 6', 20 Safar 1368 AH/21 December 1948 CE, in Al Chaidar, *Pemikiran politik*, pp. 556-7.

57 The last two letters were said to be copies of ones previously sent, which had gone unanswered and were thus deemed not to have been received.

Each letter tackled the issue in a way that was tailored to the character and position of the recipient. The letter to Roem was a direct and bare-boned request for moral, political and material support, sweetened by the hopes of this Islamic State's commanders that Roem would not let the rebellion go unknown in Republican circles.[58] The other two letters, on the other hand, went to great lengths to explain why a guerrilla movement had been organized on Mount Cupu, with Natsir even addressed as an ally:

> As a Muslim, surely you must be happy about this rebellious Muslim movement in West Java, and that the great strength that you have often mentioned as being with the Muslim group is indeed real. Unfortunately, this government, led by a leftist coalition, does not care about it, and its strength cannot be used to stop the Dutch aggression. This rebellion in West Java shows that Muslims truly love independence. With a few rifles and firm faith, the rebellion started on Mount Cupu on 17 February [1948].[59]

Hatta's letter presented him with the matter-of-fact statement that 'the future of the occupied areas lies 99% with the result of this rebellion', and that the only reason for Yogyakarta's independence was TII's activity in West Java. The Darul Islam had no naive expectations of receiving any substantial material help from the Republic. But it used this opportunity to remind the Republican leadership that it should not forget that many Indonesians were still under foreign rule, in part because of the decisions made by the Yogyakarta government, and that, as the Siliwangi Division had taken the 'good and heavy weapons' into Republican areas, the Darul Islam could not guarantee a quick victory in West Java.[60] Their requests went unheeded.

On 19 December 1948 the Dutch Army invaded Central Java, entered Yogyakarta and captured the president, the vice-president,

58 Letter to P.T. Mr. Muhammad Rum Ketua Delegasi Republik Indonesia di Yogyakarta from Pimpinan Ummat Islam Kabupaten Tjiamis KH Zainal Hasan Thoha and Tentara Islam Indonesia Bat. III Res. I Div. I Komandan Bat. III Muhammad Nur Lubis, 3 October 1948, JogjaDoc no. 150, ANRI.

59 Letter to J.M. Muhammad Natsir Menteri Penerangan Republik Indonesia di Yogyakarta from Pimpinan Ummat Islam Kabupaten Tjiamis KH Zainal Hasan Thoha and Tentara Islam Indonesia Bat. III Res. I Div. I Komandan Bat. III Muhammad Nur Lubis, 3 October 1948, JogjaDoc no. 150, ANRI.

60 Letter to P.J.M. Wkl. Presiden Republik Indonesia Drs. Mohammad Hatta di Yogyakarta from Pimpinan Ummat Islam Kabupaten Tjiamis KH Zainal Hasan Thoha and Tentara Islam Indonesia Bat. III Res. I Div. I Komandan Bat. III Muhammad Nur Lubis, 3 October 1948, JogjaDoc no. 150, ANRI. Quote also from this letter.

the head of KNIP and the Minister of Foreign Affairs.[61] This was a serious setback to the creation of an independent state of Indonesia, and it also greatly contributed to the shaping of Darul Islam-Republik Indonesia relations.

GROWING APART (DECEMBER 1948-AUGUST 1949)

Against the backdrop of these kidnappings and the collapse of the Republican government, in late December Kartosuwiryo declared a 'holy war, total war, all-encompassing people's war, against the Netherlands' to ensure the success of the Islamic revolution and the establishment of a perfect Islamic state across Indonesia.[62] The Dutch intervention gave Kartosuwiryo another opportunity to accuse the Republican government of its political failings, and at the same time to glorify the Islamic state as the only viable option for independent Indonesia.

In the following months Republican leaders conducted intense diplomatic talks with the Dutch, whilst the Siliwangi Division returned to West Java. Until mid 1949, relations between Republican agents and the DI-TII could best be characterized as an uneasy collaboration marked by the consciousness that, despite territorial divisions, resisting Dutch expansion should be their common goal.

Tentara Islam Indonesia and the Siliwangi in West Java: an uneasy cohabitation (December 1948-February 1949)

The Dutch operations prompted a new round of diplomatic negotiations, in which the Republican bargaining power was further weakened. Kartosuwiryo's response to the situation was clear:

> It will not be long before they sign a new treaty – this is the story of the Indonesian independence struggle – and this third treaty will decide the fate of the State of the Indonesian Republic. In our understanding, at that point the Republic won't be anything more than a 'Puppet State' like those the Dutch have already established a while ago: Negara Indonesia Timur, 'Negara' Kalimantan, 'Negara' Pasoendan, and so forth. Thus, with the use of weapons,

61 Ricklefs, *A history*, p. 230.

62 'Maklumat Negara Islam Indonesia no. 5', 19 Safar 1368 AH/20 December 1948 CE, AABRI DI [folii].

> the Netherlands will force the Republican government, which has already been captured, to sign a treaty according to which all the state's instruments will have to be abandoned [here anticipating the Roem-Van Royen statement of May 1949 ...]. Because of this, there is nothing for the Indonesian Islamic community, especially those living in Republican territory, to do other than to be ready to accept God's gift, to pursue a *jihad fi Sabilillah*, to oppose the enemy of Islam, the enemy of the State, and the enemy of God, and last but not least, to establish a State blessed and offered by God, an Islamic State of Indonesia.[63]

Kartosuwiryo's disappointment with the Republican government is evident. However, it would be a mistake to argue that the Darul Islam maintained an 'openly anti-Republican' attitude, as Kahin and Boland have suggested.[64]

On 21 December 1948 Kartosuwiryo declared that the struggle for the Islamic state was 'the continuation of the independence struggle, following on from and in line with the 17 August 1945 proclamation'. In this statement, Kartosuwiryo was placing the Darul Islam's struggle on the same plane as Soekarno's, rather than in opposition to it.[65] Two days later he renewed the Islamic state's 'state of war', specifying that it involved only two contenders: the NII and the Dutch government. Between the two neither cooperation nor treaties were allowed, and ongoing diplomatic contact had to be ceased.[66] Kartosuwiryo was thus pledging to continue Soekarno's struggle whilst he and his cabinet had been captured, and Republican forces were not identified as the enemy.

Following the Dutch offensive of December 1948, the Siliwangi Division crossed the Van Mook line, re-entering West Java and reigniting tensions between regular soldiers and Islamic militias, tensions about which Colonel Nasution was well aware.

63 'Maklumat Negara Islam Indonesia no. 6', 20 Safar 1368 AH/21 December 1948 CE in Al Chaidar, *Pemikiran politik*, pp. 556-7. Here Kartosuwiryo anticipated the Roem-Van Royen statement, which was signed on 7 May 1949. Regulating the transfer of sovereignty, this agreement had been heavily pushed for by the international community, as had the Renville Agreement. The international community had begun to tire of Dutch policies in the archipelago. An interesting account of these events, and of the reactions of the international community, is offered by *TIME Magazine*; see 'Regretfully obliged', 27 December 1948; 'So moves the world', 3 January 1949; 'Merdeka!', 10 January 1949; 'What about the baby?', 10 January 1949.

64 Kahin, *Nationalism and revolution*, p. 330; Boland, *The struggle of Islam*, p. 58.

65 'Maklumat Negara Islam Indonesia no. 6', 20 Safar 1368 AH/21 December 1948 CE, in Al Chaidar, *Pemikiran politik*, pp. 556-7.

66 'Maklumat Negara Islam Indonesia no. 7', 22 Safar 1368 AH/23 December 1948 CE, in Al Chaidar, *Pemikiran politik*, pp. 558-9.

The return of the Siliwangi Division to West Java stirred much commotion in DI-TII circles. In late January 1949, a new NII decree blamed Republican troops for abandoning the region and returning one year later, not as 'guests' of the Islamic state, but rather as rulers who expected to take charge of NII territory. The TNI was aware that the NII considered the return of the Siliwangi troops a breach of NII's sovereignty,[67] and saw its soldiers as a *tentara liar* (wild, illegal militia), an 'obstacle' to the Islamic revolution and an enemy of the Islamic state.[68] The 25th of January – the day of this decree – is also considered by the Republican Army as the day when 'the TNI betrayed the Tentara Islam Indonesia'. The aggression of the TNI on that day was taken as a sign of enmity towards the Tentara Islam Indonesia and the Islamic *ummah.*[69]

Even though January and February 1949 witnessed attacks on several TNI battalions by Islamic soldiers around Tasikmalaya, Ciamis, Kuningan and Majalengka, clear rules of engagement prohibited the Islamic Army from killing Republican troops, who were only to be relieved of their equipment and then dispersed.[70]

Nevertheless, cases of cooperation continued to be reported. For example, TNI and TII troops stationed in Parigi, in the South Priangan, resolved to cooperate to ensure that all soldiers had food and weapons – the people's predilection for Islamic militias remained a key element in ensuring their livelihood.[71] The beginning of the year saw cooperation in the Kuningan and Jakarta areas as well, to the extent that in Jakarta this cooperation gave rise to worries in the office of the Dutch Indies' attorney general, which had received documentation proving that the Sjarif Hidajatullah Division of TII in Central Java had obtained ammunitions and weapons from the commander of the regional police.[72]

67 'Maklumat no. 10 Siliwangi Djawa Barat', 10 April 1949, AABRI DI no. 4. *Kedatangan Tentara kita dianggap sebagai melanggar kedaulatan negara tsb* [NII] *berhubung memang Tentara kita bertugas untuk membangun kembali Pemerintah republik di Jawa Barat.*

68 'Maklumat Negara Islam Indonesia Militer no. 1', 25 January 1949, in Al Chaidar, *Pemikiran politik*, pp. 652-4.

69 'Tanggal2 bersedjarah bagi Gerombolan D.I.' [1952?], AABRI DI no. 14. *TNI melakukan penghianatan kepada Tentara Islam Indonesia.*

70 'Maklumat Negara Islam Indonesia Militer no. 1', 25 January 1949, in Al Chaidar, *Pemikiran politik*, pp. 652-4.

71 'Beknopt Politiek-Politioneel Verslag van de regentschappen Bandoeng, Garoet, Tasikmalaja, Tjiamis, Soemedang, Cheribon, Koeningan, Indramajoe, Madjalengka, Poerwakarta, Soekaboemi, Tjiandjoer en Buitenzorg, over de maand Februari 1949', AMK:RI no. 285, NA

72 'Aanbieding documenten betreffende TII- en TNI-aangelegenheden', 21 September 1949, APG no. 907, NA.

But from April 1949 onwards, the TNI reportedly joined forces with the Dutch in an attempt to clear Darul Islam pockets in West Java.[73] What changed the relationship so swiftly and so dramatically?

...and an easy divorce (February-March 1949)

On 26 February 1949 Kartosuwiryo and Oni held a conference in Langkaplancar (in the South Priangan), during which they presented the TNI with an ultimatum: the TNI could either leave the region or join the ranks of the Darul Islam, but beginning in April the only army allowed to operate in the region would be the Tentara Islam Indonesia.[74]

As the Republic readied itself for yet another round of negotiations, the Darul Islam began preparations to expand its territorial reach. In mid April, it sent a 'consul' for the NII to Sumatra with the intention of leading the local *ummah.*[75] According to a Dutch intelligence report, it is at this same time that a Javanese associate of Kartosuwiryo developed cells in the Palembang, Bengkulu, Lampung, Jambi and Tapanuli areas as well as on the west coast, and that the first contacts between Kartosuwiryo and Daud Beureueh in Aceh took place. Beureueh was a former leader of the Persatuan Ulama Seluruh Aceh (PUSA, All-Aceh Union of Ulamas) and in July 1947 he had been nominated military governor of Aceh. The Dutch also detected Darul Islam groups in South Borneo, the Moluccas and Sumbawa, and a small enclave was active in the Lesser Sunda Islands.[76] There is also evidence that Kahar Mudzakkar posed as *panglima* (commander) of the IV DI Province of Eastern Indonesia soon after the proclamation of the NII, whilst it is generally accepted that he joined the Darul Islam in early 1952.[77]

After the ultimatum, and probably as a way to justify such a dramatic change in attitude, in March 1949 Kartosuwiryo published a pamphlet on the history of the *ummah*'s struggle for independence and the secularists' track-record in diplomatic negotiations. In *ad-Daulatul Islamiyah* Kartosuwiryo drew attention to the nationalists'

73 'Beknopt Politiek-Politioneel Verslag over de maand April 1949 van de regentschappen in de Negara', AMK:RI no. 285, NA.

74 'Beknopt Politiek-Politioneel Verslag over de maand Maart 1949 van de regentschappen in de Negara Pasundan', AMK:RI no. 285, NA.

75 'Tanggal2 bersedjarah bagi Gerombolan D.I.' [1952?], AABRI DI no. 14.

76 'CMI Signalement de Negara Islam Indonesia', 21 October 1949, AAS no. 3979, NA.

77 See, for example, Van Dijk, *Rebellion under the banner of Islam*, p. 187. 'Perkembangan D.I. Djawa Barat S.M. Kartosuwiryo', AABRI DI [folii].

cooperative attitude – first towards the Dutch, then towards the Japanese, and, finally, towards the Dutch once again.[78]

To Kartosuwiryo, Soekarno's readiness to bargain with the Dutch had made a 'zoo' (*kebon binatang*) of the early independence movement: as the animals, the politicians could 'freely' move around, but they were limited by the cages and guards of the colonial administrators. Once Japan replaced the Netherlands, the zoo became a circus (*komidi kuda*), with each animal playing its part in the well-orchestrated farce of independence, tragically ended by the atomic bombings. As he himself was one of the animals in this Japanese circus, Kartosuwiryo may have felt betrayed when Japan, after having co-opted the Islamic movement in order to garner popular support, eventually entrusted the task of drafting the constitution to the secular nationalists.

Kartosuwiryo accused Sjahrir of selling out Indonesia's independence at Linggadjati, and Sjarifuddin, of leading the Republican boat through shallow waters until it ran aground on West Java in the aftermath of Renville (*Bahtera Republik terdampar*). Kartosuwiryo did not place all the blame on the Republican leaders, though, as he recognized they had been lured by the deceptions of the international community, which was interested in stalling the revolution. They had been victims of an illness that no *dukun* healer could cure – diplomacy.

When the anti-colonial Islamic revolution was spreading from Mount Cupu into the western part of Java, too many had preferred to play it safe by fleeing across the Van Mook line, working for the Dutch government in West Java, waiting passively for things to change, or seeking help from Yogyakarta. Yet, Kartosuwiryo concluded, all Soekarno and Hatta could deliver to the people were empty hopes, a second military campaign and the inevitable failure of the Yogyakarta Republic as an independent government.

Opposing reactions: Clashing military and political interests (April-August 1949)

During April, military commanders' concerns over the number of TNI soldiers that were falling victim to the Darul Islam were opposed by Masyumi and other political organizations who were instead concerned by the ruthlessness of the army's response and the future of political Islam in general.

78 Kartosuwiryo, 'ad-Daulatul Islamiyah'.

Awareness of the Darul Islam's position on the Siliwangi Division's 'intrusion' in West Java had not stopped Commander in Chief Colonel Nasution from affirming that his duty was 'to re-establish the Republican government' in the region.[79] Reporting from the Priangan, he complained that the Siliwangi Division was 'squeezed' between Dutch and Islamic troops and was suffering heavy losses.

According to Colonel Nasution, by April almost one thousand Siliwangi soldiers had been captured by the Darul Islam. Even after the local ceasefire, signed on 12 April 1949, dozens of TNI soldiers came under Darul Islam fire. In response, the division interrupted the Cirebon-Tasikmalaya road, killed a dozen Darul Islam men, burned down a factory, disturbed Darul Islam meetings in Kuningan and Ciamis, increased patrolling, hijacked two trucks and seized eighteen rifles. The following month, after being informed of Major Sentot's success in cleansing the Cirebon area, Nasution admitted that his repeated attempts to negotiate and cooperate with the Darul Islam had failed, as had those conducted by Colonel Sadikin in Tasikmalaya. A plan to eradicate the militia was now needed. Major Hardjono, in mid May, stated that the Darul Islam's unwillingness to cooperate was forcing his troops to begin purging the area.[80]

In the wake of the Roem-Van Royen Agreement, relations between the Darul Islam and the Republic had worsened. From May 1949 the ambiguities in their positions dissipated, and their differences came into sharper relief. In principle, the Islamic state was not opposed to the Republican government in Yogyakarta, but in practice it opposed Dutch interference in Indonesian politics and Dutch authority over Indonesian territory. The Darul Islam argued that West Java, as part of the occupied territories, did not fall under the control of the Yogyakarta Republic, and thus should not be forced to abide by the treaty signed by Republican leaders. In fighting the Siliwangi troops, the Darul Islam did not see itself as attacking Soekarno's Republic but, rather, as attacking the Dutch government, which was making use of Republican troops to advance its own agenda. The Indonesian Republic had become a 'puppet' in the hands of the Dutch, and was thus standing behind

79 'Maklumat no. 10 Siliwangi Djawa Barat', 10 April 1949, AABRI DI no. 4.

80 Col. A.H. Nasution on West Java and DI/TNI clashes, doc. no. 0211/pl oi/25, 26 April 1949, Pemerintah Darurat RI, 1949 [hereafter PDRI] no. 91a, ANRI; 'Darul Islam contra TNI te Tasikmalaja', Territoriaal Troepencommando East Java, 3 Mei 1949, MD:AS no. 2071, NA; Major Harjono on 'Pembersihan terhadap DI', 19 May 1949, PDRI no. 92, ANRI; 'Laporan HBKD PTTS', 23 June 1949, PDRI no. 151, ANRI.

enemy lines. Although this change in perspective had become evident to military commanders and politicians alike, Masyumi did not approve of Colonel Nasution's hard line, and party leaders pleaded with him not to attack Islamic troops and not even to enter the areas they controlled.

Regardless of the fact that the Darul Islam had no institutional link to Masyumi, the party went all out to defend the Islamic Army. They vigorously argued that the clashes with the TNI were partly in response to attacks on the part of the Siliwangi Division – attacks that had been ordered by Achmad Wiranatakoesoema and which were frowned upon by other TNI commanders – and partly a consequence of bandits roaming the border between Central and West Java, which made it difficult to establish who was TNI and who was not.

On the political front, Masyumi maintained that TNI's attacks on the Darul Islam were strengthening the Dutch scheme of 'divide and rule' and weakening popular support for the Republic across the country, and not just in those areas directly controlled by the Darul Islam. Masyumi leadership was sure that once the Dutch had left, the situation would be easily resolved by removing the source of discontent in West Java.[81]

Despite pleas for unity from Lieutenant Colonel Sudirman, who called for groups from all ideological paths to join in a holy struggle of total war (*perjuangan suci*, though not a *perang suci*),[82] and despite Masyumi's repeated attempts to mediate between the Siliwangi Division and the Darul Islam,[83] press and military reports show that by late July, and even more so from August 1949, negotiations and discussions regarding cooperation had failed. This failure was the result, on the one hand, of the Darul Islam's resentment of the Yogyakarta Republic, and on the other hand, of the TNI army's suspicion that after the communist militias had been crushed in Central and East Java in late 1948, they had heavily infiltrated the Islamic Army, especially in the Cirebon area.[84]

81 Letter from Prawoto Mangkusasmito, Pengurus Besar Masyumi, to Panglima Komando Jawa on 'Darul Islam', 9 April 1949, Kabinet Perdana Menteri RI, Yogyakarta, 1949-1950 [hereafter KabPerd] no. 150, ANRI; Letter from Muhamad Saleh, Pengurus Besar Masyumi, to Panglima Komando Jawa on 'Darul Islam', 7 May 1949, KabPerd no. 150, ANRI.

82 Letter from Panglima Komando Jawa, Lieutenant Colonel Sudirman, 9 May 1949, AABRI DI no. 4.

83 'Masjumi bemiddelaar tussen de Siliwangi en de Darul Islam?', *Indonesisch pers en radio overzicht, Java*, 12 August 1949.

84 'Communistische infiltratie in de Darul Islam', *Nieuwe Courant*, 22 June 1949. For more details on DI and communism, see Chapter 6.

DECLARING AN ISLAMIC STATE IN 'OCCUPIED' WEST JAVA (AUGUST 1949)

The Negara Islam Indonesia was rooted in the law of God and had its base in 'Medina'. As had been anticipated in the *Brosoer sikap hidjrah PSII* and in *Haloean politik Islam*, this choice of toponym pointed to the city's status as the destination of the *hijrah*, as a physical migration and a metaphoric transformation. Either way, Kartosuwiryo referred to the beginning of a new life for the *ummah*, one in full conformity with Islam. The NII extended across five regencies in West and Central Java: the Priangan (in Bandung, Garut, Tasikmalaya, Ciamis,and Sumedang districts), Cirebon (Cirebon city, Indramayu and Majalengka), Pekalongan (Brebes and Tegal), Banyumas and Bogor.

The NII had existed, *de facto*, since August 1948, when the first 'announcement' (or decree) bearing its name appeared. But the Islamic State proclamation of August 1949 represents the important transformation from a nebulously defined, idealized project to a meticulously detailed state with a blueprint for executive, legislative and judicial government institutions.

The former Masyumi branch of West Java had finally achieved the goal that the central party had set in 1945: the establishment of a republic that was based on Islam, implemented Islamic laws and directly controlled its territory. Success had only become possible in August 1949 after the 'betrayals' of the Republican government and the *ummah*'s many disappointments.

The circumstances that had enabled Kartosuwiryo and his partners to proclaim the NII were clearly explained in a political manifesto released a few weeks after the NII proclamation. In Kartosuwiryo's eyes, this text was a direct result of the Roem-Van Royen statement, which had epitomized diplomatic relations between the Netherlands and the Indonesian Republic: the ceasefire, the Round Table Conference and sustained cooperation between the two parties. Kartosuwiryo's objection to each and every point was grounded in political and historical considerations. He characterized Soekarno's authority as that of a slave who had been turned into a king by the Devil, and his political strategy as weak, disillusioned and outdated. He believed Soekarno to only be capable of selling out his country to the foreign occupier.

Kartosuwiryo pointed out that Soekarno had risen to represent the entire archipelago, even though no other leader had delegated his decisional powers to the Republican cabinet. But when bullied by the Dutch, Soekarno could do nothing more than surrender

Indonesia's sovereignty to them. The Federal Republic of Indonesia (RIS) was built on 'fake' authority, as it was a 'gift' from the colonial government and it still carried the shadow of Dutch control and supervision. Kartosuwiryo saw this dynamic as little more than a modern form of colonialism in the context of which Indonesia would only have been half-independent, as a dominion or a protectorate.

Kartosuwiryo's rejection of anything short of *de facto* and *de jure* independence was reinforced by his open condemnation of Pakistan's status as a British dominion. Soekarno's debacle had caused the end of the Republican cabinet and the collapse of the *ummah*, but Kartosuwiryo saw these events as 'a gift from God' that had empowered the Darul Islam to proclaim the Islamic state.[85]

The May ceasefire agreement was set to end hostilities on 1 August 1949. However, in Java, a fortnight passed before any real progress in ending the conflict was made. The Siliwangi Division pledged to obey the ceasefire and held meetings with local *laskar* to facilitate the transfer of authority and the troops' incorporation into the Republican Army.[86] Although the Antara news service reported that TII and TNI troops around Ciamis had initially agreed to abide by the ceasefire and would 'cooperate in wiping out irresponsible elements',[87] this solution was not embraced by every Darul Islam cell, as in the last weeks of August its militias continued to attack the Dutch, the TNI and, reportedly, also the civilian population in the Cirebon area and west of Jakarta.[88] It was in this charged political environment that Hatta left Jakarta to attend the Round Table Conference in The Hague, lasting until November 1949.

The Proclamation of the Negara Islam Indonesia

In part a result of Soekarno's weakness, the Indonesian Republic was visibly crumbling under pressure from international diplomatic efforts. The Negara Islam Indonesia was officially declared against this backdrop on 7 August 1949, during the 20th session of the *dewan imamah* in Cimampang, a meeting held in the aftermath of the Roem-Van Royen Agreement and attended by Kartosuwiryo, K.H. Gozali Toesi, Sanoesi Partawidjaja, Oni and Toha Arsjad.

85 *Manifesto politik*, Bab IV, 4.

86 'Siliwangi-divisie gehoorzaamt het cease-fire bevel', *Pedoman*, 20 August 1949.

87 *Antara News*, 23 August 1949.

88 'DI melebarken sajapnja', *Sin Po*, 26 August 1949.

Pragmatic and detailed as it was, this proclamation was still a theoretical statement that together with the 1948 Constitution presented an alternative to Soekarno's 1945 text. In Kartosuwiryo's vision the NII would evolve from a core '*Negara Basis*', named Madinah Indonesia, with only *de facto* authority over a small portion of Indonesia, into a '*Negara Kurnia Allah*' – a fully sovereign state. Solidifying the state into a permanent entity could only be obtained through a dramatic shift in the balance of power: locally, Kartosuwiryo called for an Islamic revolution; internationally, for a Third World War or a World Revolution 'more devastating and violent than the previous ones so that, God willing, the international situation will deeply change'.

Aware of the movement's current limitations, the *dewan imamah* stated that the *daulatul Islamiya*, or Darul Islam, would continue to conduct a holy war until it was transformed in the envisaged '*Negara Basis*': the NII would include the entire territory of the archipelago, be recognised as a *de facto* and *de jure* state, it would implement Islamic law, abolish slavery, and ensure that all enemies of Allah, religion and the state had left. Until these goals were met, the NII would be in a state of war (*Negara Islam dimasa perang* or *dar-ul-Islam fi-waqtil-harbi*), ruled by Islamic martial law. The time was ripe for establishing 'God's justice in this world', and Kartosuwiryo called upon the Indonesian *ummah* to pursue 'the holy duty of guarding the integrity of the NII'.[89]

The NII's criminal code

With Kartosuwiryo's formal proclamation of the NII as a political and administrative entity, what had so far been a theoretical proposal had now become a functioning state. The commitment to territorial expansion across the archipelago was supported by the efforts to provide this state with a strong legal infrastructure, including a criminal code, the *Hukum pidana*. This text dedicated considerable attention to killings, banditry and martial law, reflecting the current state of war in which the NII found itself. The code arranged the material in a semi-systematic presentation of *qisas* (retribution in equal measure), *diya* (compensation money), *ta'zir* (discretional punishment) and *hudud* (crimes and punishments mentioned in the Qur'an), following the classic *fiqhi* distinction between crimes and punishments. Here I address only the code's martial law, as its remainder is analysed in Chap-

89 'Proklamasi berdirinja Negara Islam Indonesia', 7 August 1949, AABRI DI no. 14.

ter 6 in comparison with the codes issues by the Majelis Mujahidin Indonesia (Indonesian Council of Mujahidin, MMI) in 2002 and 2005.

The NII code dedicated several articles to Islamic martial law. Its first article reiterated the fact that the 'Indonesian State' (*Negara Indonesia*) was an Islamic state currently at war and therefore subject to *hukum syariat Islam dalam masa perang.* This held four fundamental obligations, with their respective punishments. Whoever did not follow the instructions of the Islamic state, including those who did not surrender financial surplus to the treasury as contribution towards *jihad*, was to be considered a *bughat* (rebel) and punished by banishment or death (quoting Qur'an 4:58), but only if he did not rectify the situation after being taken into custody and admonished. Death was directly prescribed for the three remaining categories of offenders: hypocrites, sinners and enemies of the state. *Munafiq* (hypocrite) was the one who maintained good relations with the state's enemies, despite having been informed by the government of such prohibition (quoting Q 60:1; 9:73; 66:9). *Fasik* (sinner) was the Muslim who did not follow Islamic law; if he refused to repent, he was to be labelled an enemy of Islam and punished accordingly. Enemies of the state were all those who had 'become tools of the colonial power' in civil, military and auxiliary circumstances, unless these actions were pursued in fulfilment of orders from the Islamic government. Punishment was of two kinds: he who assisted the colonial government without bringing any disadvantage to the Islamic state was to stop all activities; but he who spied for the enemy, thus bringing direct harm to the Islamic state, was to be sentenced to death (quoting Q 4:89).

Adherence to martial law – described as one of the five pillars of *jihad* – was a *fard al-'ayn* except for the blind, crippled, sick, physically weak and those affected by infectious diseases (quoting Q 9:90).[90] All the free, sane and physically able adult Muslim males had the duty to participate in *jihad* against those who waged war on the state (defined as *orang muharib* and *kafir harbi*, infidels of war), and those who, after appropriate investigation, appeared to be supporting the enemy. It was the *imam* or *amir*'s decision whether these enemies were to be executed, exchanged for captives of war or seized goods, enslaved or, even, set free.

90 This same article is referred to in Pinardi, *Sekarmadji Maridjan*, as Q 9:91. In Pinardi, the second group exempted from participating in *jihad* is said to be *rincang*, explained as *sakit mata* (those with eye defects); however, *rincang* does not appear to exist in Indonesian, and it is likely to be a misreading of *pintjang* (the crippled).

According to the text, in times of war there were only two communities: the *ummat Negara Islam* (*ummah Muslimin*), and the infidel oppressor (*ummat penjajah*, colonizer; *ummat kafirin*, infidel). Enemies are defined as those who do not adhere to Islam, those who do not recognize as forbidden what Allah forbade, those who had broken their pledge of loyalty (*muharrib*), polytheists (*mushrik*), the *munafiq* (quoting Q 8:38; 9:12, 28, 72; 4:75), *bughat* and bandits. In addition to the more general understanding of *bughat* as someone who broke the rules of the state, this term has also acquired a very politicized connotation since the Battle of Siffin, when it was used to describe those who did not recognize the authority of the *imam*. Here the term was used for the person who refused to follow the *imam* as leader of the state, even though the community had agreed upon his nomination. Martial law allowed the arrests of those who disseminated non-Islamic propaganda, those who in so doing disturbed the peace and order of the state, those who unsettled the population, those who contributed to strengthening the enemy, and those who were suspected of being a danger to the Islamic state (quoting S. Anas, *hadith* n. 7, *Subulussalam, Muhadhanah*).

During times of peace these same crimes were punished with imprisonment or *ta'zir*. The same article also offered guidance for handling the *bughat*, who was to be arrested and lectured on Islam for the first offence and, if arrested again, sentenced to banishment or capital execution; the *fasik* was first to be advised against strengthening the enemy, and only when this had failed was he to be punished with the impounding of his wealth. Only enemies who harboured the intention of opposing the state and who planned to weaken Islam politically, or tactically, could be held in captivity.

Whilst those arrested (*ditangkap*) were to be judged by a court, those held captive (*ditawan*) were considered spoils of war and had their punishments decided by the *imam* or *amir*, whether these captives were infidel sane men, women, children, mentally insane or transvestites (*wandu*[91]). The spoils also included: (a) goods belonging to the enemy and left behind; (b) goods seized from polytheists; (c) tenants of state land; (d) goods belonging to executed apostates; (e) goods belonging to a *kafir aman* (non-Muslim who had been granted safety) with no heirs; and (f) the commercial value of infidels who traded in the country. All these goods were to be considered *fa'i* (goods obtained from the enemy, but not in battle), and to be included in the *Mushalihu'l-Muslimin* community fund.

91 Pinardi uses *banci*, an alternative, yet more derogatory, term.

The spoils acquired in battle (*ghanimah*) were to be shared between the state treasury (which received 80% of the total) and – in equal parts – among the *imam*, the poor, the orphans, those who had participated in the battle (*Ibnu'sabil*), and the community fund administered by the *imam* (each receiving 4% of the remaining 20%). Still following Shafi'i doctrine, 80% of *fa'i* was given to the Islamic state, and the rest was divided in the same fashion as the *ghanimah. Salab* (what the enemy had used in battle) was instead taken in full by those who had participated in the military action. The captives of war could be either non-Muslims (*kafir*) or apostates (*murtad*): *kafir* were condemned to become slaves and property of the state, and decisions about their future were made by the *imam* and his representatives; *murtad* had the chance to repent of the misdeed of not following the laws of the Islamic state. Failing to do so within three days meant that they were to be sentenced to death. A person could only marry a captive female *murtad* once she had observed the '*idda* waiting period of three months and ten days, which only began when approved by the *imam* or his representative, the judge.

INITIAL ATTEMPTS TO RECONCILIATION (AUGUST-OCTOBER 1949)

The Republic was committed to negotiating a compromise with the Darul Islam. During a time when clashes were still occurring, Hatta sent Muhammad Natsir to Bandung to make contact with Kartosuwiryo. Natsir had originally refused to admit that he was trying to negotiate with the Darul Islam; however, once he arrived in Bandung, Natsir decided to involve their educator and friend Ahmad Hassan of Persis, hoping that Kartosuwiryo would respect their common teacher enough to agree to a meeting and even a compromise.[92] Confronted by Ahmad Hassan, who carried a letter written by Natsir, on 10 August 1949 Kartosuwiryo explained that the Islamic state had already been proclaimed three days earlier, and that he could not undo this act. Natsir also recalls that Kartosuwiryo complained to Ahmad Hassan that the request was not 'official enough' to be taken into consideration, as it had been written on letter-headed stationary.[93] As negotiations had come to nothing,

92 *Antara News* on 1 September 1949 reported: 'When questioned about the truth of newspapers' reports that he had contacted the irregular troops of DI [Natsir said]: is it possible that within two nights can I have contacted the DI whose headquarters are not even in Bandung?'
93 Panitya Buku Peringatan Muhammad Natsir, *Muhammad Natsir 70 tahun kenang-kenangan kehidupan dan perjuangan*, (Jakarta: Pustaka Antara, 1978), pp. 185-6.

the Darul Islam established itself in the rural areas whilst the TNI maintained its hold on the cities.[94]

As the Priangan was a firmly consolidated Darul Islam area, the struggle was now mostly conducted on the north coast in the Cirebon regency. Here, in the surroundings of Tegal and Brebes, the former TNI colonel and then commander of the TII Sjarif Hidajatullah division, Amir Fatah, led groups of 200-500 men, circulated NII pamphlets and regularly engaged with the TNI.[95] The clashes continued[96] even after the Darul Islam agreed, in early September 1949, to lay down its weapons and be incorporated into the Republican Army, provided that all TNI units located in Cirebon and the East Priangan were replaced with new troops who had not previously fought against the Islamic Army.[97] By the end of the first week of September, Darul Islam troops had withdrawn from West Cirebon, but the 'Darul Islam problem' was far from solved.[98]

In September, the Dutch-language newspaper *Nieuwe Courant* called the NII proclamation 'a coup d'état in the Pasoendan', and the Semarang-based *Sulu Rakjat* condemned the Darul Islam movement for 'having nothing to do with the actual meaning of its name, "house of peace"'. Even so, Masyumi leaders Muhammad Natsir and Zainal Arifin, as well as TNI Colonel Sadikin, decided to take some conciliatory steps.[99]

Steering clear of either condemning or praising the Darul Islam, Natsir encouraged Indonesians to see the difference between those who really wanted to advance the Islamic state ideal and those who instead only sought excuses to perpetrate vandalism. He went further, holding the Dutch responsible for creating the conditions

94 'Het cease fire bevel wordt over het algemeen gehoorzaamd', in *Indonesisch pers en radio overzicht, Java*, 25 August 1949. It is worth noting that despite the fact that rural and urban areas came under different spheres of control, the press noticed that the flow of daily supplies to the civilian population was not interrupted.

95 'Daroel Islam verdrijft TNI uit desa's', *De Vrije Pers*, 27 August 1949; 'CMI Signalement de Negara Islam Indonesia', 21 October 1949, AAS no. 3979, NA.

96 'Terreur door de Daroel Islam', *De Vrije Pers*, 2 September 1949; 'Strijd tussen Darul Islam en TNI', *Nieuwe Courant*, 5 September 1949; 'Gevechten tussen TNI en Daroel Islam', *Vrije Pers*, 5 September 1949; 'Strijd Tussen TNI en DI', *De Vrije Pers*, 10 September 1949; 'Darul Islam bertempur', *Berita*, 8 November 1949; 'Daroel Islam merampok', *Sin Po*, 9 November 1949; 'D.I. terreur neemt steeds ernstiger vormen aan', *De Vrije Pers*, 12 November 1949; 'DI menjerbu', *Merdeka*, 17 November 1949; 'Sekitar activiteit Daroel Islam', *Java Post*, 15 November 1949; 'Weer een bloedbad van Darul Islam-benden', *De Vrije Pers*, 18 November 1949.

97 'De "Darul Islam" bereid de wapens neer te leggen en tot de TNI toe te treden', *A.P.B.*, 1 September 1949; 'Darul Islam masuk TNI', *Berita*, 3 September 1949. It is likely that these articles referred to local groups carrying the name 'Darul Islam', rather than the regional movement.

98 'De situatie in Banjumas en in het Indramajuse', *A.P.B.*, 6 September 1949.

99 'Darul Islam', *Suluh Rakjat*, in *Indonesisch pers en radio overzicht, Java*, 9 September 1949; 'Bij Daroel Islam heet alles: straf-maatregel in oorlogstijd', *Nieuwe Courant*, 8 September 1949.

that led to the emergence of an Islamic movement in the Priangan when they first invaded Java in July 1947, and accusing them of now conducting a 'systematic media campaign' against it.[100]

By mid September, Natsir was chairing a commission for the study of the Darul Islam, which soon concluded that the Republic should not destroy Kartosuwiryo's movement.[101] Sadikin, now commander of the Siliwangi Division, stated that the TNI would not eliminate the Darul Islam and encouraged its soldiers to surrender their weapons,[102] and Zainal Arifin, member of the KNIP for Masyumi, accused the Dutch of using the Darul Islam for their own political gains. By inflating the threat posed by the Darul Islam, Arifin argued, the Dutch were trying to convince the Republic to agree to a longer-term Dutch military presence on Java. He described the Darul Islam as a 'self-defence movement against the despotic actions pursued by the Dutch Army' and a 'small issue' for the Republic.[103] These statements further reinforced Zainal Arifin's earlier comment that 'the conflict between TNI and DI is military as much as political [...]; the DI problem is not a very difficult one, and if no third party interferes, we will solve it amongst ourselves'.[104]

One attempt to solve the Darul Islam problem peacefully at the local level had been the establishment of neighbourhood associations. The chiefs of these organizations, however, were elected, which created a system that 'fully collided with traditional *adat* institutions in West Java', according to the Dutch Secretary of State for domestic affairs. He also feared that with the current widespread presence of terrorist organizations in the territory, the chiefs could be exploited as a result of their being in control of both population and goods, thus leading to the creation of a structure 'too similar to those implemented by totalitarian regimes'. The cure, the Secretary of State concluded, would likely prove worse than the disease itself.[105]

Dutch reports from these weeks focused on the Darul Islam's violent means, even though at the same time some Republican officers continued to insist on the commonality of aims between TII and TNI. And although clashes between the two armies were still

100 'Moh. Natsir tentang Daroel Islam', *Pewarta Surabaja*, 7 September 1949; 'Moh. Natsir: Er is een Darul Islam, doch er is ook een valse Darul Islam', in *Indonesisch pers en radio overzicht, Java*, 6 September 1949.

101 'CMI Signalement de Negara Islam Indonesia', 21 October 1949, AAS no. 3979, NA.

102 'Republik tida aken berantas Daroel Islam', *Sin Po*, 19 September 1949.

103 'Membesarkan berita D.I. untuk keuntungan politik', *Harian Berita*, 21 September 1949.

104 'KNIP-leden bezoeken het gebied van Tjiamis', in *Indonesisch pers en radio overzicht, Java*, 9 September 1949.

105 'Oprichting buurtgenootschappen ter bestrijding Darul-Islam', 7 November 1949, AAS no. 3979, NA.

taking place,[106] the commander of the 3rd TNI division in West Priangan, Major Ardiwinata, stated in a letter addressed to Darul Islam troops stationed in Lamburawi: 'I am a member of TNI, but as a Muslim, I am proud of the Islamic spirit that burns in your hearts [...] The goals of the TNI, to tell the truth, are not different from the goals of the DI's fight, and it is not appropriate that we become each other's enemies [...] Don't we all want a government blessed by Allah and endorsed by the people?'[107]

In a military report written after the NII proclamation, the Darul Islam in West Java was described as a movement advancing Islamic democracy, opposing colonialist capitalism and complying with the Republic's authority.[108] In 1951 another army report argued that in 1948-49 Colonel Sadikin and the Darul Islam shared the same goal of getting rid of the Dutch and ensuring Indonesia's independence.[109]

CONCLUDING REMARKS

The Dutch invasion and occupation of West Java in the second half of 1947 had the unexpected result of 'freeing' Kartosuwiryo from Soekarno's politics, allowing him – and West Java – to pursue a different path to independence. As West Java was declared Dutch territory, the Republican agenda – now decided upon in Yogyakarta – had become irrelevant to this region. Gradually Kartosuwiryo, Kamran, Oni and K.H. Gozali Toesi realized what they had imagined and planned for years: the embryo of an Islamic state of Indonesia. Throughout this chapter we have seen the idea of such a state and its structure evolving from the Garut-based 'Defence Council' to the regional network of MOIs, followed by the expansion of the latter's control across West Java and then into Central Java, to the eventual proclamation of the Negara Islam Indonesia with a constitution and a penal code.

106 Clashes were still taking place between Islamic and regular troops, as accounted in 'Report by TNI Siliwangi', 21 October 1949, AABRI DI no. 4; 'Lapuran mingguan bulan November', TNI Siliwangi, 7 December 1949, AABRI DI no. 8.

107 Letter from Major Ardiwinata, Commander of III D. West Priangan, to Darul Islam 'brothers' in Lamburawi, 26 September 1949, AABRI DI no. 3.

108 '1. Organisasi badan perdjuangan di Jawa Barat, 1945-1948', AABRI DI [n.d.].

109 'Verslag tugas penjelesaian DI Djawa Barat', 20 July 1951, AABRI DI no. 15.
Another perspective on the changed relationship between Kartosuwiryo and the Republic can be found in B. Elson and C. Formichi, 'Why did Kartosuwiryo start shooting?', *Journal of Southeast Asian Studies* 42-3 (October 2011): pp. 458-86.

The Republic's reaction to Kartosuwiryo's actions is the parallel thread woven throughout this chapter and at the heart of the next. As encapsulated in Boland's and Kahin's statements, this relationship is generally understood as Darul Islam's opposition to the Republic. Post-independence state-controlled narratives, expounded in Chapter 6, also propagated the idea that, in the eyes of the Republican state, Kartosuwiryo and the Darul Islam were 'the enemy within'. However, it is quite clear their relationship was more complicated: in 1948 TNI and TII attempted to coordinate actions on the ground, TII commanders reached out to Republican ministers arguing they fought the same battle, and several Masyumi leaders in the Republic's territory were also inclined towards creating an Islamic state.

The separation of the political paths taken by the Pancasila Republic and the Islamic State in mid 1947 had helped smooth the edges of the secular nationalists and the religious factions. But the political re-unification of Java after the second Dutch invasion in December 1948 precipitated a situation in which Kartosuwiryo openly accused Soekarno of being a weak leader and a puppet of the colonial masters. Within the Republican ranks, commanders and politicians were not all of the same mind. Opposing military and political interests left the relationship between the Republic and the Darul Islam undefined throughout 1949 and well into the 1950s, as we shall see in the next chapter.

5

The 'War of the Roses'
The Islamic state and the Pancasila Republic (1949-1962)

[The government] should not consider [the Darul Islam] an enemy, rather like a father his son. Regardless of how naughty the son, if taught a lesson he should not be beaten to death, rather given a lecture, or dealt just one blow, drenched in affection. It is similar with a domestic rebellious movement.[1]

Disillusioned by the Republic's acquiescence to Dutch demands, under pressure by the TNI's operations in West Java and let down by Masyumi's inability to make political Islam relevant in parliamentary politics, on 7 August 1949 Kartosuwiryo and the *dewan imamah* had officially proclaimed the establishment of the Negara Islam Indonesia.

As shown in the previous chapter, Masyumi's political leadership and some elements of the TNI reached out to Kartosuwiryo's NII in the following months to find a political solution to what had become known as the 'Darul Islam problem' (*soal Darul Islam*). This chapter follows the relationship between the Islamic state and the Indonesian Republic in the aftermath of the surrender of Dutch sovereignty, focusing in particular on how the transformation from the federal RIS to a unitary state affected NII's attitude and activities.

Diplomacy had dictated the rhythm of Indonesian politics for years, with treaties followed by ceasefires followed by their infringement. Some provinces in the archipelago were slowly warming up to the idea of a federal Republic under the patronage of the House of Orange, but the population of West Java – regardless of its allegiance to the Islamic state – remained unimpressed by the Roem-Van Royen agreement, which, far from confirming the country's independence, had established the Negara Pasoendan as an instrument of The Hague.

1 Kasman Singodimedjo, chairman of Masyumi, 'DI anaknja, Masjumi ajahnja', *Harian Ra'jat*, 20 September 1955.

The Dutch were buying the allegiance of civil servants and politicians, and Republican leaders were settling the details for the transfer of sovereignty. Yet, despite its opposition to the Dutch-sponsored state, its frustration at the Republican leadership's diplomatic approach and its anger at the Siliwangi Division's re-entry in 1948, the Darul Islam was not yet univocally antagonizing the Republican government and army.

If one were to believe the image of Darul Islam that has been dominant since the 1960s (a topic I explore in the next chapter), it would be easy to think that as early as 1948-49 the Siliwangi Division and Republican leaders, concerned with restoring law and order, openly condemned the Darul Islam as a destabilizing force, an agent of the Netherlands and a terrorist movement exploiting and oppressing the people of West Java. On the contrary, archival sources clearly show that the scattered occurrences of cooperation that had dotted 1948 continued through 1949, and that, until the mid 1950s, military commanders and political leaders (mostly, but not exclusively, from Masyumi) suggested that the Republic should put its efforts into finding a political solution to the Darul Islam problem.

SHIFTING APPROACHES: BETWEEN NEGOTIATION AND CONDEMNATION (1949-1954)

The 'Commission for the solution to the Darul Islam problem'

At the end of 1949, two years after the conception of the Majelis Oemmat Islam and the organization of the Islamic Army, the NII was well established in West Java and in Republican areas. Following the second Dutch attack on the Indonesian Republic, in December 1948, Kartosuwiryo appointed a TII consul for the Republican territory,[2] the Central Java branch of Masyumi was transformed into an MOI, and, in early March 1949, an *imam* was appointed to the Majelis Islam in Solo.[3]

In mid 1948 the Darul Islam had expanded well into Central Java under the command of Amir Fatah, and groups had been established in the Banten area, including Malingping, in west-

2 'Pemerintah NII – Petikan daripada Piagam2 Imam no. 200/PNII/I/48, 12 December 1948, JogjaDoc no. 218b, ANRI.

3 Letter from Madjlis Islam daerah Surakarta to Imam Negara Islam Indonesia, 9 April 1949, KabPerd no. 150, ANRI.

ern Java.[4] But its influence had gone further than this, with the dispatching of an NII consul to Sumatra. Although the CMI had identified some Darul Islam groups outside Java as early as October 1949, it would take a few more years before the DI-TII established other structured branches and battalions, with their own distinctive characteristics there. The Aceh rebels, for example, only openly declared their participation in the NII in 1955.

By the time that colonial rule in West Java was coming to an end, in early September 1949, the press had already exposed the inability of the Dutch to respond to Darul Islam's attacks.[5] As the Islamic militias, which were now defined by the media as 'bandits', were disseminating terror[6] and clashing with other soldiers,[7] the vice-president of the Pasoendan state was counting on TNI's support to solve the problem.[8]

According to a military source, the intensification of Darul Islam's activities was aimed at 'improv[ing] their [Darul Islam's] situation before the transfer of sovereignty to the RIS, meaning before the region's control [was] to be transferred to the TNI'.[9] The ramping up of activities should be read in both political and military terms. On the one hand, it represented the Islamic state's attempt to conquer as much territory as possible from the Dutch, so as to appear stronger against the Republic of Yogyakarta. On the other hand, the Islamic Army felt more comfortable attacking colonial soldiers, rather than fellow Indonesians.

Months passed, marked by contrasting opinions and the absence of a coherent approach towards the Darul Islam, as illustrated in the previous chapter. Then, at its West Java congress – in which only the Banten, Jakarta, Bogor and Cirebon branches participated – Masyumi made it clear that it disagreed with Kartosuwiryo, even if the party was far from condemning his entire movement. K.H. Wahid Hasjim stated that

> every Muslim has to strive for the establishment of an Islamic state, and Masyumi, as an Islamic political party, agrees with the institution of an Islamic state. It doesn't just agree with it, but it also has to apply itself towards its achievement. What Masyumi doesn't agree with, in regards to the 'Preparation for an Islamic State of Pasoen-

4 'Rapport', Politie Bantam, 8 October 1949, APG no. 998, NA.

5 *Antara News*, 2 September 1949 and 20 October 1949.

6 'Soal TNI dan DI – Petjajaan anggota Parl. Pasoendan', *Berita Indonesia*, 29 November 1949; 'DI menjerbu – 100 rakjat mendjadi korban', *Berita Indonesia*, 17 November 1949.

7 *Antara News*, 3 November 1949, 9 November 1949, 15 November 1949 and 18 November 1949 (in Cirebon, Indramayu and Garut).

8 *Antara News*, 2 September 1949.

9 'Tentara Belanda menggempur DI', *Berita Indonesia*, 7 December 1949.

> dan', is not its Islamic foundation, but rather the fact that a separatist movement in West Java uses the banner of Islam when the general population wants instead West Java to be a region within the [federal] state.[10]

On this same occasion, the party renewed its commitment to the 'parliamentary way' of establishing Indonesia as an Islamic state,[11] and a week later the national congress in Yogyakarta issued a resolution requesting that the RIS form a 'solution commission' (Komisi/ Panitya Penyelesaian Darul Islam) that would 'look for the best way to settle the Darul Islam issue and all that is linked to it'.[12]

At the transfer of sovereignty, Soekarno named Mohammad Hatta, Ide Agung Gde Agung of Bali, Sultan Hamengkoeboewono IX of Yogyakarta and Sultan Hamid II of Kalimantan as *formateurs* of the first federal cabinet. This body was not to represent party politics, but rather was meant as a 'work cabinet', representing Masyumi, PNI, the Christian party and several others.[13] More important than the cabinet's wide-spread ideological representation, though, was the fact that the Indonesian Republic of Yogyakarta retained the majority of seats, whilst the remaining sixteen states and territories only accounted for a minority.[14] This imbalance was to play a crucial role in the following months, as the Republic of Indonesia (Yogyakarta) pressed the case for the dismantling of the federal structure in favour of a unitary one.[15]

As Masyumi's prediction that the Darul Islam would dissolve had not come true with the final transfer of sovereignty and the subsequent withdrawal of the Dutch – nor had the movement relented in its violence – the Darul Islam became a problem for the new Indonesian state. Throughout 1950, politicians across the spectrum issued comments on what the government and parties should do about it.

10 'Separatisme – mendjalankan move baru dng. nama Islam', *Berita Indonesia*, 12 December 1949. The outlook of the federal state and the dynamics surrounding its establishment have been expounded in great detail by Kahin, *Nationalism and revolution*, pp. 391-445.

11 'Masjumi menghendaki Negara Islam dengan djalan parlamenter', *Warta Indonesia*, 10 December 1949.

12 'Resolusi Kongres Masjumi tentang DI', *Warta Indonesia*, 22 December 1949.

13 The cabinet featured four Masyumi ministers (Finance, Education, Religious Affairs and one without portfolio), three PNI ministers (Labour, Communications and Information), one minister from the Christian Party and seven more without affiliation.

14 East Indonesia held the Interiors' and Information seats, Pasoendan the seat for Social Affairs and West Borneo had one minister without portfolio. But the remaining eleven seats were occupied by Republican ministers.

15 Herbert Feith, *The decline of constitutional democracy in Indonesia* (Ithaca: Cornell University Press, 1962), pp. 46-100.

The debate about a proper 'solution' to the problem of the Darul Islam was opened in December 1949 by Masyumi, which issued a resolution advocating the political option. Masyumi's position was quickly endorsed by the temporary government of Garut, which then demanded the formation of a commission to ensure that the Darul Islam was transformed into a civilian organization.[16] The following month in Ponorogo, Muhammadiyah and Nahdatul Ulama members of Masyumi took a more extreme position, openly condemning the movement as 'unhealthy' and un-Islamic because of its violent methods, and criticizing it for drawing its ideology from 'outside of the boundaries of what is deemed acceptable by the party'.[17]

In March 1950, the Minister of Religious Affairs, K.H. Wahid Hasjim, was compelled to spell out to President Soekarno that only the Darul Islam had turned its back on the 1945 proclamation. The rest of the Islamic community of the Priangan supported the proclamation and had repeatedly affirmed its commitment to the Republican government. Hasjim stressed that the bulk of the Islamic community should thus be protected from any form of violence, both at the hands of the Army and the Darul Islam.[18]

The government appeared strongly committed to a political compromise, as Mohammad Hatta and the now Minister of Defence Hamengkoeboewono IX had attempted for months to get in touch with Darul Islam's local leaders, as well as with Kartosuwiryo himself. The government went as far as establishing a 'contact commission', under the jurisdiction of the Ministry of Interiors. In early 1950 the vice-mayor of Yogyakarta announced that, between December 1948 and late 1949, Hatta sent two letters to Kartosuwiryo: one from his exile in Bangka and one after he had returned to Yogyakarta. Hatta had asked if the Darul Islam and the Republic could elaborate a common strategy of defence against the Dutch; if Kartosuwiryo was interested in receiving a Republican medal for combat; and if he would reconsider his position on the Republic once an independent state of Indonesia was established. These letters apparently went unanswered.[19]

16 'Mosi badan perwakilan sementara Kabupaten Garut', 7 January 1950, Kabinet Presiden Republik Indonesia Serikat 1949-1950 [hereafter RIS], no. 85, ANRI.

17 'Suara Masjumi terhadap Darul Islam', Kantor Polisi Kabupaten Ponorogo, 16 January 1950, KabPerd no. 150, ANRI.

18 'Nota oleh seorang '*ulama* dikirim dari Menteri Agama RIS K.H. Wachid Hasjim kepada President RIS tentang ummat Islam di Priangan dan soal Darul Islam', 21 March 1959, RIS no. 97, ANRI.

19 'Ichtisar gerakan DI/Kartosuwiryo', Kementerian Dalam Negeri Yogyakarta, 24 July 1950, KabPerd no. 150, ANRI.

The 'solution commission' was not making any evident progress. Between late March and early May 1950, several members were replaced (including Colonel Sadikin, whose position was assigned to the less politically involved Colonel Wijono), but still the commission was making no progress. The Islamic parties began openly questioning the competency of the commission and complaining that the RIS government should be more committed to a political solution while limiting the military attacks conducted by the Army against the Darul Islam – an issue that had also been raised at the KNIP meeting.[20] The Ministry of Religion kept redrafting the list of members of the Panitya Penyelasaian Darul Islam; by August 1950, nothing had been achieved.[21]

'Silently resorting to great military force'

Meanwhile, the movement for a unitary state was gaining enough political support in Jakarta that in March 1950 the Hatta Cabinet issued an emergency decree stating the possibility for federal states and territories to merge into the Yogyakarta-based Republic of Indonesia. Republican propaganda in favour of the unitary state was articulated in the rhetoric of the country's colonial legacy. This discourse was marked by the condemnation of arbitrary boundaries, a heavy and confusing administrative apparatus and, above all, the suppression of the spirit of nationalism that had driven the revolution.

The process of unification did not proceed smoothly, as demonstrations ensued in both pro- and anti-unification camps, which often deteriorated into violence. Even though some territorial entities had been incorporated into the Republic as early as January 1950, other regions – such as West Java, Aceh, South Maluku, Kalimantan and South Sulawesi – continued to fight for autonomy until the late 1950s and mid 1960s (or even later, as in the case of Aceh). By May 1950 the Hatta Cabinet had concluded that, in Herbert Faith's words, 'A unitary state had to be achieved quickly'.[22]

20 'Sikap PSII terhadap penjelesaian soal Darul Islam', 4 May 1950, RIS no. 107, ANRI. 'Kutipan pertanjaan-pertanjaan anggauta-anggauta badan pekerdja Komite Nasional Pusat kepada Pemerintah untuk didjawab pada harti-pertanjaan sidang ke-V tahun 1950; mengenai Kementerian Dalam Negeri, dari anggauta W. Wondoamiseno (PSII)', KabPerd no. 150, ANRI.

21 An early draft of the members of the Panitya Penyelesaian Darul Islam (Commission for the solution of the Darul Islam) was prepared by the Ministry of Religious Affairs (11 June 1950), but subsequent drafts (8 July and 8 August 1950) show the (attempted) collaboration of the ministries of the Interiors, Religious Affairs, Information and Social Affairs. All in KabPerd no. 150, ANRI.

22 Feith, *The decline*, p. 68.

The first statement to openly condemn the tactics of the cabinet and the army against the Darul Islam was issued by a small group named Angkatan Muslim Sedar, or Amusa, about which little is known. The Amusa statement argued that such treatment should be reserved for Westerling and his APRA troops (Angkatan Perang Ratu Adil, Army of the Just King), which were a 'deviation' and had nothing in common with the 'holy aim' of Kartosuwiryo's Darul Islam, the essence of whose struggle should be valued.[23] In a similar tone, Masyumi accused the government of ignoring its requests to approach the Darul Islam with 'peace and compromise' and instead 'silently resorting to great military force'. The government was blamed for giving too much autonomy to the army, more often than not endangering the civilian population.[24]

In May 1950, PSII leader Wondoamiseno – representing the working committee of KNIP – questioned the RIS parliament on its approach to the Darul Islam. Wondoamiseno strongly criticized the government's decision to use military force and the army's inability to limit civilian casualties. He voiced his disapproval of the fact that Muslims in the Priangan and Pekalongan had stopped praying and attending mosques for fear that soldiers would arrest those displaying the kind of 'pious' attitude to religion that might mark them as Darul Islam sympathizers. Wondoamiseno concluded by requesting that the government make public the numbers of those arrested and their arrest reports to determine whether they had really been Darul Islam members or not.[25] At around the same time, the PSII's frustration towards the government reached its peak. After recognizing that the party's institutional and individual support for a peaceful solution had generated no results, PSII's central committee resolved to instruct its branches and members to remove themselves from any bodies that had been set up to solve the Darul Islam problem, thereby rejecting any further responsibility for the problem or for its solution.[26]

23 'Angkatan Muslim Sedar "Amusa", perihal Darul Islam dipolisionil', General Secretary S. Ridjaluddin, 24 March 1950, KabPerd no. 150, ANRI. The APRA was led by Captain Westerling, a defecting Dutch officer who first led rebels in South Sulawesi and then moved to West Java, where in January 1950 they occupied Bandung. For more on the APRA, see Chapter 6.

24 'Statement Masjumi tentang perisitiwa "Darul Islam"', Ketua Dewan Pimpinan Partai Masjumi Moh. Natsir, 23 April 1950, KabPerd no. 150, ANRI.

25 'Kutipan pertanjaan-pertanjaan anggauta-anggauta badan pekerdja Komite Nasional Pusat kepada Pemerintah untuk didjawab pada harti-pertanjaan sidang ke-V tahun 1950; mengenai Kementerian Dalam Negeri, dari anggauta W. Wondoamiseno (PSII)', KabPerd no. 150, ANRI.

26 'Sikap PSII terhadap penjelesaian soal Darul Islam', 4 May 1950, RIS no. 107, ANRI.

The duty to restore peace

As attempts to negotiate were failing, and as the army was (successfully) conducting small-scale anti-Darul Islam operations between March and early May 1950, the areas of Tasikmalaya and Pekalongan saw a number of DI-TNI clashes and Darul Islam attacks on the civilian population, and combatants were being arrested in large numbers. At the same time, though, the press highlighted that in East Priangan, where the population was particularly poor, the Darul Islam's scheme of land re-distribution had ameliorated the general living conditions of the local population, further reinforcing the conviction that the Darul Islam 'issue' could only be solved through a political compromise.[27]

But the Islamic groups were not the only ones to be disappointed. Cries for a political solution were coming from many sides, especially after the Yogyakarta police had underlined that this would have been facilitated by Kartosuwiryo's diminishing strength. Wali Alfatah – the Masyumi leader and political representative for Central Java who was in favour of an Islamic state – agreed to embark on a mission to meet Kartosuwiryo at his headquarters in June 1950. However, he never succeeded in meeting Kartosuwiryo, and was instead held captive for several weeks by Darul Islam soldiers. Upon his release in late June, he commented that the *imam* would not accept a diplomatic solution and that only military force could bring the problem to an end.[28]

In the same month, Hamengkoeboewono IX planned a personal and unofficial visit to the areas affected by Darul Islam in Tasikmalaya. Soon after his return, Hamengkoeboewono IX reminded the population that the army's role was to maintain order in the country, regardless of whether the enemy included peasants, labourers or religion itself. The TNI was thus ordered to cut all supply lines to Darul Islam headquarters. Despite the parties' lack of faith in the efficacy of the parliament, a Republican official encouraged PSII and Masyumi to cooperate with the government to bring the Darul Islam to an end.[29]

Because Kartosuwiryo seemed uninterested in a dialogue with the representatives of the Republic unless Soekarno first recog-

27 'Ichtisar gerakan DI/Kartosuwiryo', Kementerian Dalam Negeri Yogyakarta, 24 July 1950, KabPerd no. 150, ANRI.

28 'Missi sdr. Wali Alfattach', Kementerian Dalam Negeri Yogyakarta to Minister of the Interiors RI in Yogyakarta, 10 June 1950, KabPerd no. 150, ANRI.

29 'Ichtisar gerakan DI/Kartosuwiryo', Kementerian Dalam Negeri Yogyakarta, 24 July 1950, KabPerd no. 150, ANRI.

nized the NII, the conviction built up amongst the public that he was not going to accept any compromise. The Chinese-Indonesian newspaper *Sin Po* suggested that after all the effort the Darul Islam had put into keeping the Dutch at bay, it would never agree to give up the areas it controlled; nor would the population be keen on TNI regiments taking their place, as the Islamic militias still enjoyed much support. An even bleaker picture was drawn by an official in Pekalongan, who argued that the Darul Islam would not be terminated by either military force or political compromise, as it was there to stay.

Eventually, on 30 June, the RIS cabinet issued a declaration published in *Kedaulatan Rakjat* stating that it 'respected the DI's ideology as one of the political streams (*aliran*)', but adding that if the movement caused disorder in society, the government had the duty to restore peace.[30]

The unitary state: 'A modern form of colonialism'

Between May and July 1950, the federal Republic and the Republic of Indonesia in Yogyakarta formed a joint committee to work on a constitutional text for the unitary state. The two ministerial cabinets approved a draft, but their respective parliaments did not ratify it. Reiterating the 'temporary' character of the 1945 Constitution, this document did not provide a timeline for elections; it appointed Soekarno president of the new Unitary State of Indonesia (Negara Kesatuan Republik Indonesia), and it retained the Yogyakarta Republic's majority in parliament. After reshuffling the Pasoendan cabinet, warranted by the local leadership's alleged involvement in the Westerling case, the supporters of the Yogyakarta Republic eventually outnumbered pro-federation representatives by 20 members.[31]

The unitary state was declared on 17 August 1950, marking the quinquennium of Soekarno's proclamation of independence, and thus symbolically casting this Unitary Republic in the legacy of the Yogyakarta Republic. Soekarno's 'Bersatu kembali' speech, celebrating the birth of the unitary state, prompted a direct answer from the Islamic state. The proclamation of a unitary state was a

30 'Ichtisar gerakan DI/Kartosuwiryo', Kementerian Dalam Negeri Yogyakarta, 24 July 1950, KabPerd no. 150, ANRI; Statement Masjumi tentang peristiwa "Darul Islam"', Ketua Dewan Pimpinan Partai Masjumi Moh. Natsir, 23 April 1950, KabPerd no. 150, ANRI; 'Sikap PSII terhadap penjelesaian soal Darul Islam', 4 May 1950, RIS no. 107, ANRI; 'Soal Darul Islam dan pembersihan jang telah diadakan', Menteri Pertahanan RIS, 8 May 1950, KabPerd no. 150, ANRI.

31 Feith, *The decline*, pp. 46-99.

heavy blow to the Darul Islam as Kartosuwiryo and his colleagues still aspired to establish an Islamic state, at the very least in West Java, with its authority recognized within the federal structure. The fact that Kartosuwiryo continued to hold on to this goal is evidenced by the Darul Islam's attempt to make a connection with Wiranatakoesoema and the 1948 Masyumi congress.

The NII's information office in Pekalongan replied to Soekarno's speech by stating that the unitary Republic was 'a modern form of colonialism', both political and economic. According to the NII, this transformation was in opposition to the principles of the 1945-49 revolution, the very revolution that Soekarno pointed to as the kernel of this new state. Hence, 'it is impossible for the Islamic guerrilla to surrender its weapons', because doing so would be the greatest betrayal to the Indonesian people.[32]

A new round of negotiations

Muhammad Natsir was appointed to form the first cabinet of the unitary state in September 1950. This cabinet's first priority was internal security, and, consistent with his August 1949 attempt to negotiate with Kartosuwiryo, Natsir once again refused to take a strong stand on the Darul Islam. In November Natsir called for a general amnesty for all armed guerrillas.

Perhaps hopeful that a Masyumi government would take a positive attitude towards the issues of the Islamic state and the Darul Islam's achievements in the independence struggle, around the same time Kartosuwiryo sent letters to both Soekarno and Natsir, arguing that political Islam was the only weapon the Republic had to fight communism, as they were 'ideological enemies'. Emphasizing that nationalism could be co-opted by leftist agitators, Kartosuwiryo suggested that the Republic should be transformed into an Islamic state.[33]

This proposal was never taken seriously, but Al Chaidar has suggested that in December 1950 Natsir attempted once again to make contact with Kartosuwiryo, this time via a former PSII colleague, Kiyai Muslich. Kartosuwiryo refused to receive the *kiyai,* but instead entrusted him with a personal letter for the Prime Minister. In this letter, Kartosuwiryo offered the NII's absolute support if Natsir

32 'Sambutan seruan PR Bung Karno (Presiden) pd. tg. 17 August 1950 tentang: "Bersatu Kembali" jg. disiarkan oleh Kementerian Penerangan RI', Jawatan Penerangan NII daerah Pekalongan, RIS no. 131, ANRI.

33 'Nota rahasia' from Kartosuwiryo to Soekarno, 22 October 1950, in Boland, *The struggle of Islam,* pp. 244-9.

were to use his authority to 'add the letter "I" to the RI', so as to transform the Pancasila state into the 'Republik Islam Indonesia'.[34]

Sporadic attempts to negotiate continued in the years to come, but they were to little avail, as Kartosuwiryo was committed to defending the 'sacred right' (*hak suci*) of the Islamic *ummah* to live in an Islamic state. If the Republic was not ready to recognize the NII as an autonomous state, then he 'could not be responsible for the fate of the Indonesian state and people, in front of neither the Tribunal of History, nor the Tribunal of God'.[35] These kinds of statements by Kartosuwiryo only further polarized Masyumi and the secularists. The former reiterated its dedication to an Islamic state through democracy and parliamentary debates – thus signalling its commonality of goals with Kartosuwiryo – whilst the latter were strengthened in their conviction that the solution to the Darul Islam lay in decisive military action.

Natsir's dedication to diplomacy with the Darul Islam was transformed, in January 1951, into accusations that the Darul Islam had infiltrated Masyumi. Natsir had to explain that attempting to make contact with Kartosuwiryo and his lieutenants had been a strategy to reach a political solution and not an indication of complicity. Within a few days, Isa Anshary, the chairman of the West Java branch of Masyumi, issued a 'freeze' on the Garut party branch on account of military attacks against Masyumi's members, accused of collaboration with the Darul Islam.[36] Natsir remained convinced that the Darul Islam 'problem' – as well as the unrest in South Sulawesi and Sumatra – could only be solved through political action and eliminating the 'source of disappointment', as the use of military force had initiated a vicious cycle that was slowly dragging the country into civil war.[37]

Soekiman's 'more resolute way'

Natsir was unwilling to cooperate with the nationalist PNI, and his cabinet fell within six months of its installation. Soekarno then requested that the second cabinet, eventually formed by another Masyumi leader, Soekiman, should be truly a coalition cabinet. The

34 Al Chaidar, *Pemikiran politik*, p. 116.

35 'Nota rahasia kedua' from Kartosuwiryo to Soekarno, 17 February 1951, in Boland, *The struggle of Islam*, pp. 250-5.

36 'Masjumi tidak di-infiltrasi oleh Darul Islam', *Berita Masjumi*, 12 January 1951; 'Tentang infiltrasi DI dalam Masjumi' and 'Masjumi Garut dibekukan', *Berita Masjumi*, 19 January 1951.

37 Muhammad Natsir, *Capita selecta* (Jakarta: Abadi-Yayasan Capita Selecta, 2008), vol. 2, pp. 48-50, 66-8, 230-5, 272-4, 275, 331, 340-5, 371-2, 381-2, 392-8, 422-3; vol. 3, p. 26. These articles and speeches were delivered between 12 May 1951 and 11 November 1956.

resulting coalition was characterized by smoother inter-party relations, a decisive anti-communist outlook and a clear antagonism between the government and the army. This tension mostly arose as a result of the army's realization that its role was shrinking while post-revolution Indonesia developed into a constitutional democracy.

These tensions were not eased even by Soekiman's tougher approach to the Darul Islam. The cabinet's early days were marked by the pride that 'this [Soekiman's] cabinet will address the issue of security in a more resolute way, which will be felt by the people when compared to the previous cabinet, which endeavoured to end the DI problem with politics'. To this statement Natsir replied: 'The cabinet saw the Darul Islam as one aspect of the more general guerrilla problem [...] but I was not qualified to determine how to end it. Whether [the solution] was political, or military, or military-political depended on the experts.'[38]

Despite his stronger disposition towards a military solution, Soekiman did not manage to launch an anti-Darul Islam military operation, as he had to focus instead on the other rebellions that had suddenly reawakened in mid 1951. Most strikingly, the agreement that Natsir had reached, after months of negotiations, with Kahar Mudzakkar in South Sulawesi, and which sanctioned the incorporation of his battalions into the Republican Army, came undone. On the eve of the ceremony, Mudzakkar fled to the mountains with his men, a group that was estimated to number around 20,000.[39] In the meantime, the 426 Battalion of the Central Java TNI Division, disappointed with the direction taken by the Republic, mutinied *en masse*, swelling the rank and file of the Darul Islam.[40]

Soekarno's Pancasila national state and its opponents

Essentially an administrator's cabinet, Soekiman's government did not last long, but subsequent attempts to form a politically coherent cabinet headed by a charismatic leader also failed. After two months of negotiations, Soekarno resolved to let Wilopo (of the PNI) form another coalition government. Between its inauguration in April 1952 and its fall in June 1953, this cabinet saw many changes in the national climate. Political Islam was weakened by Nahdatul Ulama's decision to leave Masyumi, the Communist Party succeeded in overcoming the legacy of the Peristiwa Madiun

38 'Soal DI: Suatu bagian dari masalah gerilla', *Berita Masjumi*, 16 May 1951.

39 Feith, *The decline*, pp. 172, 212-3.

40 Markhaban Fakkih, 'Golongan santri dan peristiwa 426 di Klaten' (thesis, Universitas Gadjah Mada, Yogyakarta, 1970).

(Madiun Affair) and became a supporter of Soekarno and army hierarchies were reorganized after the 17 October affair.

As noted, Masyumi had emerged during the Japanese occupation from the merging of various political and non-political Islamic organizations. During its reorganization after 1945, NU members had been relegated to the Majelis Sjoero on account of their legal expertise. In 1949, however, this organ had been transformed from a legislative body into an advisory committee, stripped of its legal authority. NU's final split from Masyumi resulted primarily from two main factors. First, NU's political aspirations had been repeatedly frustrated: in the two Masyumi cabinets, NU had only been assigned the Ministry of Religious Affairs, and in 1952 NU had been deprived of this ministry as well. Second, there continued to be a great difference between modernist and traditionalist understandings of the religion-politics nexus which entailed quite different strategies for achieving the Islamization of state and society.

Soon after the split, the NU re-constituted itself as a political party and joined forces with the PSII, the Sumatran Persatuan Tarbiah Islamiyah (Perti, Islamic Tarbiyah Union) and a smaller Islamic party from Sulawesi, to form the Liga Muslimin Indonesia (League of Indonesian Muslims). Aside from supplying an alternative to Masyumi's vision of Islam and politics, the formation of the league overall weakened the Islamic front in parliament. In the 1955 elections, Masyumi would finish second, after the PNI, whilst the NU would finish third, closely followed by the PKI.

The Communist Party underwent much transformation in the 1950s. Dipa Nusantara Aidit, representing the younger generation, had returned to Indonesia soon after the end of the revolution, and in 1951 succeeded in assuming the party's leadership. Gradually playing down his connections with Moscow, Aidit espoused nationalism. By 1953 the party had become openly supportive of Soekarno, and in 1954 it embraced the Pancasila. It was this very step that raised concerns within Muslim circles and marked a change in Islamic groups' approach to the state philosophy.[41]

Masyumi's and Nahdatul Ulama's worries rose in the following years, and not just because the first principle of the Pancasila – the belief in the one and only God – was being emptied of its religious value gradually becoming acceptable even to communists, but also because Soekarno had abandoned his professed ideological neutrality. In late January 1953, during a visit to Amuntai, South Kalimantan, Soekarno declared that 'the state we want is a national state consisting of all Indonesia. If we establish a state based on Islam, many areas

41 Feith, *The decline*, pp. 225-46; Nasution, *The Islamic state in Indonesia*, pp. 91-9.

whose population is not Islamic, such as the Moluccas, Bali, Flores, Timor, the Kai islands, and Sulawesi, will secede'.[42] Whilst in Makassar the following year, Soekarno explained that the first *sila* should be understood to include also 'the animist belief in spirits and ghosts'.[43]

The 1953 speech made in the Muslim town of Amuntai resonated across the religious spectrum, not least because of the looming elections. When Soekarno was asked to elaborate further on the Amuntai statement, he solemnly replied that the Pancasila already represented a compromise and that what Indonesia needed now was unity, not debate. Not only would a national state refrain from opposing Islamic precepts, he argued, but because Islamic texts include no explicit basis for democracy or elections, Muslims should not be able to say, 'My party has the larger numbers, I must win'. Laying the foundations for his *konsepsi* (vision), Soekarno added that democracy was just a means, not a goal in itself, and what the people needed was a 'democracy with leadership'.[44]

These declarations also reassured non-Muslims that even though Soekarno was a Muslim who often welcomed others with the Islamic greeting *as-salam 'alaykum* and mentioned the Qur'an and *hadith* in his speeches, the Indonesian Republic was a national state based on the Pancasila. Reactions to the Amuntai speech ranged from 'Soekarnoists' praising his political *savoir-faire* in ensuring that the nation would not collapse into a civil war, to religious political leaders condemning the statement. Isa Anshary accused Soekarno's speech of being un-democratic, un-constitutional and in open conflict with Islam. Anshary's comments were followed by the NU chairman's refutation of the president's statement that 'an Islamic government would not concern itself with the unity of the people'. Another reaction came from the Front Muballighin Islam in Medan, which argued that Muslims did not reject the Pancasila, but felt this was an 'incomplete' ideology. Perti argued that the issue of *dasar negara* (foundation of the state) should be surrendered to the constitutional assembly 'in a democratic fashion', without necessitating presidential intervention. Finally, the GPII sent a letter to Soekarno stressing that he was misleading Indonesians about the true meaning of Islam, that he was not teaching them the principles of democracy and that ultimately he himself was planting the seeds of separatism.[45]

42 Feith, *The decline*, p. 281.

43 Soekarno's speech was given in Makassar in May 1954, as reported in Nasution, *The Islamic state in Indonesia*, p. 99.

44 Feith and Castles (eds), *Indonesian political thinking*, pp. 164-70; quote from p. 170.

45 All the above visions are recorded in Sajuti Melik's booklet, *Negara nasional ataukah Negara Islam* (Yogyakarta: Kedaulatan Rakjat, 1953), pp. 10-4.

The greatest impact of the Amuntai speech was felt in Aceh, where in March the crowd received the president with banners reading, 'We love the president, but we love religion more'.[46] These banners suggested that if creating an Islamic state would have driven away non-Muslim regions, Soekarno's Pancasila state would have the opposite effect, leaving Islamic regions no choice but to separate themselves from the state. The 'Manifesto of the Atjeh Rebels' issued by Daud Beureueh in 1953 seemed to confirm this view; because the Pancasila was taking over the law of God, Beureueh argued, 'we shall therefore be the ones to secede from a state that is based upon nationalism'.

Showing some similarities with Kartosuwiryo's approach, the manifesto went on to describe not 'a state within the state', but rather a separate state entirely: 'We have always seen the Republic as a golden bridge to the Islamic state, but it has now become an obstacle [....] We urge the Republic not to use arms in dealing with our problem, we will resist with whatever arms we have.'[47]

The relation between Soekarno and Daud Beureueh was an uneasy one as ethnicity, religion and regionalism all played key roles in defining the links between Jakarta and Aceh. Rebellion in the westernmost province of the archipelago broke out in 1950 after the central government refused to allow Aceh to be a self-standing province and forced its merger into North Sumatra. This act stripped Aceh of its territorial identity, which its population had also defended at length against the Dutch, and caused changes in the military hierarchies, as local troops were replaced by non-Acehnese ones. Internal tensions developed between the *uleebalang* as traditional bearers of authority and the new hierarchies instituted in the post-proclamation years.

Religion was not the primary reason for disagreement, but, as Aspinall has argued, Soekarno's failure to establish Islamic law in Aceh 'laid the foundation for the fourth great myth of modern Acehnese history: that of the broken promise'. Hence, the tensions between Islamic, ethnic and territorial identities tipped the balance, leading Daud Beureueh to join Kartosuwiryo's DI-TII in Aceh and pushing him to declare Aceh a 'federal state' within the NII in 1955.[48]

46 Feith, *The decline*, p. 346.

47 Feith and Castles (eds), *Indonesian political thinking*, pp. 211-3; quotes from p. 212 and p. 213.

48 Aspinall, *Islam and nation*; see pp. 31-4 on the Darul Islam. The quote is from p. 31. Aspinall's main argument is that there was no sense of national identity in Aceh before the twentieth century, and this absence mostly emerged from four 'myths' of local history: the golden age of the seventeenth-century Sultanate; the heroic struggle for self-preservation; Aceh as backbone of Indonesia's national liberation; and the myth of the broken promise.

'Final operations' against the enemies of the state

Following the fall of the Wilopo Cabinet, at the end of July 1953 Ali Sastroamidjojo formed the first government without Masyumi and with NU as an independent party. The Nahdatul Ulama was growing rapidly thanks to its social and political characteristics: for one, it had deep roots in Java's countryside, an area that would be key to the party's electoral success in 1955; for another, Wahab Chasbullah, the party's chairman, had been a close friend of Soekarno's since the 1920s, a factor that was to play an important role in the evolution of NU's strategy. In the months leading up to the formation of the Sastroamidjojo Cabinet, the NU was divided on the issue of participation. Chasbullah's pragmatic view, based on the argument that participation in the government and contribution to politics was a religious duty, eventually prevailed. The hardliners – a faction that took a better-defined shape in the following years as Chasbullah became increasingly supportive of Soekarno's policies – argued instead that as an Islamic party, the NU had the 'moral imperative' to oppose Soekarno's 'undemocratic' reforms to establish the 'Guided Democracy'.[49]

The new cabinet set as its first priority the restoration of order and security. During his proclamation speech on 17 August 1953, Soekarno reiterated the importance of ending the Negara Islam Indonesia, now considered the major threat to the fledgling nation. This goal was to be pursued by applying every tool of the state, including both diplomacy and armed repression. On this occasion Kartosuwiryo and his Darul Islam were defined as 'enemies of the state', and within days the Prime Minister officially called for the forced termination of the Darul Islam, which was now defined a rebellion.

The speech provoked a direct response from the TII, which pointed to Soekarno's statement as a manifestation of his weak authority and his waning influence on the Indonesian people. What more, TII accused Soekarno of indirectly legitimizing communist activities against the Negara Islam Indonesia.[50] Muhammad Natsir formulated an equally indignant response: to First Deputy Prime Minister Wongsonegoro's call for a *komando terakhir* (final operation), Natsir replied that nothing short of rifles, bombs and mortars had been used in attempting to solve the problem over

49 Greg Fealy, 'Wahab Chasbullah', in Barton and Fealy (eds), pp. 1-41.

50 'Pendjelasan singkat mengenai 1. Program Kabinet RIK tentang keamanan, 2. Pidato Presiden RIK, menjambut peringatan Proklamasi 17 Agoestus 1945', Colonel S. Mughny TII, 1953?, AABRI DI no. 10.

the past two years, and yet the gap between the Republic and 'the disappointed' had only widened.[51]

The 1955 elections were aimed at forming both a parliament (in September) and a constitutional assembly (in December). Upon the return of the PKI at full force, the constitutional debate on the ideological foundations of the state began to shift, revolving now around three main options: the Pancasila, Islam and Social-Economy (this latter was inspired by socialist economic principles and democracy). In this environment, the debate that ensued from the Amuntai speech quickly became a central aspect of the electoral campaign.

In April 1953 a conference of *ulama* in Medan issued a *fatwa* stating that it was *haram* (forbidden) for Muslims to vote for a candidate who did not work for the implementation of Islamic laws, even if he represented a religious party. Isa Anshary, who had established an anti-Communist front to counter the increasing influence of PKI, went as far as declaring that it was *haram* to equate the belief in the One and Only God with animistic beliefs, and labelled communists as *kuffar* who should not be buried as Muslims. But Natsir, on the other hand, supported the Pancasila as an ideology that included most Islamic principles.

On the other side of the fence, the PKI fully embraced the Pancasila and accused Masyumi of 'imperialism' for its attempt to impose Islam, while the nationalists propagated the idea that an Islamic victory would signify the complete abandonment of the Pancasila, the substitution of the Indonesian flag with the crescent and star and the replacement of the anthem *Indonesia Raya* with a song commemorating Muhammad's migration to Medina.[52]

THE DEMISE OF MASYUMI AND DARUL ISLAM (1955-1962)

Political defeat

The campaign and election process have been thoroughly discussed by Herbert Feith, and this is not the place to repeat that endeavour.[53] It is sufficient to note that the results of both parliamentary and constitutional deliberations played key roles in shaping the future of political Islam in Indonesia in theory and in practice. Nation-

51 Natsir, *Capita selecta*, vol. 2, pp. 48-9.

52 Nasution, *The Islamic state in Indonesia*, pp. 99-103.

53 Herbert Feith, *The Indonesian elections of 1955* (Ithaca: Modern Indonesia Project, Cornell University, 1957).

alists and communists fared better than expected, whilst Masyumi entered the parliamentary arena as the defeated contestant. In 1950 Masyumi had been the largest party in parliament, but the Nahdatul Ulama's secession had taken away most of its support in East Java and had generally fragmented the 'Muslim vote'.

Masyumi won the greatest number of votes in almost all the provinces, but, as about half of the total votes were cast in Java, losing the east and central regions transformed Masyumi into the party of the 'non-Javanese' and left this Islamic party in second place.[54]

As Soekarno openly placed his bet on the Pancasila, political alliances and power relations were reshaped. NU changed its initial anti-Pancasila stand, and Masyumi was left to pursue the struggle for an Islamized Republic alone.

The efforts of the Islamic intellectuals took several forms: between 1949 and 1956 some of them published structured proposals for an Islamic state of Indonesia, while others were engaged in more subtle attempts to show how Islamic societies across the world had incorporated religious principles into their constitutions. In 1951 the Bandung publisher Al Ma'arif printed the first volume of a compilation of constitutions from Muslim states, including Afghanistan, Iraq, Iran and Turkey. A second volume was released in 1955 by the bigger, Jakarta-based (and Masyumi-connected) publisher Bulan Bintang, with the addition of the constitutions of Egypt, Saudi Arabia, Syria, Transjordan and Pakistan. The new introduction to the second volume bears witness to how greatly the political context had changed between 1951 and 1955. After opening with a criticism of the fact that the 'temporary' constitution had yet to be validated by the Indonesian people, Zainal Abidin Ahmad, a Sumatran modernist, goes on to introduce the book as a reference for

54 In the parliamentary elections PNI obtained 22.3% of the votes, Masyumi 20.9%, NU 18.4%, PKI 16.4% and PSII 2.9%, and the same breakdown was maintained in the Constituent Assembly. As per the regional differences, NU was by far the leading party in East Java with 34.1% (Masyumi 11.2%, PNI 22.8% and PKI 23.2%) and South Kalimantan with 48.6% (Masyumi 31.9% and PNI 5.9%). PNI won the majority in Central Java (33.5%, PKI 25.8%, NU 19.6%, and Masyumi 10%) and West Nusatenggara (37.1%, Masyumi 21.1%, NU 8.3% and PKI 5.3%). But Masyumi obtained the most votes in all other constituencies: West Java (26.4%), Greater Jakarta (26%), South Sumatra (43.1%), Central Sumatra (50.7%), North Sumatra (36.4%), East Kalimantan (25.7%, closely followed by PNI with 25%), West Kalimantan (33.2%), North and Central Sulawesi (25.1%, closely followed by PSII with 22.9%), South and Southeast Sulawesi (40%), Maluku (35.4%, closely followed by Parkindo with 32.8%). The other exception was East Nusatenggara, where the Catholic Party won 40% of the votes. Feith, *The Indonesian elections*, pp. 66-72, 78-9. Nasution has noted that Islam and communism were both victorious when their numbers are compared with the situation in the provisional parliament, as they had gained fifty-seven and twenty-two seats, respectively. On the other hand, nationalists and socialists suffered a heavy blow, with their presence falling by eleven and nine seats, respectively. Nasution, *The Islamic state in Indonesia*, p. 107.

members of the future constitutional assembly, Indonesia's Islamic leaders, 'as well as all those who follow Islamic ideology'.[55]

Masyumi was fighting the battle for political Islam on two levels. First, it was still lobbying for a political accommodation of the Darul Islam, refusing to label the movement an enemy of the Republic. And second, it held its ground in the constitutional assembly, supporting the formation of a state based on Islam.

In late 1955 the Republican government was still undecided on how to bring the Darul Islam to an end. The new Prime Minister, Burhanuddin Harahap, rejected Ali Sastroamidjojo's approach and called instead for the second general amnesty in five years.[56] Similarly, Kasman Singodimedjo argued that this rebellious movement should not be labelled an 'enemy', but rather should be considered to be the 'naughty son' who would make no progress if he were beaten to death; the state should, then, 'hit' this son with one blow 'drenched in affection'. The news was quickly disseminated, meeting with much discontent in army circles, especially in West Java where the Siliwangi soldiers often clashed with Islamic troops.[57]

Singodimedjo was not the only politician who believed that the Darul Islam was not a rebellion. At the 1955 Masyumi congress, Mohammad Roem argued that the DI, TII and Daud Beureueh were the party's allies in the fight for an Islamic state in Indonesia.[58] In the mid 1950s Isa Anshary declared that the 'Ummat Islam should not support a government which is not the NII', and K.H. Chalid Hasjim of the Nahdatul Ulama proclaimed that Muslims who did not strive for the NII were hypocrites who lived in ignorance (*jahiliah*).[59]

The interventions of the Islamic parties were not enough, though, and without the collaboration of the army and the other parties, the amnesty failed to solve the problem. When Ali Sastroamidjojo was called to form his second cabinet in March 1956, he once again proclaimed that he would end the Darul Islam with force, and this time Masyumi did not oppose the decision.[60]

55 L.E. Hakim, *Konstitusi negara2 Islam* (Bandung: Al Ma'arif, 1951), pp. 5-6, and Hakim, *Konstitusi negara-negara Islam* (Jakarta: Bulan Bintang, 1955), pp. 4-5. Zainal Abidin Ahmad is further discussed in Chapter 6.

56 *Harian Ra'jat*, 13 August 1955, in Muhammad Isa Ansyori, 'Respons Masyumi terhadap gerakan Darul Islam di Jawa Barat (1949-1960)' (thesis, Universitas Pajadjaran, Jatinangor, 2007, p. 86).

57 'DI anaknja, Masjumi ajahnja', *Harian Ra'jat*, 20 September 1955.

58 *Harian Ra'jat*, 26 September 1955, in Ansyori, *Respons Masyumi*, p. 87.

59 'Berkas mengenai Negara Islam Indonesia, Mazuki Arifin no. 366', in *Gerakan separatisme Indonesia tahun 1945-1965* (Jakarta: Arsip Nasional Republik Indonesia, 2003), pp. 36-7.

60 *Harian Ra'jat*, 12 March 1956, in Ansyori, *Respons Masyumi*, p. 88.
It ought to be noted that regardless of these statements, this cabinet was particularly inconsequential on several fronts, including finding a solution to the Darul Islam problem.

The results of the constitutional elections mirrored the parliamentary vote, making Masyumi's loss even more decisive, as the party registered a further decline of more than 100,000 votes. And in turn, the success of PNI, PKI and NU was all the more resounding, eventually leading to a highly fragmented assembly.

Until the early 1950s Islamic intellectuals had put considerable effort into combining the principles of the Pancasila with Islam, but following Soekarno's speeches in Amuntai and Makassar, many of these same intellectuals began to feel the Pancasila could be understood in too many ways. The debates in 1957 and in 1959 focused on the necessity to choose whether Islam or the Pancasila would be the foundational state ideology. The latter was seen as acceptable by the nationalists, communists, socialists and Christians, but the former was considered compulsory by most politically minded Muslims, with some also arguing that it would be 'undemocratic' not to choose Islam because of the nation's Muslim majority.

Natsir, in his *Islam sebagai dasar negara,* affirmed the superiority of Islam as foundation of the state, capitalizing on the risks of secularism (as it lacked a higher, otherworldly authority) and on the vagueness of Pancasila (which could be rooted in any ideology, including communism). He insisted that Islam was an overarching system that would guide Muslims in their worldly lives and into the afterlife. In making such an argument, as Michael Feener has aptly pointed out, Natsir 'counter[ed] what he perceived to be tendencies within contemporary Indonesia to limit discussions of Islam strictly to religious and ritual matters'.[61]

The two years of the constitutional assembly provided a stage for numerous ideological debates. On the one hand, the Islamists feared that the position of the 'belief in the One and Only God' in the Pancasila was theologically weak, and they generally looked down on the Pancasila for being an empty concept that could be moulded into anything; they considered both of these points proven by the PKI's acceptance of the Pancasila. On the other hand, the secularists brought to the fore examples of oppressive and violent Islamic governments in Indonesia, in both former and present days, including the Darul Islam of West Java.[62]

In February 1957 Soekarno began to develop his *konsepsi* – a political system 'closer to Indonesian traditions', which was soon to become the *demokrasi terpimpin*, or 'Guided Democracy'. Seeking

61 Muhammad Natsir, *Islam sebagai dasar negara* (Jakarta: Pimpinan Fraksi Masjumi dalam Konstituante, 1957); R. Michael Feener, *Muslim legal thought in modern Indonesia* (Cambridge: Cambridge University Press, 2007), p. 87.

62 Nasution, *The Islamic state in Indonesia*, p. 110.

to return to the 1945 Constitution, which also guaranteed stronger powers to the president, Soekarno proposed to the assembly that the Jakarta Charter be accepted as a 'historical document'. Masyumi and NU opposed this solution, unless the charter were to be included in the constitutional text. The debate was thus frozen for decades to come.[63]

The political developments of the following months marked the end of both the constitutional democracy experiment and the Islamic state ideal in Indonesia, neither of which would be resumed until some forty years later, after the fall of the Suharto regime in 1998. Until then, Islamic groups would play a role primarily limited to the social life of Indonesians whilst lobbying from the sidelines for change in legislation, thus attempting an only gradual Islamization of the country.

In his *konsepsi*, Soekarno proposed a four-party coalition cabinet inclusive also of the communist PKI, which had been excluded from mainstream politics since the Madiun Affair. As power became increasingly polarized between Soekarno and the army (especially after Hatta's resignation), the Communist Party was to be a buffer, supported by one and repressed by the other.[64] The *konsepsi*'s second point was the creation of a national council composed of functional groups that proportionally represented all ethnic groups and thus sanctioned Javanese predominance. Such a national council would implicitly counter the divisiveness of the parties' ideologies.

Darul Islam and the regional rebellions

The second chapter of Ali's premiership ended dramatically within a year of its inception with the proclamation of a nationwide state of war and emergency. This was soon followed by martial law in March-April 1957. Military commanders had their powers renewed after having been sidelined in the post-revolution era, and regional civilian authority was further weakened. In Jakarta, political parties could not find common ground, and their activities were being closely monitored and restricted, whilst army officers thrived and lobbied for more power. After the proclamation of martial law, as Suwiryo failed to form a cabinet, Soekarno appointed himself – as 'citizen' Soekarno – to form 'an emergency, extra-parliamentary,

63 Feith, *The decline*, pp. 578-97.

64 This was especially the case as the United States of America was pressuring Soekarno to put a lid on the Communist Party in mid 1958. With the implementation of press control, journalists' arrests and restrictions on May Day celebrations, the army became the main arm of anti-communist policies, transforming the previous triumvirate into a *de facto* duumvirate.

business cabinet', in which only PNI, Nahdatul Ulama, the Christian Party and PSII were represented. With Djuanda as Prime Minister, the country was led by an informal triumvirate of Soekarno, Djuanda and Nasution.

The main reason behind the return to power of army officers in Jakarta was the string of regional rebellions that had been challenging the central authority. The peak of political instability was reached in December 1956, when Hatta, a Sumatran, resigned, leaving non-Javanese leaders without representation in the government. The rebellions stretched from North Sumatra to Sulawesi and East Indonesia and, as explained in the preface, these were connected to the Darul Islam in different degrees.

In early March 1957 the army commander for Sulawesi and East Indonesia announced a state of siege and proclaimed a regional government independent from Jakarta. In this way, the army inaugurated the Perdjuangan Semesta (Permesta, 'Total Struggle') movement. None of the actors on stage made attempts at reconciliation, allowing the conflict to escalate. In late November 1957 Soekarno was victim of an attempt on his life in Jakarta, and regional commanders, as well as prominent Masyumi leaders, were accused of involvement.

Masyumi had had a 'soft' attitude towards the Darul Islam because of its ideological commitment to the Islamic state, but the party had been open in its condemnation of the use of violence. So far as the regional rebellions were concerned, though, Masyumi had been supportive all along. This fitted with its new 'non-Javanese' outlook, as well as its opposition to Soekarno's *konsepsi* – which the party saw as anti-constitutional – and its frustration at having been left out of Soekarno's 'work cabinet'.

By the end of the year, Muhammad Natsir, Sjafruddin Prawiranegara and Burhanuddin Harahap had joined the rebellion in Sumatra, and in February 1958 they announced the formation of the Pemerintah Revolusioner Republik Indonesia (PRRI, Revolutionary Government of the Republic of Indonesia), under Sjafruddin's leadership. Van Dijk mentions that in April 1958 Permesta and Mudzakkar's Islamic state signed an agreement 'to cooperate in opposing Indonesian as well as international communists who were influencing and manipulating the Soekarno group'.[65] Towards the end of 1959 and in early 1960 the PRRI joined with DI Aceh and changed its name to Republik Persatuan Indonesia. Van Dijk has described this alliance as a 'coalition of losers', but for Herbert Feith and Daniel Lev this step

65 Van Dijk, *Rebellion under the banner of Islam*, p. 211.

represented the rebellion's alliance with the Darul Islam within a federal scheme.[66]

The backlash instigated by the proclamation of the PRRI contributed to the reshaping of government politics in the years to come. The ensuing repression eliminated all outspoken enemies of Soekarno and those officers who might have challenged the authority of Nasution and his faction. It also allowed for the return of communism as an influential political ideology, and eventually isolated Masyumi, thus eclipsing the possibility of a fulfilment of the *ummah*'s aspirations for an Islamic state.

None of those rebellions had, at their inception, links to the Darul Islam. However, both the PRRI and Permesta established strategic links to the Darul Islam in their respective areas. Each group retained its own primarily regional identity, and the ideological links between PRRI and DI in Aceh, and Permesta and DI in Sulawesi, are still unclear.

I suggest that the major difference between Kartosuwiryo's Darul Islam in West Java and its offshoots in other regions lay in the original spark. Daud Beureueh in Aceh, Kahar Mudzakkar in South Sulawesi and Kiyai Hadjar in South Kalimantan all decided to join Kartosuwiryo's Darul Islam after respective rebellions were already ongoing. Under each leader, these regional rebellions were framed in Islamic terms, in more or less detail, only after having become involved in Kartosuwiryo's Islamic state project.[67] In West Java the process was reversed, as the platform for an Islamic state had first been developed and implemented when there was no unitary national government to challenge.

OPERATION 'ANNIHILATE'

The weakness of the unitary Republic and the presence of a strong, regionalized army led to the collapse of the parliamentary system, giving birth to the 'Guided Democracy'. After seven short-lived min-

66 Van Dijk, *Rebellion under the banner of Islam*, pp. 336-7; Herbert Feith and Daniel S. Lev, 'The end of the Indonesian rebellion', *Pacific Affairs*, 36-1 (Spring 1963): pp. 32-46 .

67 For an overview of Darul Islam-linked rebellions across the archipelago, see Van Dijk, *Rebellion under the banner of Islam.* On the situation in South Sulawesi, see Barbara Sillars Harvey, 'Tradition, Islam and rebellion, South Sulawesi 1905-1965' (PhD thesis, Cornell University, 1974); Harvey, *Permesta. Half a rebellion* (Ithaca: Cornell Modern Indonesia Project, Cornell University Press, 1977); Esther Velthoen, '*Hutan* and *kota*: Contested visions of the nation-state in Southern Sulawesi in the 1950s', in Samuel Hanneman and Henk Schulte Nordholt (eds), *Indonesia in transition: Rethinking 'civil society', 'region' and 'crisis'* (Yogyakarta: Pustaka Pelajar, 2004), pp. 147-74. For the Aceh case, see Aspinall, *Islam and nation.*

isterial cabinets composed by *formateurs* appointed by Soekarno, the one parliamentary election – held ten years after the proclamation of independence – never resulted in the establishment of a cabinet. Instead, the constitutional assembly was dissolved, and by decree Soekarno re-instated the 1945 Constitution, without amendments, in 1959.

It is this transition that the Army Historical Office sees as pivotal in allowing the convergence of political and military views on the Darul Islam, as well as the development of an organized and systematic response to the rebellion. The order to begin the Gerakan Operasi Penumpasan (Operation 'Annihilate') against the DI-TII/SMK - as it was commonly referred to - was issued in 1958 (with Peraturan Pemerintah no. 59), but the first few months of the operation were dedicated to studying the movement and elaborating an anti-guerrilla strategy.

The 'passive-defensive' approach, based on stationary deployment of troops, was abandoned in 1959, and the Siliwangi Division moved onto an 'active-offensive' technique that made use of mobile units. When it became evident that Republican troops – including additional battalions from the Diponegoro and Brawijaya divisions – were unable to overcome the TII, in 1960 the civilian population was forcibly co-opted to participate in the Pagar Betis operation. The operation's name, which means 'Human Fence', is a direct reference to its primary technique. Civilians were arranged in a long line, each man standing 5-10 metres away from the other, to form a net that would slowly proceed upward from the base of the mountain, cutting supplies and isolating Darul Islam units. An additional advantage for the regular soldiers was that the Islamic militias were now forced to fire upon civilians; the Human Fence also worked as a human shield. The operations spanned between December 1959 and 1965 in West and Central Java, peaking in 1962, when most of the leaders, including Kartosuwiryo, were arrested or executed.[68]

Military documents suggest that in late 1961, the army and the Minister of National Security, General Nasution, set out detailed instructions for the categorization and treatment of surrendering rebels. The list of names shows how the military were making political decisions. Importantly, whoever had been involved in the regionalist rebellions was labelled *persona non grata*. The available list include former rebels of national calibre who enjoyed broad influence on the people, regional leaders who had become

68 Dinas Sejarah TNI, *Penumpasan pemberontakan D.I./T.I.I.*, pp. 124-5; details on the *pagar betis* operation are from Van Dijk, *Rebellion under the banner of Islam*, pp. 124-5.

intellectuals in the rebellion and who also had a broad influence in their regions and regional followers who had local authority. The list featured prominent Masyumi and army figures suspected of plotting the attack on Soekarno in Jakarta, including Muhammad Natsir, Colonel Zulkifli Lubis and Burhanuddin Harahap, as well as the officers involved in the Permesta and PRRI rebellions, and Darul Islam leaders Kahar Mudzakkar, Daud Beureueh and Kartosuwiryo (all of them listed as 'national leaders').[69] Even in late 1962 Sjafruddin, Muhammad Natsir, Zulkifli Lubis and Daud Beureueh were kept under surveillance and under house arrest as political prisoners; the only exception was Kahar Mudzakkar, who had not surrendered and had once again fled to the jungle.[70]

Kartosuwiryo was captured on 4 June 1962 by Colonel Ibrahim Ajie. The stories about this encounter are many, manufactured on both sides to further substantiate divergent myths and legends. After an accelerated trial, Kartosuwiryo was executed on 12 September 1962, without his family ever seeing either the body or the grave.

CONCLUDING REMARKS

The Darul Islam and the Indonesian Republic conducted their activities in a similar manner, opposing Dutch colonial authority and building an independent nation-state for the Indonesian people. Ideological differences between secular nationalists and Islamists, during their rapprochement, had been lessened in favour of these common goals; even after the departure of the Dutch, relations between the Darul Islam and the Indonesian Republic were not clear-cut. Masyumi and PSII went to great length to promote a political solution to the 'Darul Islam problem' and to limit the army's intervention in the Priangan.

The proclamation of the unitary state in 1950 and Soekarno's increased favouritism towards a spiritual understanding of the Pancasila, which by then would include the communists in his coalition, resulted in the emergence of substantial and structured antagonism. Coupled with calls for national unity and pressure to 'restore peace' – especially after the regional uprisings in Sumatra

69 'Instruksi Menteri Keamanan Nasional no III/B/0056/61, General TNI A.H. Nasution, AABRI DI no. 33.

70 'Saran dalam bidang Follow up Keamanaan, masalah pemberontakan dan gerombolan jang menjerah', AABRI DI no. 33.

and Sulawesi – Soekarno was encouraged to take a stronger stand against the Darul Islam.

By the time Indonesians were called to the ballots in 1955, ten years after the 'temporary' constitution had been proclaimed, political Islam was between a rock and a hard place. Masyumi had lost the NU, its non-Javanese outlook had led it to support the regional rebellions and its founding ideology pushed it to favour the Darul Islam. These factors contributed to its political demise.

By the end of the decade the army had regained its political power, and on the issue of the Darul Islam it now had the upper hand against those calling for a political solution. In June 1962 Kartosuwiryo was captured and Darul Islam activities slowly petered out.

From rebellion to martyrdom?

> *I am a child of DI-TII who is ready to sacrifice himself for Islam. Remember, oh mujahidin of Malingping, how our imam, S.M. Kartosuwiryo, built and upheld and proclaimed the independence of the Islamic state of Indonesia with the blood and lives of martyrs, not by relaxing and fooling around the way we do today. If you are serious about seeing the glory of the buried Islamic state of Indonesia rise again, shed your blood so that you won't be ashamed to face Allah, you who acknowledge yourselves to be children of DI-TII.*[1]

Kartosuwiryo was executed in September 1962. His death was announced through a military communiqué, his body never released to the family and the place of his burial never made known. In the late years of Soekarno's premiership, after thirteen years of armed rebellion, Kartosuwiryo's body was not the focus of the public attention that would many years later be lavished on the coffins of the Bali Bombers Imam Samudera and Ali Ghufron, which were accompanied to Tenggulun, East Java, by large crowds in 2009.[2] Kartosuwiryo's memoirs, if they existed, were not published, and the media only reported on his execution at a later date. Even today there is little certainty regarding the location of his burial, and after half a century of silent grieving, his grandchildren are publicly demanding DNA tests on a grave on Onrust Island, off the northern shores of Jakarta, which could be Kartosuwiryo's final resting place.[3]

This snapshot is symbolic of the changing debates about Kartosuwiryo, which rest at the centre of four broadly delimited stages in the development of public attitudes towards political Islam: condemnation, reconciliation and glorification; it is only since 2010 that works have appeared testing a fourth approach that aims at balancing the previous ones, a trend for the most part spearheaded by non-politicized authors.

1 Last Testament of Iqbal, alias Arnasan, alias Acong, October 2002. I am grateful to Ms Sidney Jones of the International Crisis Group, Jakarta, for sharing this document.

2 'Govt, media blamed for bombers' martyrdom', 10 November 2009, *The Jakarta Post.*

3 'Still a mystery after 45 years', in 'Kartosoewirjo', special edition, *Majalah Tempo,* 24 August 2010, p. 46.

In this final chapter I reflect on how the Darul Islam and Kartosuwiryo's actions were received and represented from 1947 until today. This is the final step in developing my argument on the contemporary relevance and legacy of the Darul Islam and Kartosuwiryo to Indonesian politics and Indonesian Muslims' identity.

SPECULATIONS AND THE RHETORIC OF BETRAYAL (1948-1950)

Kartosuwiryo's call for a holy war in West Java, it will be recalled, was first received positively by Minister of Defence Kasman Singodimedjo, who had given thanks to God for the bravery of Kartosuwiryo's actions.[4] Yet, as the Indonesian Republic was gradually taking shape and relations between the regular army and the Islamic militias were worsening by the day, the Indonesian press in 1949 started condemning these 'wild troops' for creating disorder and undermining the nation-building process. We should read both press and intelligence reports published in the late 1940s and early 1950s against this backdrop, which has been explored in the previous two chapters.

Throughout the first months of 1948, the Dutch struggled to understand and to keep pace with the transformations of the West Java branch of Masyumi and its armed wings. At the same time, the name 'Darul Islam' occasionally appeared in Republican police reports. Even when officials had a sense of Darul Islam's and Kartosuwiryo's activities, they often misunderstood the group's nature and motives. In fact, the Darul Islam were not the only irregular troops, and the similarity in tactics made it extremely difficult for observers to ascertain who was behind the sabotaging of infrastructure.[5]

In 1949 and 1950, public discourse about Darul Islam's violence focused on the idea that the religious movement had been hijacked. In October 1949 Muhammad Natsir suggested that there were two 'kinds' of Darul Islam in Java – one truly committed to the country's independence and freedom from colonial domination, and the other one only interested in destabilizing the already fragile status quo.[6]

4 'Keterangan ringkas tentang Perang Sabil S.M. Kartosuwiryo', JogjaDoc no. 243, ANRI. See Chapter 3.

5 'Laporan No. 9/6/48 Perihal Darul Islam dll.nya didaerah Jawa Barat', 29 June 1948, JogjaDoc no. 203, ANRI.

6 'Daroel Islam ada toelen dan palsoe?', *Sin Po*, 26 October 1949.

Even so, Dutch and Republicans could not agree on who was behind the supposed hijacking. The Dutch argued that it was an act of the communists, whilst the Indonesian press was keen on downplaying this possibility in favour of reading the D.I. as a 'Dutch Infiltration'.

Darul Islam and communism

The strings between the Darul Islam and communism were, on paper, tied very tightly. The first connection between the groups was drawn in June 1948. Yet it would only be after the Madiun Affair of September 1948 that Islamic and communist militias were portrayed in Dutch military reports as two faces of a single enemy, ready to cooperate to bring down the Republic. These reports considered Cirebon and Indramayu's Darul Islam troops to have the strongest communist character, with the PKI and the Darul Islam occasionally even sharing their headquarters.[7] But it is evident that this was a localized reality, as in the south TII and PKI militias were conducting a war of propaganda aimed at garnering broader support at each other's expenses.

Dutch intelligence services noted the Darul Islam swelling in the aftermath of the Madiun Affair. After the Siliwangi Division had withdrawn from West Java in February-March 1948, these Republican soldiers were stationed just outside of Surakarta. By mid September the tensions between Republican forces and anti-government communist troops, whose stronghold was in Central Java, had escalated to a point of no return. PKI and the socialist Pesindo militias, estimated to number between 5,000 and 10,000 men, gathered in Madiun on 18 September, took control of the key points in the city and announced the formation of a new National Front (Front Nasional) government.

Musso – a prominent leader of the PKI in the 1920s, who had recently returned from Moscow after living more than twenty years overseas – was unable to counter Soekarno's calls for unity and Nasution's military attacks. The rebels were pushed out of the city and dispersed into the countryside, sparking violence between communists and PNI-Masyumi sympathizers. Musso was killed on 31 October. Amir Sjarifuddin was arrested and later executed by the Dutch because of his involvement in the events. Meanwhile Aidit fled for China, only to return a few years later to become Secretary General of PKI.

7 'Daroel Islam', 5 June 1948, APG no. 1002, NA; 'Rapport van Bk. Bandoeng inzake Islamitische stromingen in de residenties Priangan en Cheribon', AIntel, no. 1705, NA.

In the aftermath of Madiun, Tan Malaka's 'national communism' became the only politically viable form of communism in Indonesia, at least until the second Dutch military aggression. Tan Malaka was eventually captured and executed by the TNI in February 1949.[8] It would take another five years before communism could re-establish itself as a political force in Indonesia.

The first references to communist infiltrations in the Darul Islam ranks appeared in September 1948, when the Dutch uncovered both communist and Islamist literature and military badges in the same households in Ciawi. This discovery led the Dutch to argue that the communists, following their strategy of infiltration, had succeeded in taking over the Islamic movement. They drew further evidence from the Darul Islam's effort to redistribute land among the peasants,[9] and the family connections between the Darul Islam and the left-wing Bamboe Roentjing militias. This much had already been suggested by the Indonesian press in April 1948.

The Dutch speculated that the Darul Islam had expanded into East Java, establishing a second Darul Islam group in the Ponorogo-Besuki-Jember area; this area had been hijacked by communists in September 1949 and had a different agenda and leadership than Kartosuwiryo's (actual) Darul Islam group in the Garut and Tasikmalaya districts.[10] The Indonesian press responded to this theory by claiming that it was not a hijacking of the movement, but rather the case that the 'red' guerrilla were using the Darul Islam label to garner popular support and to provoke a greater political impact.[11]

In the following months this argument gained strength from additional speculations on Kartosuwiryo's past, advanced by the Indonesian army and Dutch information services: he was now portrayed as a 'well-known communist and a prominent PKI leader in the Southeast Priangan since 1928'. This came as something of a surprise to the Dutch, as the report continued mentioning that 'it is utterly incredible that someone who has been a communist in the very dangerous years between 1928 and 1942 would now be a

8 Ann Swift, *The road to Madiun*, (Ithaca: Cornell Modern Indonesia Project, 1989).

9 KNIL report on 'Dar-ul-Islam beweging', 2 September 1948, AAS no. 2752, NA; 'Verbindingen tussen de 'Dar-ul-Islam'-beweging o.l.v. S.M. Kartosoewirjo en de Tan-Malaka-aanhang', 21 April 1949, AAS no. 2753, NA.

10 'Ponorogo: Daroel Islam', *De Vrije Pers*, 19 September 1949. The Dutch also attempted to argue that the Darul Islam had institutional presences in Panarukan, Jember and Mojokerto, but they also admitted that a plot to establish a Darul Islam group in Bondowoso had been uncovered in time to be stopped: 'And today here there is a communist government, and this is a strong one.' *Logbericht*, Soerabaja, 17 october 1949.

11 'Tak ada DI di Madiun Ponorogo?', *Trompet Masjarakat*, 5 October 1949; 'Lebih dikwatirkan provokatief daripada DI', *Trompet Masjarakat*, 12 December 1949.

convinced religious politician'.[12] The life of Kartosuwiryo was rewritten, and the origins of communism in Java were inextricably linked with the history of Sarekat Islam.

In this re-invented genealogy, the Sarekat Islam had initially been divided between Agoes Salim's cooperating group and the SI *hijau* ('green' SI), which in 1926 gave life to the Sarekat Rakyat and Alimin's PKI in Cirebon. But Salim's group also split, with Abikoesno and Kartosuwiryo taking the path of non-cooperation. In the aftermath of the first Dutch invasion, Masyumi and the Soeffah (Kartosuwiryo's educational institution) were transformed into the Majelis Islam in West Java to challenge the Dutch.[13] In the light of Masyumi's mobilization of peasants and farmers, the party's favourable disposition towards the left wing (*sayap kiri*) and Tan Malaka's allegedly strong influence on several Masyumi leaders (including Wondoamiseno, Wahid Hasjim, Kartosuwiryo, Abikoesno, Wali Alfatah and Soetan Akbar),[14] the Dutch had irrevocably established the connection between the Darul Islam and Tan Malaka's group.[15]

The Dutch connected the dots: Masyumi's roots in Sarekat Islam's Islamo-socialism, the individual backgrounds of party leaders, the overlapping of the military and political goals of the two factions, the labelling of Darul Islam actions as radical and anarchist, the Darul Islam and PKI's common interest in socio-economic justice and land distribution, and the infiltration of communist militias into the (apparently) emerging Darul Islam in East Java became solid foundation for their speculative argument.

The religious character of the Darul Islam was then described as a smokescreen, which at the beginning of the Cold War seemed a more logical assumption than rejecting entirely the possibility of a leftist infiltration, especially as 'it could be assumed that the majority of the people in this country do not see the difference between communism or socialism and the social dimension of Islam'.[16]

In 1950 the Dutch intelligence agency declared that all depended on local leaders and alliances, and as much as West Java

12 'Rapport betreffende MI, NII, TNII', 17 October 1948, APG no. 997, NA.

13 'Stukken betreffende verhoudingen tussen Communisme en Islam in Nederlands-Indië', AIntel no. 1706, NA.

14 'Verbindingen tussen de "Dar-ul-Islam"-beweging o.l.v. S.M. Kartosoewirjo en de Tan-Malaka-aanhang', 21 April 1949, AAS no. 2753, NA.

15 Harry Poeze has also pointed to the cooperation between the Darul Islam and the Gabungan Lasjkar Rakjat in West Java. See his *Verguisd en vergeten: Tan Malaka, de linkse beweging en de Indonesische revolutie, 1945-1949* (Leiden: KITLV Uitgeverij, 2007), p. 1523. See also 'Verbindingen tussen de "Dar-ul-Islam"-beweging o.l.v. S.M. Kartosoewirjo en de Tan-Malaka-aanhang', 21 April 1949, AAS no. 2753, NA.

16 'Stukken betreffende verhoudingen tussen Communisme en Islam in Nederlands-Indië', AIntel no. 1706, NA.

(especially Cirebon) had a strong communist influence, the roots of this cooperation were an opportunity and not ideological.[17] In more recent times, the intellectual and writer Ahmad Tohari has suggested that the height of Darul Islam violence in the early 1960s, especially in Central Java, was connected with communist guerrillas readying themselves for the alleged coup of 1965.[18]

The DI: A scheme of '(D)utch (I)nfiltration'

The Indonesian press was unimpressed by the Dutch argument, and, as mentioned above, it often found valid counter-evidence to the 'communist Darul Islam' argument. The press instead argued that behind the group's expansion, and behind its most violent acts, were Dutch officers who were exploiting the current situation to destabilize the Republic and retain control over the colony.

During the 1945-49 period, some Dutch officers deserted the Royal Army to join Indonesian soldiers in support of various rebellious movements in the archipelago. The best known case is that of Captain 'Turk' Westerling, who had earned notoriety during his deployment in South Sulawesi and who, after the transfer of sovereignty, became the leader of an anti-Republican, pro-regional government army in West Java – the aforementioned Angkatan Perang Ratu Adil, or APRA. Mostly because of the territorial overlapping of Darul Islam and APRA activities, in early 1950 the Republican Army and the press became convinced that the two were working together. What is more, they believed that behind the Darul Islam's antagonism against Soekarno were the Dutch.

At the opening of the RIS parliament in February 1950, Soekarno 'blamed the groups that are staining the name of Islam with cruel and violent actions'. And Tempo magazine glossed:

> What the President meant was the Darul Islam. Who pursues these cruelties though, whether it is really Kartosuwiryo's Darul Islam or

17 On the issue of Darul Islam and communism as discussed above see also: 'Communistische infiltratie in de Darul-Islam', Regentschapskantoor Garut, 6 July 1949, AAS no. 2753, NA; CMI Publication No. 97, 18 November 1948, AAS no. 3977, NA; 'Kort Overzicht van de houding van de Islam met betrekking tot de huidige politieke ontwikkelingen', 29 April 1949, in AMK Geheim 1901-1940: KVG no. F33, NA; 'Aantekeningen bij CMI publicatie van 5 Mei 1949 nr. 4797. Exh 10 Mei 1949, Kab Lett Z 42-2206, 1 June 1949, AAS no. 2754, NA; 'Nota', Batavia Police Commissar, 31 July 1949, AAS no. 2753, NA; 'Negara Islam Indonesia', 1953, AABRI DI; 'Nota betr. Darul Islam en Westerling, 2 February 1950, AMK Geheim 1901-1940: KVG no. T8, NA.

18 Ahmad Tohari, *Lingkar tanah, lingkar air* (Yogyakarta: LKiS, 1999), and interview with author, 31 April 2008, Purwakarta.

> a '(D)utch (I)nfiltration', is difficult to tell, perhaps because members of the DI-Kartosuwiryo pursue violent acts too, as its members have received incorrect information and thus bear a grudge towards those who are now considered their enemies.

The article continued that

> it is known that at the beginning the DI was against the TNI because it felt abandoned in the occupied areas after the first Military Action [the July 1947 Dutch invasion] – yet the TNI had only abandoned some pockets. This resistance will increase, mostly because of the dangerous rumours that vilify the TNI. This is not an impossible development in the context of the propaganda conducted by reactionary groups like Westerling, which indeed envisage fragmentation and animosity amongst us.[19]

In the following years this argument was further refined, and as more NII documents showing the involvement of former Dutch officers became available, the government grew increasingly convinced that foreign, reactionary elements had infiltrated the regional uprisings. In 1956 it was even speculated that following protests from within the Darul Islam leadership, Kartosuwiryo could have been replaced as *imam* by Van Kleef, a former KNIL officer who had been in the ranks of the Darul Islam since 1949.[20]

Almost thirty years later, in 1977, a Siliwangi publication interpreted the Darul Islam as an extension of the colonial attempt to destabilize the newly established Republic, mildly admitting a possible underlying religious motive for the movement.[21] One year later, the head of the Siliwangi Division, General Nasution, published his multi-volume history of the independence struggle, in which he openly attacked Kartosuwiryo as the internal enemy in the struggle against colonial oppression.[22]

19 'Bhinneka tunggal ika harus merupakan kenjataan', *Majalah Tempo*, 26 February 1950. Soekarno's quote also from Tempo.

20 Kementerian Penerangan, *Republik Indonesia*, pp. 213-35; 'Gerombolan di Djawa Barat', 28 September 1956, AABRI DI no. 23. More on Van Kleef's involvement in the Darul Islam can be found in Jackson, *Traditional authority and national integration*, pp. 428-32.

21 The book included a picture of Westerling's troops entering Bandung with the caption: 'On 23 January 1950, the APRA troops of the Just Prince entered Bandung to experiment with the establishment of the Islamic state of Indonesia (NII) with Bandung as capital city or to try to bring down the Pasoendan puppet state conceived of by Van Mook.' Madewa, *Esa hilang dua terbilang*, p. 92.

22 Abdul Haris Nasution, *Sekitar perang kemerdekaan Indonesia* (Bandung: Angkasa, 1978) pp. 15-6.

MISSING IDEOLOGICAL REACTIONS TO KARTOSUWIRYO'S NII

The previous chapters showed that in the late colonial period and during the revolution, the Islamic state was seen as a viable platform for shaping the indigenous nation-state. It was not until around 1949 that the two trajectories of political Islam that had co-existed since the Japanese departure went their own separate ways: one became an engaged armed movement (the Darul Islam), alternately opposed and ignored by the other, the political front (Masyumi and its affiliates).

Masyumi's early calls for an Islamic state in 1945 had resonated across the country, and suggestions of an Islamized republic continued throughout the 1950s, as the party reiterated these calls until it was banned in 1960. Between 1948 and 1956, the debate on an 'Islamic state of Indonesia' thrived, both in magazines such as *Aliran Islam* (Bandung) as well as in book-length publications, often printed by Masyumi's printing houses in Bandung and Jakarta.

Yet one would be mistaken in thinking that Kartosuwiryo's NII found support, or became an inspiration, among these intellectuals. Whilst the party was fighting a political battle to ensure a diplomatic solution to the 'Darul Islam problem', those theorizing possible hybrids for an Indonesian Republic rooted in Islam, to be pursued through parliamentary consultation, did not acknowledge the developments that were taking place in West Java. Kartosuwiryo's theoretical elaboration and practical implementation of an Islamic state prompted no reactions, even as Masyumi ideologists were theorizing alternative options for an Indonesian Republic based on Islam. Kartosuwiryo's activism and writings, which until 1946-47 were part of Masyumi's apparatus, had been sidelined since he began his work towards creating an Islamic state in 1948.

In the following paragraphs I introduce briefly alternative conceptions of the Islamic state as elaborated by two political leaders. One is from the already mentioned Persis leader Isa Anshary; the other is from Masyumi intellectual Zainal Abidin Ahmad, who moved in the same circles as Kartosuwiryo in West Java. They tackled the same issues and had the same long-term vision for Indonesia. Yet it appears that Kartosuwiryo's blueprint of an Islamic state was neither embraced nor condemned, but rather ignored by these politicians.

Kartosuwiryo's experiment was not appreciably different from what these Masyumi intellectuals would suggest. However, their decision to 'stay in the game' implied a compromise, especially as the political climate continued to change. The fundamental difference lay in the political circumstances surrounding the drafting of these works, rather than in their religious-ideological stand. I suggest that it is because of these historical circumstances that Kartosuwiryo turns out to be more relevant to twenty-first century reformulations of Islamic polity than to his own contemporaries.

Isa Anshary first published *Falsafah perdjuangan Islam* in 1949, subsequently reprinted in 1951. In this booklet Anshary addressed issues pertaining to the Islamic state, including its foundations, its theological underpinnings and its form, making use only of Islamic sources.[23] Anshary advocated the need to establish the Indonesian Republic on local cultural references (meaning Islam) rather than on foreign ideologies (Pancasila).

Engaging with the Pancasila, however, he strongly favoured making the underlying reference to Islam more explicit: he had a firm conviction that the sovereignty of God (*ketuhanan*) could only be understood in a state based on the Qur'an and *sunnah* that aimed to guide its citizens to salvation in this world and the next. The constitution's statement of *ketuhanan*, then, should have included a clear reference to Islam in order to guarantee the validity of the laws of God and to prevent people from 'thinking that they can have their own interpretation'.[24]

Zainal Abidin Ahmad (1911-83) was a Masyumi leader, a Sumatran of Minangkabau origins and the editor of *Pandji Islam* throughout the 1930s. His first systematic work was published in 1949 in Jakarta as *Konsepsi tata negara Islam*, re-printed as *Konsepsi negara Islam* (1952), and further expanded into *Bentuk negara Islam* in 1956, which included the original of 120 pages, plus 300 more.[25]

Different from Anshary, Zainal Abidin relied in equal measure on Western and Islamic thinkers, and he used both traditions to build his argument in favour of an Islamic state. Offering a glorified version of Western democracies, Zainal Abidin envisioned a binary structure, in which the Caliph represented the political authority and the Darul Islam was its socio-economic counterpart.

23 Anshary, *Falsafah perdjuangan Islam* (Medan: Saiful, 1951).

24 Anshary, *Falsafah*, pp. 172-5.

25 Zainal Abidin Ahmad, *Konstitoesi negara, pendjelasan landjoet tentang oendang-oendang dasar negara Republik Indonesia* (Bukit Tinggi: Poestaka Islam, 1946); *Konsepsi tata negara Islam* (Jakarta: Sinar Ilmu, 1949); *Konsepsi negara Islam* (Bandung: Al Ma'arif, 1952) and *Membentuk negara Islam* (Jakarta: Widjaya, 1956). In the meantime, Zainal Abidin Ahmad was also publishing about Islamic economics, and in the 1960s he translated Farabi's *Ideal city*: Zainal Abidin Ahmad, *Dasar-dasar ekonomi Islam* (Jakarta: Sinar Ilmu, 1950; 2nd ed. Jakarta: Pustaka Antara / Aida, 1952); Zainal Abidin Ahmad, *Negara utama (madinatu'l fadilah)*, (Jakarta: Djambatan, 1964; 2nd ed. Jakarta: Kinta, 1968).

In the introduction to its first edition, Zainal Abidin defined the Islamic state as 'an issue which long ago became an aspiration' for the Indonesian nation, and it is 'just because of the lack of understanding and knowledge of its form and modes, that at times we sense hesitation amongst our leaders'. Hence, he had engaged in this endeavour 'so that [this book] may reach the level of being studied in schools', as well as being read by the general public.[26]

Zainal Abidin expressed, in his 1952 *Konsepsi negara*, an understanding of the existing Republic as substantially resembling an Islamic state, but one in which institutions could be reformed to become stronger through their religious affiliation. Hence, in regards to the much debated principle of *ketuhanan*, Zainal Abidin expressed a different understanding of 'culture' from Isa Anshary, arguing that Soekarno's 'cultural *ketuhanan*' was 'a *ketuhanan* that holds firm tolerance', and 'a *ketuhanan* whose character and external features offer the people freedom to follow any religion they like'. This *ketuhanan* would be fully acceptable within the framework of an Islamic state. Further, he praised the Indonesian Republic for laying 'an important stone' in building a religious foundation for the state by establishing the Ministry of Religious Affairs and re-affirming the Pancasila itself.[27] Yet, in the same text he offered suggestions for strengthening the religious character of the constitutional text, the structure and foundation of the state, its institutional features, the election of the head of state, the structure of religious bodies and of the education system, and more.[28]

As domestic politics and the position of political Islam in Indonesia were changing, in 1952 Zainal Abidin had modified his approach. In the second revised edition of 1956 those instructions had disappeared, substituted by a general recommendation to draft a constitutional preamble 'briefly identifying the ideology and basics principles that will become the *hukum abadi* [eternal laws] of the state'.[29] In this changed political environment, Zainal Abidin was testing intellectual avenues to affirm that the Indonesian Republic already was, substantially, an Islamic state.

Zainal Abidin's efforts to frame the current state as Islamic were made clearer in 1956, when he argued that 'there is no obstacle for each state to have its own slogan as *dasar negara*, so long as it doesn't undermine the four pillars [*amanah*, *keadilan*, *ketuhanan*, *kedaulatan*

26 Ahmad, *Konsepsi tata negara Islam*, 'Introduction' (*Pendahuluan untuk tjetakan ke II*).
27 Ahmad, *Konsepsi negara*, p. 43.
28 Ahmad, *Konsepsi negara*, p. 107.
29 Ahmad, *Konsepsi negara*, p. 107; Ahmad, *Membentuk negara*, p. 100.

rakyat[30]] we have mentioned [as fundamental for an Islamic state], so it is not wrong if the Indonesian state recognizes the Pancasila mentioned in the constitution'.[31]

The minimum standard for a sound Islamic state was identified as having both a Muslim president and a majority Muslim population that would have the largest presence in the national and regional government bodies. To these two criteria Zainal Abidin added that Islam must be acknowledged as the ideology of the state, which already included the elements of an Islamic government. Yet he allowed that these Islamic elements might bear a different name (Pancasila, for example), so long as the law of the state does not contradict Islamic laws and the constitution guarantees *mushawarah* (consultation) and democratic principles.[32] Arguably, in 1956 the Indonesian Republic was close enough to Zainal Abidin Ahmad's proposed Islamic state.

Zainal Abidin's writing consistently reflects the contemporary political situation of his time. As such, it is worth noting that in the context of the constitutional assembly Zainal Abidin argued that it was not enough to have Islam as 'founding ideology of the state', and that more substantial steps needed to be taken to consolidate the position of Islam in the Indonesian state. To support his argument, he cited the opinions of Islamic scholars on various Islamic constitutions, including those of Medina, the Abbasids, Turkey and Egypt.[33]

BUILDING THE IMAGE OF A 'STERILE REBEL'

In the decades between 1950 and the mid 1990s, the Soekarno regime, the army and the New Order – with the tacit complicity of Islamic organizations – pursued a campaign aimed to portray the Darul Islam as a group of bandits who had attacked Dutch and Republican soldiers in equal measure, terrorizing the civilian population and destabilizing the country. Whether the Darul Islam was a channel for extended Dutch infiltration, communist activities or local grievances mattered little to the propagandists, and their explanations did not touch upon the movement's Islamic nature. In this environment, public discourse focused on the rhetoric of

30 Safety, justice, belief in God, people's sovereignty.
31 Ahmad, *Membentuk negara*, p. 76.
32 Ahmad, *Membentuk negara*, pp. 159-66.
33 Ahmad, *Membentuk negara*, pp. 14-5.

national betrayal. Indonesian commentators depicted Kartosuwiryo as driven by self-interest and personal ambitions for political power, and his religiosity was labelled as 'mystical'. Kartosuwiryo's character was entirely sterilized of its ideological motivations, while the Darul Islam became associated with violence and, ultimately, with defeat.

Before outlining this second phase, however, I first turn to the Darul Islam's initial appearance in Western academic discourse and, arguably, to the last instance of Kartosuwiryo's being defined as a politician rather than a rebel or a martyr. In 1950 Van Nieuwehuijze described the Darul Islam as a movement that ignored calls for unity in the anti-colonial struggle in favour of outright confrontation in striving to establish an independent state of Indonesia solely based on Islam.

For Van Nieuwehuijze, 'the *dār ul-Islām* ideal is fulfilling the same function in Javanese society that is performed by revivalist movements in primitive societies [...] Amidst a socio-spiritual life that has been experiencing a deep shock, [the common man] is groping for values that possess certainty and permanence', while the 'supernatural authority' – a pattern of pre-Islamic societies – is embodied by the Islamic customary authority of the *ulama*.[34] Here Kartosuwiryo was described as a Muslim politician dedicated to the anti-Dutch struggle, the leader of a terrorist movement and possibly a crypto-communist, for whom Islam is the common referent for an alternative paradigm to Western domination.

Condemnation: Mysticism, violence and defeat

As Indonesia was slowly settling into being an internationally recognized independent nation-state, the Ministry of Information led the first attempt to produce a national historiography project, publishing a series of volumes illustrating the history of each province. The volume on West Java appeared in 1953. Here the Darul Islam's activities are described as 'rotat[ing] around the individual aspirations of Kartosuwiryo', a man driven by feelings of political disappointment, fanaticism, religious dogmatism and adventurism.[35]

A *pseudo-figurant* (or 'fake leader') who used Islam as a tool to achieve governmental aspirations and who relied on political

34 C.A.O. van Nieuwenhuijze, 'The Darul Islam movement in Western Java', *Pacific Affairs* 23-2 (1950): pp. 181-2.

35 Kementerian Penerangan, *Republik Indonesia*, p. 232. In the same year volumes also appeared on Sumatra (North, South and Central), Sulawesi, Sunda Kecil and East Java.

opportunism to rally popular support, Kartosuwiryo is an evil person, for whom it 'is better to die than to face defeat'. Kartosuwiryo emerges as a man dedicated to increasing his personal power, and for whom Islam is merely an instrument for gathering support. On this foundation, the ministry initiated a parallel discourse to Kartosuwiryo's motives: that of villagers' resistance and opposition to the Darul Islam.[36]

This same position was also taken by Western scholar Karl D. Jackson in the 1970s. A behavioural political scientist, Jackson argued that villagers in West Java decided whether or not to join the Darul Islam according to patterns of traditional authority, mirroring their village leaders. Islam, Jackson argued, was integral to the Darul Islam only so far as 'it supplie[d] groups that [we]re heterogeneous in their religious beliefs with a panoply of symbols that [could] be used to legitimize the leadership and ignite political action'.[37] I shall not dwell further on this piece of scholarship, as Ruth McVey has systematically deconstructed Jackson's methodology and arguments, pointing to his inappropriate choice of applying a 'laboratory-like experiment' to a social movement. Jackson had rooted his study in a survey of more than 200 questions to a sample of villagers not really representative of the Priangan population, a choice that for McVey highlighted how Jackson did not have a comprehensive understanding of Islam or of Sundanese society.[38] Jackson was, however, not the only scholar who opted to ignore the importance of Islam in Kartosuwiryo's activities and ideals on the basis of his 'mystic hence unorthodox' beliefs, as already discussed in the Preface and Chapter 1.

In the aftermath of Kartosuwiryo's capture and execution in 1962, the army and the government conducted a campaign presenting the Darul Islam as a terrorist movement supported by anti-nationalist and anti-Republican forces, whose costs were borne most heavily by the civilian population. Its religious-political goals and Kartosuwiryo's ideological depth were systematically flattened, and in combination with the absence of public debate on the subject, Kartosuwiryo slowly began to emerge as what I describe as a 'sterile rebel'.

36 Kementerian Penerangan, *Republik Indonesia*, pp. 218, 234-5. On p. 262 the picture of a village gathering bears the following caption: 'The Islamic community of Ciparay, under the leadership of its religious scholars, gathers in large numbers to cleanse the area of elements of the Darul Islam group that stir trouble.'

37 Jackson, *Traditional authority and national integration*, p. 126.

38 Ruth Thomas Mcvey, 'Reviewed work: Traditional authority, Islam, and rebellion: A study of Indonesian political behavior by Karl D. Jackson,' *Pacific Affairs* 54-2 (1981).

Unlike the Dutch authorities in the 1920s-40s and Islamist activists in the 2000s, who highlighted the religious quality of Kartosuwiryo's actions, Indonesian commentators throughout the 1960s slowly erased religion from the picture. Earlier suggestions that Kartosuwiryo was a fanatic Muslim were quickly superseded by suggestions that he had markedly mystical tendencies. Amak Sjariffudin stressed how Kartosuwiryo was seen by his followers as a receiver of the *wahyu Cakraningrat Sadar,* bearer of the title of 'Representative of God to the entire Islamic community', and thus holder of traditional symbols of authority; this status was also demonstrated by him carrying a *keris,* a *cundrik,* and amulets.[39] Sjariffudin's is the first description of Kartosuwiryo that unveils the underlying complexity, and perhaps even the internal contradictions, of his character as an Islamic leader.

The mixture of mysticism and religious fanaticism would become a recurrent theme; more importantly, it would become the foundation for arguing that Kartosuwiryo was not genuinely committed to an Islamic state. Because of his lack of formal religious education, his ignorance of Arabic and his own followers' belief in supernatural forces (elements first brought to light in a 1964 army-sponsored biography written by Pinardi), Kees van Dijk and Deliar Noer have argued that Kartosuwiryo was 'a dedicated sufist'. Because 'Sufism is almost the direct opposite of modernism', he 'definitely does not seem to fit into [Sarekat Islam's modernist] atmosphere', Van Dijk sentenced in 1981.[40]

The various political and scholarly approaches were supplemented by visual representations constructed by the military for wider public consumption. These memorabilia, pictures and graphic dioramas were publicized in museums and publications, and were often dedicated to highlighting the struggle against the Darul Islam.

One such museum is the Siliwangi museum in Bandung, which was opened in 1966 by Kartosuwiryo's captor, Ibrahim Ajie. The museum's collection focuses on the rebellion in West Java, highlighting the destruction carried out by the militias and the social involvement of the army in the post-conflict period. The most interesting pieces held here are the personal belongings of Kartosuwiryo and his wife at the time of their capture: he was reportedly holding a *keris* and a *golok,* whilst she was wearing a *baju-sarong* outfit. A large drum is placed right at the entrance to the gallery with a caption

39 Amak Sjariffudin, *Kisah Kartosuwirjo,* pp. 7, 20-1.

40 Van Dijk, *Rebellion under the banner of Islam,* pp. 8, 27-8, 391-6; Noer, *The modernist Muslim movement,* p. 148.

stating that it was used to call Darul Islam soldiers to prayers. From this we can infer that the curators aimed to depict the couple and their followers as traditional Javanese and Sundanese characters, rather than as 'orthodox' or 'fanatical' Muslims.

At the same time that mysticism was being used to undermine Kartosuwiryo's dedication to the Islamic state ideal, the more general propaganda campaign continued to focus on the Darul Islam's betrayal of nationalist aspirations, as well as on its indiscriminate violence against civilians and on the defeat of a weak local movement by a strong unitary army.

After 1968 several publications commemorated the struggle of the Siliwangi troops in West Java against external and internal enemies, and attempted to belittle the Darul Islam movement's religious motivations, while emphasizing its violent overtones. With hardly an exception, Kartosuwiryo's character and personal dimension were absent from these books, as the focus shifted to the negative impact of the rebellion on the civilian population.

Yet, his name and face have remained omnipresent. The cover of *Album peristiwa pemberontakan DI-TII di Indonesia* summarized the numerous tales of the Darul Islam's terror that for years had been fed to the public: trains are derailed, villages ransacked and burnt down, peasants are running away with their newborns, while the TNI is bravely fighting the rebels. Kartosuwiryo's face is printed at the top of the page together with Daud Beureueh's, representing their similar leading role in such destruction.

These books show readers how dangerous the Darul Islam was, how violent and immoral their actions had been and how dedicated the Republican TNI was to reconstructing the affected areas in the 1960s. They also show how weak the movement had become, as the rebels' headquarters are pictured as shacks in the jungle and their leaders as either dead, defeated or captured. Since the mid 1950s, pictures of bloody militias have been shown next to healthy Republican soldiers. When Kartosuwiryo was included in the picture, he was usually portrayed as either bed-ridden or next to Colonel Ibrahim Ajie, invariably looking sick and emaciated from fighting, starvation and illness.[41]

41 The peak of TNI propaganda was reached with an exhibit of pictures showing Siliwangi soldiers rebuilding roads, schools and mosques all over the Priangan region, the heartland of the rebellion. Interestingly, these images of the army's role in rebuilding the region are not present in the army's own publications, but instead dominate the scene in army museums. Other symbolic images include those of Kartosuwiryo being 'returned to civilization' as his hair is cut, and those of him facing the reading of his death sentence. Madewa, *Esa hilang dua terbilang*.

In its first decade, the New Order regime dedicated considerable attention to separating the social and political dimensions of Islam. Throughout the 1970s political Islam became the *bête noire* of the regime, whilst at the same time Suharto pushed individual piety as an anti-communism policy. The building of mosques and the encouragement to attend sermons under repressive rule transformed these places of worship into the only available spaces for youths' and dissidents' gatherings and discussion. When these local manifestations of Islamic piety met with the ongoing international Islamic revival, the radicalization of Islam – whether political or spiritual – was almost inevitable.

On the other hand, the government merged all Islamic parties into the Partai Persatuan dan Pembangunan (PPP, Unity and Development Party) to ensure that religious groups would not benefit from the elimination of communism and to capitalize on the different souls of the religious movement. The senior leadership of Masyumi still advocated some combination of state and religion, whilst the younger generation called for a renewal of Islam, arguing that the Islamic state was now a mirage.[42]

The results of the elections of 1977 were not appreciably different from those of 1971 in number: the Golkar government party maintained its 62% majority; the nationalists, rearranged into the Partai Demokrat Indonesia, or PDI, slid from 10% to 8.6%, and the PPP Islamic party was still just under 30%. Yet, in the time between the two elections, Golkar's approach to Islam had changed dramatically. As R. William Liddle has pointed out, 'In 1971 Golkar had had a strongly anti-Islamic image and had actively cultivated the support of the abangan [nominal Muslims], who fear a theistic state should political Islam come to power. By 1977 Golkar had many local Islamic teachers in its camp [...] and used them to counter PPP arguments that Muslims were obliged to choose the Ka'abah,' meaning voting for the PPP.[43]

In the long term, the New Order's support for Islamic piety and its repression of its political expressions backfired, much as similar Dutch efforts had in the late colonial period.

Reconciliation: keep your friends close, but your enemies closer

The campaign that for decades had condemned Kartosuwiryo and his movement as anti-Republican and anti-national came to a halt

42 Hefner, *Civil Islam*, pp. 100, 126.

43 R. William Liddle, 'Indonesia 1977: The New Order's second parliamentary election', *Asian Survey* 18-2 (February 1978): pp. 175-85; quote on p. 181.

in the early 1980s. The denunciation of Kartosuwiryo was first softened and then suspended. When it was replaced years later, it was with a new critique that distinguished between the means and the goals of the struggle, bearing witness to Suharto's attempted reconciliation with Islamic groups in the late 1980s and mid 1990s.

Before this new wave of critiques, however, in 1983 Suharto announced the *asas tunggal* policy, according to which all organizations and parties had to affirm their foundation in the Pancasila. Whilst this policy was intended to eradicate Islam from politics – NU, for example, refused to abide by this principle and withdrew from politics – its unintended outcome was that now religion could no longer be confined to one party (the PPP), and religiously informed politicians could now spread their influence across the political stage. Several Nahdatul Ulama leaders lent their support to Golkar during the electoral campaign of 1987, and the PPP lost more than 10% of its votes.[44]

The 1980s were marked by three important phenomena: the religious revival, the secularists' increasing interest in democratic reforms and the military's mild opposition to Suharto. During this time, Suharto began to see conservative Muslims as suitable new allies, and the New Order changed its attitude towards Islam.

The tension between the ideological and violent aspects of the Darul Islam are probably best represented in the ABRI museum Waspada Purbawisesa, the Museum of Eternal Vigilance. This museum was opened in Jakarta in November 1987 by Suharto, with the objective of 'present[ing] some of the historical facts surrounding the cruelty of DI-TII terrorism' and with the intention of 'building and placing on a solid foundation the nation's determination to preserve the Pancasila and the 1945 Constitution'.[45] The museum exhibits charts, maps, pictures, archival documents, miniatures and memorabilia laid out in such a manner as to establish an intelligible framework for the TNI operations against the Darul Islam across the archipelago.

Katharine McGregor has claimed, in her *History in uniform*, that 'a visitor to the Museum of Eternal Vigilance is provided with only one motive for the Darul Islam rebellions: the establishment of an Islamic state'.[46] However, as a visitor I did not have the same impression, and the group's religious motivations do not appear as evident

44 Hefner, *Civil Islam*, pp. 167-8. PPP went down from 27.8% in 1982 to 16% in 1987

45 Museum Waspada Purbawisesa, *Museum Waspada Purbawisesa: Buku panduan*. 3rd ed. (Jakarta: Markas Besar Angkatan Bersenjata RI, Pusat Sejarah dan Tradisi ABRI, 1997 [1995]), p. iii.

46 Katharine E. McGregor, *History in uniform: Military ideology and the construction of Indonesia's past* (Singapore: NUS Press, 2007).

as its violent means. Within a few years after the museum's opening, the story was to change. Despite there being very little evidence to indicate the Darul Islam's dedication to the Islamic cause, the guide to the building, published in the mid 1990s, describes Kartosuwiryo as having been committed to the Islamic state since 1938 and contextualizes the Darul Islam's actions within the framework of the Islamic political cause and the anti-colonial struggle.[47] I suggest that this change, which in the long term helped the elaboration of alternative, positive visions of the movement, was the result of the state's new relation with Islam. By the early 1990s, Suharto had relaxed limitations to public displays of religion and had strengthened his own Islamic credentials. The regime allowed headscarves and increased the offering of religious subjects in state schools, widened the powers of Islamic courts and recognized the Palestinian Authority. The presidential family went on *hajj* and supported the opening of the first Islamic bank. Catholic officers were replaced by 'Green Generals', more sympathetic towards Islam. Also, the conservative Ikatan Cendekiawan Muslim Indonesia (ICMI, Association of Muslim Intellectuals) was established.[48]

Yet an underground rapprochement had already started as early as the 1960s. Under the cover of New Order repression, political Islam had come to represent the new enemy, but as the autocratic regime required a careful balancing of forces, the secret services orchestrated occasional releases of pressure. This great scheme of co-optation was doomed to fail, as former members of the Darul Islam were not prepared to be played as puppets and sought instead to take advantage of the movement's guided reorganization to reconnect with each other and regain their strength.

The Darul Islam had been officially disbanded in 1962, when the movement's top leaders signed a Joint Proclamation (*Ikrar Bersama*) acknowledging that they had been 'wrong and misguided' and affirming their allegiance to the Republic. Yet the quashing of the rebellion and the curbing of the Islamic state dream did not imply the total disappearance of the movement. In the 1960s the army made occasional use of its militias, as was the case during the alleged coup of 30 September 1965, for example, when former Darul Islam members in West Java and northern Sumatra were given weapons to attack suspected communists. In the words of a Darul Islam veteran, 'Between 1962 and 1968, the Islamic state of Indonesia was buried by the worldly facilities that the enemy provided'.[49]

47 *Museum Waspada Purbawisesa*, p. 2.

48 Schwarz, *A nation in waiting*, p. 175.

49 Jones, 'Recycling militants', pp. 2-3.

As Suharto was consolidating his newly acquired power, the disbanded Islamic Army offered an appealing pool of unofficial military supporters, especially as their collaboration was granted on the expectation that Islam would substitute communism as the new ideological ally of the state.

In the early 1970s the New Order continued to press forward with its co-optation policies, and the Badan Koordinasi Intelijen Negara (BAKIN, National Intelligence Coordination Body), under Ali Moertopo's guidance, became involved in the reconstruction of the NII leadership. In 1973 Daud Beureueh was made a military commander, and the following year he became *imam*. Yet once the movement's resurrection had been secured, tensions were quick to emerge. Daud Beureueh's policy of 'diplomacy and consolidation' caused the first split in 1976, when Gaos Taufik – a former Hizboellah and Darul Islam member from Garut – deemed the times ripe to re-open a *jihad* front and created Komando Jihad as a jihadist re-embodiment of Kartosuwiryo's group. Moertopo's creation had released itself from the tight embrace of the government: at the end of the decade power struggles fragmented the organization, and Adah Djaelani – a first-generation fighter from West Java who had been co-opted by BAKIN in the early 1960s – bypassed Daud Beureueh and rose to the position of *imam*. He then reinstated Kartosuwiryo's sons and original associates back into the *dewan imamah*.[50]

The fragmentation of this new Darul Islam did not lead to the fading of its activities, but rather to their proliferation. By the late 1970s Komando Jihad had expanded its operations to Sumatra and Flores, leading the police to crack down on the entire organization between 1979 and 1982. Adah Djaelani was also arrested, and by 1986-87 it had become clear that the movement could not proceed without an acting *imam*. The election of Masduki transformed yet again the outlook of the Darul Islam, most importantly by fostering the development of its international connections. In the changed context of the mid 1980s, Abu Bakar Ba'asyir and Abdullah Sungkar often travelled to Afghanistan and the Middle East. The goal of an Islamic state of Indonesia evolved into that of a transnational caliphate.[51]

In the years that followed, this jihadist soul of the Darul Islam alienated the sympathies of those committed to the socio-reli-

50 Jones, 'Recycling militants', p. 22.

51 Jones, 'Recycling militants', pp. 2-3. For more details on Darul Islam's re-embodiments in the 1970s-90s, see Quinton Temby, 'Imagining an Islamic state in Indonesia', *Indonesia* 89 (April 2010): pp. 1-36.

gious advancement of the *ummah*, including the *usroh* movement, inspired by the Egyptian Muslim Brotherhood. This jihadist faction eventually became the Jemaah Islamiyah in 1993. The Darul Islam movement was, overall, rarely weakened by these splits, as it was able to absorb their impact by multiplying and differentiating its strategies and priorities. It gave birth to the cell-based *usroh* movement, the institutional Majelis Mujahidin Indonesia and the international jihadist Jemaah Islamiyah: in the words of a Darul Islam member, 'The Darul Islam is a house with many rooms, enough for all the factions'.[52]

In late November 1997, seventeen activists were arrested in Solo on the heels of a number of other arrests in West and Central Java. During the raid, the police reportedly found only one book, and it was about Kartosuwiryo and his struggle. Interviewed on the issue, a commentator declared: 'This NII that we have now cannot be separated from the first NII.'[53]

What has kept these various factions under a single roof is Kartosuwiryo's project of establishing a Negara Islam Indonesia. The deep desire to revive Kartosuwiryo's memory and goals has led to his public re-interpretation as hero and model in the post-Suharto era.

Glorification

From 1962 onwards, the Indonesian government and military apparatus worked hard to erase the memory of Kartosuwiryo as a nationalist politician as well as a religiously inspired leader, instead promoting a single image of him as a separatist rebel whose actions were directly aimed at fragmenting the unitary republican state. However, since the end of the New Order regime in 1998, we have witnessed a proliferation in alternative visions of this 'enemy of the state', now often portrayed as a martyr.

I have suggested that the transformation of the portrayal of the Darul Islam and Kartosuwiryo – from enemy of the nation, to absentee, to dedicated Muslim – should be read as mirroring the transformations in public attitudes towards Islam. As noted above, the government's sterilization of Kartosuwiryo was heralded by the obliteration of his religious dimension (of both his character and his movement's rebellion) and his gradual disappearance from public discourse in the 1970s-80s. Yet in the long-term, this

52 Darul Islam members' saying in Jones, 'Recycling militants', p. 31.
53 *Panji Masyarakat*, 'Impian para pendukung Kartosuwirjo', 24 November 1997, pp. 16-8.

approach of the New Order created an empty space, ready to be filled once the state and its tight-fisted control of public narratives had been weakened.

Suharto's attempts to invert the decades-old outright condemnation of the Darul Islam had not gone far enough: public discourse was still saturated with negative depictions of the struggle when the relaxation of restrictions on the press, the increasing reach of the Internet and the growing use of blogs allowed the proliferation of alternative visions of history in the post-*reformasi* era. These developments ultimately resulted in the emergence and rapid spread of hagiographical depictions of Kartosuwiryo's life.

This literature ought to be seen as one aspect of a more general process of the re-Islamization of the public sphere that has been taking place since 1999, and is deeply embedded in the political agendas of groups interested in a religious revival. In fact, the authors who have been involved in rehabilitating Kartosuwiryo's memory are often the same actors who have been active in the effort to implement sharia law and to resurrect visions of an Islamic state. As the name of Kartosuwiryo has gradually disappeared from government-sponsored materials – he is barely mentioned in Indonesian text books, for example – these positive depictions of his life and legacy have contributed to creating an aura of respect and admiration for him, which in turn has led to the creation of a new role model, a hero and martyr for Islam.

The first author who has looked at Kartosuwiryo from this new perspective is Al Chaidar, a former member of the new Darul Islam movement in Jakarta and supporter of the Islamic state project, who graduated from Universitas Indonesia (Depok, Jakarta) in 1996 having written a thesis on the Islamic state ideology in Southeast Asia. Al Chaidar has produced several titles on the theory of the Islamic state and Kartosuwiryo's experiment. Yet he has not taken the opportunity to offer a critical assessment of Kartosuwiryo's ideology and actions, limiting his scope instead to describing events in a supportive and apologetic tone.[54]

Another productive author has been Irfan Awwas, the secretary of the Majelis Mujahidin Indonesia (MMI, Indonesian Coun-

54 Al Chaidar, 'Ideologi Negara Islam di Asia Tenggara: Telaah perbandingan atas terbentuknya diskursus politik Islam dalam gerakan-gerakan pembentukan negara di Indonesia dan Filipina pasca kolonialisme' (thesis, Universitas Indonesia, Jakarta, 1996); Al Chaidar, *Wacana ideologi negara Islam* (Jakarta: Darul Falah, 1998); Al Chaidar, *Pemikiran politik*; Al Chaidar, *S.M. Kartosoewirjo: Pemberontak atau mujahid* (Jakarta: Suara Hidayatullah, 1999); Al Chaidar, *Sepak terjang K.W.9 Abu Toto menyelewengkan N.K.A.-N.I.I. pasca S.M. Kartosoewirjo*, revised ed., vol. 1, 'Serial musuh-musuh Darul Islam '(Jakarta: Madani Press, 2000).

cil of Mujahidin). He was also the editor-in-chief of *Arrisalah,* until the magazine was shut down and Awwas sentenced to nine years in prison for activities associated with the NII movement.[55] Among others, Awwas has written on the figure of Kartosuwiryo in 1999 and on the Islamic state ideology in 2007; another book, published the following year, compares Kartosuwiryo, Daud Beureueh and Kahar Mudzakkar as NII leaders.[56] Many periodicals have also engaged this newer perspective on Kartosuwiryo's legacy. One example is a magazine titled *Majalla Darul Islam,* edited by Al Chaidar, which is specifically dedicated to issues related to the establishment of an Islamic state of Indonesia and the spread of Kartosuwiryo's writings and ideology. *Sabili,* edited by Herry Nurdi, similarly dedicates itself to spreading Kartosuwiryo's writings and incorporates numerous contributions from both Awwas and Chaidar.[57]

As is clear from the books' titles and the authors's backgrounds, these publications fed into the propaganda for an Islamic state and did not criticize any aspect of Kartosuwiryo's struggle. Both Chaidar and Awwas, despite holding the benefit of privileged information and networks, failed to provide a complete assessment of Kartosuwiryo's leadership and character. Blinded by their personal beliefs, they avoided acknowledging the violent aspects of the Darul Islam's operations, univocally blaming all actions of terror on infiltrated army soldiers or communist militias.

Kartosuwiryo emerges as the patron of the Islamic state, a man who gave his life for its ideals and their realization and who fell victim to secular forces. In representing him as such, though, Kartosuwiryo's advocates have made the same mistake as New Order propagandists: hiding certain aspects of the story, the integrity of the authors and the truthfulness of their accounts have been called into question, thus alienating the sympathies of those who might be inclined towards considering Kartosuwiryo an Islamic nationalist and an important figure in the independence struggle. This

55 Noorhaidi Hasan, *Laskar Jihad: Islam, militancy, and the quest for identity in post-New Order Indonesia* (Ithaca: Southeast Asia Program Publications, Cornell University, 2006), pp. 18-9. I am grateful to Martin van Bruinessen for suggesting that probably the very first attempt at 'glorification' was an article in *al-Ikhwan* magazine later to become *Arrisalah,* likely written by Irfan Awwas himself in the early 1980s.

56 Irfan Awwas, *Menelusuri perjalanan jihad S.M.Kartosuwiryo: Proklamator Negara Islam Indonesia* (Yogyakarta: Wihdah Press, 1999); Irfan Awwas, *Jejak jihad S.M. Kartosuwiryo.* 3rd ed. (Yogyakarta: Uswah, 2007); Irfan Awwas, *Trilogi kepemimpinan Negara Islam Indonesia* (Yogyakarta: Uswah, 2008).

57 Herry Nurdi, 'S.M. Kartosoewirjo: perlawanan dari Malangabong', *Sabili* 11-9 (2003).

vision, in fact, is now embraced by liberal secular publishers such as Gramedia and Tempo (see below).

In the post-*reformasi* context, amid heavy criticism of the army and within the framework of a surging Islamic consciousness, condemnatory portrayals of Kartosuwiryo have been shunned in favour of new ones. In an effort to bring him forward as a model of Islamic leadership in contemporary Indonesia, Islamist authors actively adjust representations of Kartosuwiryo's religiosity to conform with renewed standards of orthodoxy, often denying or ignoring the mysticism that had been relevant to his leadership in 1940s-50s Java.[58]

KARTOSUWIRYO AND CONTEMPORARY VISIONS OF ISLAMIC LAW IN INDONESIA: THE HUKUM PIDANA OF 1949 AND THE MMI CODE OF 2005

The congress that gave birth to the MMI was opened by Irfan Awwas under the banner of being the 'first national congress of *mujahidin*'. It was attended by some 2,000 people from different backgrounds and organizations, all interested in calling for full implementation of sharia law and rejecting anything that was against Islam. The leadership of the movement was for several years shared between Irfan Awwas, as chairman of the executive committee, and the senior Hadrami cleric Abu Bakar Ba'asyir, nominated *amir ul-mujahidin*. Ba'asyir, alongside Abdullah Sungkar (a key figure in the Jemaah Islamiyah), was crucial in creating a network of like-minded activists through the establishment of the conservative *pesantren* al-Mukmin in Ngruki, near Solo, in the early 1970s. However, according to Noorhaidi Hasan, during Ba'syir's and Sungkar's more than twenty years of self-imposed exile in Malaysia, it was Irfan who had ensured the revival of the efforts to establish a caliphate and an Islamic state by constituting once again the Negara Islam Indonesia.[59]

The use of NII terminology is neither generic nor casual, as recent research has brought to light the genealogical connections between Kartosuwiryo's Darul Islam movement in West Java and the Islamist groups that emerged between the 1970s and today.[60]

58 Awwas, for example, in reporting Kartosuwiryo's psychological evaluation subtly censors the sentences that suggested that Kartosuwiryo's mysticism was an aspect of his intelligence.

59 Noorhaidi Hasan, *Laskar Jihad*, pp. 18-9, 47.

60 See the recent work done by the International Crisis Group in Jakarta; Martin van Bruinessen, 'Genealogies of radical Islam in post-Suharto Indonesia' (2002), Utrecht University Website, at http://www.let.uu.nl/~Martin.vanBruinessen/personal/publications/ genealogies_islamic_radicalism.htm; Greg Fealy's ongoing research; and Quinton Temby's doctoral research.

Based on the connections already highlighted between Kartosuwiryo and contemporary Islamist circles, I also advance the hypothesis that the MMI's sharia code, drafted in 2002 (and re-drafted in 2005), should be analysed in comparison with the 1948-49 NII's Criminal Code, the *Hukum pidana.*

Tim Lindsey and Jeremy Kingsley have argued that the MMI code finds its origins 'beyond Indonesia's shores', more specifically, in Malaysia, where the Islamist Parti Islam Se-Malaysia (PAS, Pan-Malaysian Islamic Party) party ratified sharia criminal codes in Kelantan in 1993 and in Trengganu in 2003. They further suggest that Zia ul-Haqq's legal reforms in Pakistan and Saudi Arabia's Wahhabi *madhhab* influenced, in more and less direct ways, the drafting of the code.[61] It is my contention, instead, that even though it is admissible that Malaysia and Pakistan had a political influence on the MMI, there was no need for Lindsey and Kingsley to look so far away, as a substantially similar criminal code had been compiled by Kartosuwiryo in Java in 1949, which mostly reflected a traditional Shafi'i interpretation of *fiqh.* In addition to geographical proximity, during my research I have noticed that the ideological connections with, and respect for, Kartosuwiryo and the NII amongst Indonesia's sharia-minded activists is still strong, and his texts are widely read and circulated. According to the introduction to the 2005 code, the MMI had set up a Komisi Khusus (Special Commission) to produce a text that would enable 'each Muslim to easily understand the matters of the Islamic criminal code, so as to be ready to support an integral enforcement of *Syariat Islam*'.[62]

The two formative texts of Kartosuwiryo's NII were the Constitution and the Criminal Code. I suggest that differences in these two documents, issued one year apart from each other, reflect a change in political priorities, a consequence of the transformed military context and the changing relationship between the Islamic state and the Indonesian Republic. With the Constitution, Kartosuwiryo gave the NII a political-administrative structure, the same goal pursued by Masyumi intellectuals in the 1950s. But with the Criminal Code, Kartosuwiryo shifted the focus away from governance and

61 T. Lindsey and J. Kingsley, 'Talking in code: Legal Islamisation in Indonesia and the MMI *shari'a* criminal code', in Peri Bearman et al. (eds), *The law applied* (London: I.B.Tauris, 2008), pp. 295-320; quote on p. 309.

62 'Proposal for a Criminal Code for the Republic of Indonesia adjusted to accord with the Syari'ah of Islam', issued by the central headquarters of the Majelis Mujahidin, Jl.Veteran no. 17, Jogjakarta, Indonesia. I have here used the English translation of this 2002 draft, kindly provided by Jeremy Kingsley. Fauzan Al-Anshari, *KUHP Syariah dan penjelasannya* (Jakarta: Departemen Data dan Informasi MMI, 2005).

towards the day-to-day lives of the Islamic state's citizens. The same concern is at the root of the MMI's effort to draft a criminal code based on Islamic precepts, and the issue of the government's structure is not touched upon.

The reasons for Kartosuwiryo's establishment of the NII before the achievement of a 'perfect' Muslim society can be found in the peculiar political context of 1949; as noted above, the Darul Islam originally called for a gradual transformation of West Java's society into an Islamic state. The doors to implementing this project had opened with the anti-colonial struggle, only to be shut by the Dutch invasion of West Java and the later inclusion of this region in the Pancasila Republic. At that point, all which the Darul Islam could concern itself with was the regulation of the daily lives of those resident in the areas it controlled.

Half a century later, with the fall of the Suharto regime and the opening of the debate on what direction Indonesian politics should take, the majority of Islamic groups began their campaign for a stronger, more formal presence for religion in society, without an open challenge to the Republican structure. With the restoration of democratic institutions, Islam has made a comeback in parliament, and with respect to constitutional amendments, the question of the Jakarta Charter and sharia law once again came under the spotlight between 1999 and 2002. Interestingly, of the twenty-one Islam-based parties allowed to compete in the general elections of 1999, only four campaigned for the transformation of the Indonesian Pancasila Republic into an Islamic state, but fourteen lobbied for the inclusion of Qur'anic laws into the civil and criminal codes. They have channelled their efforts towards drafting a criminal code in compliance with the sharia, but not necessarily as part of a state based on Islam.

This trend helps make clear why MMI has insisted that legislation be based in the sharia, which would be considered more acceptable and therefore potentially more influential, rather than that the government be entirely Islamic. None of the proposed amendments passed, and the Jakarta Charter was officially rejected in August 2002. However, since 2000 several local regulations, or *peraturan daerah*, have been passed at the provincial and district levels to introduce legislation in accordance with sharia.[63]

63 Robin Bush, 'Islam and constitutionalism in Indonesia', in David Linnan (ed.), *Legitimacy, legal development and change: Law and modernization reconsidered* (Surrey, UK: Ashgate, 2012); Robin Bush, 'Regional Sharia regulations in Indonesia: anomaly or symptom?', in Greg Fealy and Sally White (eds), *Expressing Islam: religious life and politics in Indonesia* (Singapore: Institute of Southeast Asian Studies, 2008), pp. 174-91.

Thus, the MMI code fully ignores the question of the government's form or its ideological foundations, focusing instead on legal regulations to be followed by 'every citizen on the territory of the Unitary State of the Republic of Indonesia'. This compilation of a sharia-based criminal code was first drafted after the August 2000 foundation meeting, and later presented as the *Garis-garis besar Syariat Islam* in July 2002, when parliament was yet again discussing a constitutional amendment to re-introduce the Jakarta Charter.[64]

Where pre-1948 Kartosuwiryo, and Zainal Abidin Ahmad and Isa Anshary in the 1950s, had been concerned with the structure of a state that could harmonize Islamic principles with the needs of a modern state, the MMI and post-Roem-van-Royen-Agreement Kartosuwiryo solely focused on establishing a comprehensive Islamic law, demanding that the Indonesian state approximate it, paying little attention to government structure.

It is therefore because of historical circumstances that Kartosuwiryo turns out to be more relevant to twenty-first century reformulations of Islamic polity than to his own contemporaries writing in the 'consolidation' years.

Comparing the Codes: Crimes and punishments

Reflecting the classic distinction between crimes and punishments, both the NII and MMI codes offer a presentation of *qisas*, *diya*, *ta'zir*, and *hudud*. It is indicative of the respective socio-political context that the NII code focuses mostly on killings and banditism, and the MMI's on sexual offences.

In the NII text *qisas* is obligatory for the crime of killing a person that the law does not allow to be killed, and for the wounding that impairs reasoning capabilities (quoting Qur'an 5:45). *Diya,* instead, could be requested if the heirs of the victim were to give forgiveness, or in case of non-impairing wounding. *Ta'zir* is prescribed for the killing of a person who it was lawful to kill, but who was killed before the *imam* or his representatives had passed the sentence.

Shafi'i jurisprudence prohibited applying *qisas* for the killing of a *dhimmi,* and such offence is punished in the NII code by light compensation (*diya mukhaffafah*). *Qisas,* however, is also forbidden in this code on the father of the victim, a practice that is otherwise usually allowed by the Shafi'i and Maliki schools.[65] Another discrep-

64 'Proposal for a Criminal Code'. Fauzan Al-Anshari, *KUHP Syariah.*

65 J. Schacht, *Ḳiṣaṣ*, EI2.

ancy is in the distinction applied to 'intentional', 'unintentional', and 'apparently intentional' killings, as mainstream Shafi'i legal thought does not require the intention to kill for *qisas.*[66] According to the NII text 'light compensation' was permitted for intentional killing when apologies were offered to - and accepted by - the relatives of the victims, and the same punishment is prescribed for unintentional killing - either 100 camels or 16,000 golden *dinar.* The amputation of a single limb equalled 50 camels in compensation, two body-parts 100 camels, and a wound on the head 5 camels. In the MMI code these internal distinctions in compensation have disappeared, replaced instead by differentiations between compensation for a male Muslim victim, a female Muslim, and a *kafir*: the *diya* is fixed at 100 camels, 1,000 golden *dinar,* or 12,000 silver *dirham* for the life of a Muslim male or the loss of two limbs, while it is half for a Muslim woman, and the sum is further halved if the victim is a non-Muslim (and no differentiation is made between a *dhimmi* and a *kafir*).

Hudud offences are those crimes that break the limits (Arabic *hadd, hudud*) of what God has allowed. Tradition regards these offences as having fixed, unchangeable penalties, as these are God's own right. Illicit sexual intercourse (*zina'*), false accusation of *zina'* (*qadhf*), drinking alcohol, theft and robbery, and apostasy (*irtidad, murtad*) are all mentioned and discussed in the two texts. Both prescribe stoning for a married adulterer, although the NII code also includes the possibility of heavy compensation to be made in the case of the married adulterer, and 100 lashes (or banishment) in punishment for the unmarried one.[67] The NII sanctions discretional punishment for bestiality and sodomy, with the latter reflecting the Hanafi school rather than the Shafi'i,[68] whilst the MMI assimilates sodomy to *zina'* and changes the punishment for bestiality from *ta'zir* in 2002 to stoning in 2005. It should not surprise that the MMI code includes several additional articles on unacceptable sexual practices when compared with Kartosuwiryo's text. The inclusion of articles on lesbianism, necrophilia, and incest, as MMI's efforts to pass an Islamic criminal code, cannot be discerned from the general attempt of Islamist groups to impose

66 J. Schacht, *Ḳatl,* EI2.

67 'Proposal for a Criminal Code', point no. 17; Fauzan Al-Anshari, *KUHP syariah,* point no. 16; *Qanun asasy Negara Islam Indonesia,* AABRI DI no. 9, point no. 12.1.
Another discrepancy between Pinardi's copy and AABRI DI no. 9 regards the crime of *zina'.* Unless it was a typo, in Pinardi (who, in my opinion, uses a later text) the code appears to deal with the crime of adultery in a more progressive way, as article 18 does not suggest stoning, banishment, or imprisonment as forms of punishments.

68 R. Peters, *Zina,* EI2.

Muslim standards of moral conduct, as also evidenced by the anti-pornography bill that was passed in 2009. For *zina'* accusations, the *Hukum pidana* required four male witnesses who had witnessed the sexual act (*kelihatan masuk dan keluarnya*) for the specific intention of testifying in court. The MMI code, on the other hand, requires no such burden of proof; in both codes he who accuses without satisfying the requirements is to be punished with 80 lashes.

The NII code punishes the drinking of alcohol with 40 lashes according to Shafi'i tradition, but the MMI incorporates Caliph Umar Ibn al-Khattab's decree that the lashes number up to 80, thus stipulating a punishment between 40 and 80 lashes; plus, in 2005, the addition of death penalty for he who is convicted for a fourth time.[69] An interesting deviation from traditionally accepted jurisprudence, and an indication that this NII code was adapted to local understandings, is an article specifying that he who drank *arak* or other kinds of alcohol as a medical treatment and under the suggestion of a doctor should be exempted from the punishment. It should also be noted that neither the NII nor the MMI codes prohibit gambling.

The MMI code bears witness to the deep transformations in Islamic practice since the religious revival of the 1980s, as the evidence of cultural adaptation present in Kartosuwiryo's code, including the categorization of *wandu* and the permission to drink alcohol whenever prescribed by a doctor, have disappeared.

In the NII code, the article on robbery and theft (here described as *baigal dan pencurian*) prescribed execution by crucifixion for he who accidentally kills during a robbery, simple death for he who kills without seizing the goods, amputation of the right hand and left foot for he who robs without shedding blood, and *ta'zir* for he who scares travellers without causing any damage. Amputation was also the punishment for a person who stole up to ¼ of a *dinar*, a prescription that reflects Shafi'i tradition. Finally, he who killed while defending himself (*daf'ul-sial*), his belongings, or his wife's honour was exempted from punishment. In the NII code, as well as in the MMI ones, apostasy is treated in full accordance with, and acknowledgement of, books of *fiqh* (*sebagaimana jang termaktub dalam kitab2 Fiqih*): in the event that the order to repent went unheard, the apostate was to be punished with death.[70]

Comparing the treatment of *hudud* crimes and punishments it is evident that between 2002 and 2005 the MMI had further radicalized its position: the act of theft (*sariqah*) is punished in 2002

69 'Proposal for a Criminal Code', point no. 27; Fauzan Al-Anshari, *KUHP syariah,* point no. 13.
70 'Proposal for a Criminal Code', point no. 28; Fauzan Al-Anshari, *KUHP syariah,* point no. 10.

with the amputation of the right hand and left foot for the first and second offences respectively, and with 'beating with a piece of wood or imprisonment for a term determined by the judge to give the convicted the opportunity to repent to God' for the third and subsequent ones. In 2005, however, the last clause is replaced with three more, specifying the amputation of left hand and right foot for the third and fourth offences, and eventually death for the fifth-time offender. In Kartosuwiryo's code this latter clause prescribes banishment, and the offence itself is referred to as *pencurian*.[71] The second *hudud* crime taken into consideration by the MMI is *hirabah*, which is explained as civil disturbance and seems to correspond with the NII's *baigal* in its description of both offence and punishment.[72]

Although scattered throughout the text, the NII code offers detailed regulations to meet most needs of society, focussing on those particularly relevant for a society in a state of war. Muslim fighters were allowed to withdraw when outnumbered, as preventing damage should take precedence over the acquisition of benefits (quoting Q 8:1, 15). When fighting the infidels, Muslims could retreat if outnumbered 10 to 1 or 2 to 1 by the enemy (quoting Q 8:65-66). Those who withdrew from the battlefield under any other circumstance were to be banished (quoting Q 8:16). The last article prescribed that the corpses of infidel enemies (as well as apostates) were to be buried for hygienic reasons; those executed whilst pronouncing the *shahada* were to be considered Muslims, and thus attended to as prescribed. Finally, Muslims who had died in battle or within 24 hours of being wounded were to be considered *shahid dunia akhirat*, or martyrs.

BEYOND CONDEMNATION AND GLORIFICATION

In addition to the views of Kartosuwiryo expressed in the sections above, in recent years efforts have been made to bring the complexities of Kartosuwiryo's career back under the spotlight. A first attempt to achieve balance can be seen in a 2006 publication titled *Kearifan guru bangsa: Pilar kemerdekaan* ('The fathers of the nation: Pillars of independence'). In this illustrated volume, Kartosuwiryo

71 'Proposal for a Criminal Code', point nos.10-11; Fauzan Al-Anshari, *KUHP syariah,* point no. 27; *Qanun asasy Negara Islam Indonesia,* AABRI DI no. 9, point no. 21.

72 'Proposal for a Criminal Code', point no. 14; Fauzan Al-Anshari, *KUHP syariah,* point no. 12; *Qanun asasy Negara Islam Indonesia,* AABRI DI no. 9, point no. 21.

is represented alongside Amir Sjarifudin, Muhammad Husni Thamrin, Hadji Misbach, Mohammad Hatta, Soekarno, Tan Malaka and other leading representatives of the revolution, for the first time placing him in a wider hall of fame.

Kartosuwiryo is the subject of two chapters, titled 'Before the Darul Islam' and, 'A sad sequence', which point to the evolution of his approach to politics. The author singles out the pivotal shifts in Kartosuwiryo's career, from being Tjokroaminoto's disciple, to his move to West Java and his rising concerns for peasants' grievances and anti-colonial feelings which were channelled in the Darul Islam, to his eventual establishment of the Soeffah. Kartosuwiryo's understanding of Islam is represented as Arab-inspired, and the Soeffah as a work-camp whose strict regime caused his political failure, imprisonment and, eventually, cost him his life. The importance of this work lies in the fact that Kartosuwiryo is placed amongst officially recognized nationalist leaders, yet the simplification of his character has omitted his mysticism, in favour of highlighting an 'Arab orthodoxy'.[73]

A reflection is necessary on the most recent engagement of a 'mainstream' publication with Kartosuwiryo and the Darul Islam's history and legacy. In 2010 the special 'Independence Day' issue of *Tempo* was fully dedicated to Kartosuwiryo, covering everything from his political career to his contemporary following. These articles were reprinted in 2011 as a booklet that was part of a Gramedia book series 'Islamic leaders of the early independence period' (*Tokoh Islam di awal kemerdekaan*), which also included volumes on Daud Beureueh, Muhammad Natsir and Wahid Hasjim.[74]

What is noteworthy here is the editors' choice of two different covers for the Indonesian and English editions of the *Tempo* issue, which points to the difficulty that a renowned liberal magazine faces in attempting to ensure compliance with local and international understandings of political Islam in the twenty-first century.

While the Indonesian cover has Kartosuwiryo looking assertive, with the title 'Kartosuwiryo: Dreaming the Islamic state', the English edition features a pensive and troubled-looking Kartosuwiryo with the title, 'Kartosuwiryo: An impossible dream'.[75] This divergence shows not too subtly how the magazine intended to offer what the readership expected: for the Indonesian audience, the editors neither condemned nor glorified the struggle for political

73 Suryana Sudrajat, *Kearifan guru bangsa: Pilar kemerdekaan,* (Jakarta: Erlangga, 2006).

74 Tempo, *Kartosoewirjo, mimpi negara Islam.* Seri buku Tempo: Tokoh Islam di awal kemerdekaan (Jakarta: Gramedia, 2011).

75 *Majalah Tempo,* August 18-24, 2010; English and Indonesian editions.

Islam, while for the Western audience they made a strong statement about the infeasibility of achieving an Islamic state in the past as well as today.

CONCLUDING REMARKS

Kartosuwiryo's memory – and its management – are emblematic of Indonesia's Islamic identity. Whether we look at family connections, territorial expansion or historical and ideological references, Kartosuwiryo and the Darul Islam are constant elements in the Islamist as much as the secular discourse. Yet the dominant image of Kartosuwiryo and the Darul Islam is a magnified one, of Kartosuwiryo as *imam* of the Negara Islam Indonesia, commander of the Tentara Islam Indonesia and crafter of an anti-Pancasila unitary Republic movement. But this is a picture only representative of a part of his political life. Those who hail him as a martyr and a hero differ from those who call him an enemy of the state or a terrorist only in perspective; both sides see Kartosuwiryo through their own self-interested filters. But Kartosuwiryo's historical relevance lies in his advocacy of non-cooperation with the Dutch, his dedication to an unshakably nationalist movement committed to absolute and uncompromising freedom from colonization and his framing the struggle for independence in Islamic terms. His legacy, however, is inextricably linked with the violent turn of his movement, because of which Islam lost its chance to become a prominent factor in national politics.

The violent evolution of the Darul Islam tainted the image of Islam as a political ideology, further pushing away the chance to realize an Islamic state. The portrayals of Kartosuwiryo and his movement need to be analysed amidst the changing context of Indonesian politics, from the revolution and Soekarno's subsequent consolidation of the Pancasila state, through the army's rising power and co-optation policies and Suharto's rapprochement with Islam and eventual fall, to the emergence of a new wave of Islamization of Indonesia's society.

The political development of Indonesia as an autocratic, non-confessional state, in which the army held control over the government and society for most of its existence, led to such a crystallization of understandings of Kartosuwiryo's actions and goals that his complexities were eventually reduced to an over-simplified dichotomy that could only be challenged after the passing of several decades and dramatic political transformations.

Conclusion
The development of political Islam and the making of the Indonesian state

This book has explored the development of political Islam in twentieth-century Indonesia by following the life, career and legacy of Sekarmaji Marjan Kartosuwiryo. My goal has been twofold: on one hand I have attempted to reassert the religious motivations behind the Darul Islam movement and to explore Kartosuwiryo's legacy for contemporary Islamists. On the other hand, this reassertion of Islam as the main stimulus for what became a rebellious movement has formed the core of my explanation for the failure of political Islam in the 1950s. The contested identities of both the Darul Islam and Kartosuwiryo himself shaped Indonesian Muslims' political attitudes throughout the twentieth century and beyond.

Born into a traditional Javanese family, to a father employed in the colonial administration, Kartosuwiryo failed as a student in medical school. However, he soon grew to become an important figure in the anti-colonial movement in the 1930s. It is unclear why he first joined the religious Sarekat Islam in 1927; he may have been attracted by Tjokroaminoto's charismatic leadership and his Islamo-communist conviction, or perhaps by Agoes Salim's commitment to the Islamic ideal. Regardless, Kartosuwiryo developed a strong sense of socio-economic justice, which he would soon frame in religious terms and translate politically into his efforts towards the establishment of an independent Islamic state. His relationship to the pan-Islamic project oscillated between post-Ottoman Caliphate transnational aspirations and more pressing anti-colonial goals, as nationalism became increasingly paramount. Alongside his conviction that only Islam could be 'the' solution were his distrust of cooperation, secularism and overall 'neutrality' – all key elements, incidentally, of Soekarno's platform since the late 1920s.

The Japanese invasion is an unquestionable landmark in Indonesia's modern history; in addition to the economic disaster brought on by the war effort, Japan empowered the masses with a national consciousness, which lay the foundations for the 1945-1949 revolution. And the impact of Japan's initial predilection for the Islamic movement, which had been mostly due to its grass-roots networks, could not be undone when Japan entrusted the preparations for independence to Soekarno's faction. Masyumi was strong, grounded and ready to fight. The Hizboellah and Sabilillah troops were better trained and more motivated than the Republican soldiers, believing that they were striving on the path of God, and Masyumi's organization and its platform for an Islamic state formed the backbone of anti-Dutch resistance in West Java.

Kartosuwiryo had affirmed his willingness to collaborate with the Japanese, and even after the Dutch had returned, he participated in formal politics, supporting Masyumi's commitment to creating an Islamic state via parliamentary consultation. But the July 1947 invasion could not be ignored. Similarly, the forcible inclusion of West Java into the unitary Republic in August 1950 demanded a reaction.

In 1948 Kartosuwiryo led the restructuring of the West Java regional branch of Masyumi at a time when there was no central branch with which to coordinate activities. But in the following years the struggle for the survival of the Negara Islam Indonesia became identified with the 'external' regions' dissatisfaction with Soekarno's centralized control.

The 1949 proclamation of the NII state and its ensuing struggle for self-preservation and expansion should be seen as an attempt to bring Indonesia – or, at least, parts of it – under the control of an independent Islamic nation-state. The alternative, as Kartosuwiryo argued, would be a Dutch-supported puppet state, which could too easily fall prey to communist forces.

In the 1950s Masyumi and PNI had divergent political orientations, parliamentary discussions were in constant stalemate, the government seemed incapable of progress on any front and the Communist Party was on the rise as a result of Soekarno's support. Cabinet members continuously bickered, and military officers were frustrated at their reduced powers, as Indonesia began attempting to establish itself as a constitutional democracy after the war. Elections were slow to come and ministerial cabinets fast to fall. And all the while, Soekarno held tight to his presidential role.

The temporary character of the Pancasila constitution began to vanish in the face of ongoing political and military instability, frustrating the hopes of those who wished for Islam to be officially recognized as the founding principle of the nation, and exacerbating the position of the Darul Islam. During the revolution relations between the Republic and the Islamic state had oscillated between explicit cooperation, recognition of a common goal and clashes on the battlefield; in the 1950s Masyumi and, crucially, Muhammad Natsir, promoted a diplomatic solution to 'the Darul Islam problem' and the regional rebellions. But the Islamic party had already been weakened by the Nahdatul Ulama's secession in 1952 and its poor electoral performance in 1955; its siding with the revolutionary governments of Sulawesi and Sumatra paved the way for Masyumi's final disbandment in 1960.

Soekarno quickly tired of the constitutional assembly and the debate on Islam, Pancasila and Social Economy. Emboldened by the communists' support, his renewed co-optation of the military and the decline of Masyumi, in 1957 he disbanded the assembly, restored the 1945 Constitution, and implemented his *konsepsi* for a 'Guided Democracy'. Meanwhile, in 1959, the cabinet officially abandoned the 'political solution' to the Darul Islam problem, and the army began to elaborate a military strategy to end what was now defined a 'rebellion'.

In the early 1960s political Islam seemed to have no future in Indonesia, the Darul Islam was quashed and the most prominent leaders of Masyumi were arrested. These developments eventually facilitated the creation of an overall perception of political Islam as a danger to the Republic, an idea that had been advanced by Soekarno as early as 1953 in Amuntai.

In the years preceding Soekarno's Guided Democracy, Islamic intellectuals had dedicated considerable effort to drafting alternative solutions to the Pancasila state, hopeful that Islam could become the foundation of an independent democratic Indonesia. Yet they never acknowledged Kartosuwiryo's experiment, the NII had no influence on their work and the impact of the Darul Islam was now found in the public's suspicion of, and negative attitudes towards, political Islam. Since the 1960s Kartosuwiryo and the Darul Islam had been portrayed as enemies of the Republic – terrorists who were only interested in destabilizing the country and its government, who were led by disenchanted politicians and guerrilla commanders who wanted more power and cared little about Islam.

Ignored, misread as communist, and eventually labelled as separatist and anti-Republican, the Darul Islam movement and its leadership were condemned to oblivion, allowing for the consolidation of a non-Islamic, broadly non-confessional, state. It was only in the aftermath of Suharto's fall that Islamists' revisionist efforts 'rescued' the memory of Kartosuwiryo's religious and political goals from Soekarno's and Suharto's propagandist agendas, even if only to coat his endeavours with apologetic awe and respect, thus giving new life to the forefather of Indonesia's Islamism.

Appendix
Articles and pamphlets authored by S.M. Kartosuwiryo

Articles (in alphabetical order)

'Aniajaan dan siksaan', *Fadjar Asia*, 26 September 1928
'Anti-nationaal dan anti-persatoean', *Fadjar Asia*, 19 November 1928
'Bahaja jang mengantjam roeh dan djiwa ra'iat djadjahan', *Fadjar Asia*, 14 February 1929
'Baitoel-mal pada zaman pantjaroba dan tarich bait-al-mal zaman Rasoeloellah clm dan choelafa-oer-rasidin r.a.a.', SMIAI, 28 June 1943
'Bangsa dan bahasa', *Fadjar Asia*, 8 May 1928
'Bank Nasional', *Fadjar Asia*, 27 August 1928
'Barisan moeda', *Fadjar Asia*, 6 February 1929
'Bekal bathin dalam perdjoeangan', SMIAI, 1 March 1943
'Belanda keboen jang soeka mempermainkan anak isteri orang', *Fadjar Asia*, 6 June 1929
'Beloem djoega mengerti!!', *Fadjar Asia*, 16 July 1929
'Benteng Islam', SMIAI, 1 September 1943
'Berbagai-bagai penangkapan', *Fadjar Asia*, 30 July 1929
'Berekor pandjang (pers dan politiek)', *Fadjar Asia*, 2 July 1929
'Bertoekar fikiran: Agama dan politiek', *Fadjar Asia*, 3 April 1928
'Bertoekar fikiran: Agama dan politiek II', *Fadjar Asia*, 4 April 1928
'Boekan memboeta toeli, malahan membabi boeta', *Fadjar Asia*, 1 March 1929
'Boekan merintangi, melainkan tidak toeroet', *Fadjar Asia*, 4 September 1929
'Boekan oekoeran kita', *Fadjar Asia*, 24 June 1929
'Boekan sifat lelaki', *Fadjar Asia*, 15 July 1929
'Boepati dan agama Islam', *Fadjar Asia*, 21 April 1930
'Congres PCI jang pertama I', *Fadjar Asia*, 3 August 1929
'Congres PCI jang pertama II', *Fadjar Asia*, 5 August 1929
'Damai doenia', *Fadjar Asia*, 23 July 1928
'Ditjari-tjari dan direka-reka', *Fadjar Asia*, 17 November 1928

‘Djawaban kepada Fadjar Asia’, *Fadjar Asia*, 13 May 1929
‘Doenia dan acherat, *Soeara PSII*, November 1937
‘Faham koeno dan faham moeda’, *Fadjar Asia*, 12 September 1928
‘Fardl-oel-‘ain dan fardl-oel-kifajah dalam Islam’, SMIAI, 1 May 1943
‘Gara-gara hari lebaran’, *Fadjar Asia*, 3 April 1928
‘Hadji Agoes Salim ke Geneve’, *Fadjar Asia*, 30 April 1929
‘Halangan PMI Solo’, *Fadjar Asia*, 28 June 1929
‘Hendak damai ataoekah mengganggoe?’, *Fadjar Asia*, 30 April 1930
‘I’tibar madjazy dan ma’any’, SMIAI, 15 July 1943
‘Indonesia Raja dan… kerbaoe’, *Fadjar Asia*, 6 August 1929
‘Irrigatie meroesak pertanian?’, *Fadjar Asia*, 9 October 1928
‘Islam dan kemerdekaan’, *Fadjar Asia*, 23 July 1929
‘Islam dan nasionalisme’, *Fadjar Asia*, 24 May 1929
‘Islam terantjam bahaja’, *Fadjar Asia*, 9 February 1929
‘Islamisme, nasionalisme dan internasionalisme I’, *Fadjar Asia*, 3 November 1928
‘Islamisme, nasionalisme dan internasionalisme II’, *Fadjar Asia*, 7 November 1928
‘Keamanan dan ke’adilan’, *Fadjar Asia*, 15 September, 1928
‘Keber’atan ra’iat’, *Fadjar Asia*, 27 April 1929
‘Keliroe sedikit’, *Fadjar Asia*, 7 November 1928
‘Kemadjoean Islam’, *Fadjar Asia*, 3 April 1928
‘Kepentingan ekonomi di dalam perdjoeangan kita’, *Fadjar Asia*, 3 September 1928
‘Kewadjiban oemmat Islam menghadapi “doenia baroe”’, SMIAI, 15 May 1943
‘Koerban poenale sanctie’, *Fadjar Asia*, 27 July 1929
‘Kongres Liga’, *Fadjar Asia*, 25 April 1929
‘Kongres P3KI kedoea’, *Fadjar Asia*, 10 August 1929
‘Lagi ditembak mati’, *Fadjar Asia*, 31 July 1928
‘Lagi tentang oelil amri’, *Fadjar Asia*, 24 May 1930
‘Lahir dan bathin’, *Fadjar Asia*, 29 October 1928
‘Lain doeloe, lain sekarang!’, *Fadjar Asia*, 11 September 1929
‘Lain pemandangan tentang tooneelstuk Troenodjojo’, *Fadjar Asia*, 7 December 1928
‘Liga melawan imperialisme dan PSI-Hindia Timoer’, *Fadjar Asia*, 12 November 1928
‘Liga, Perhimpoenan Indonesia dan kita’, *Fadjar Asia*, 31 August 1929
‘Main-kokolijo’, *Fadjar Asia*, 18 May 1929
‘Ma’loemat’, *Fadjar Asia*, 11 September 1929
‘Ma’loemat’, *Fadjar Asia*, 14 November 1929

'Ma'loemat LT-PSI Indonesia', *Fadjar Asia*, 20 April 1929
'Mana hak ra'iat?', *Fadjar Asia*, 8 June 1929
'Matjam2 rintangan, *Fadjar Asia*, 30 April 1929
'Memang koerang adjar!', *Fadjar Asia*, 25 June 1929
'Memboeta toeli', *Fadjar Asia*, 29 January 1929
'Menoedjoe ke arah dar-oel-Islam dan dar-oes-salam', SMIAI, 15 March 1943
'Moelai sadar akan hak2nja', *Fadjar Asia*, 16 February 1929
'Moenafeqah?', *Fadjar Asia*, 4 April 1928
'Naik tiang pengantungan', *Fadjar Asia*, 25 July 1929
'Nasib ra'iat Tjitjoeroek', *Fadjar Asia*, 11 May 1929
'Neutral, onpartijdig dan kemoenafikan', *Fadjar Asia*, 14 June 1929
'Obat pemboengkam moeloet', *Fadjar Asia*, 17 July 1929
'Orang Lampoeng boekan monjet, tetapi jalah manoesia belaka!', *Fadjar Asia*, 10 June 1929
'Pandai tapi koerang 'akal', *Fadjar Asia*, 3 April 1928
'Partij Allah pasti menang', *Soeara PSII*, November 1937
'Pengharapan jang choesjoeq', *Fadjar Asia*, 3 October 1928
'Pendjiar perchabaran palsoe', *Fadjar Asia*, 22 June 1929
'Perajaan 1 Mei', *Fadjar Asia*, 6 May 1929
'Perajaan 1 Mei, semboengan Fadjar Asia kemarin', *Fadjar Asia*, 7 May 1929
'Perajaan Maulud Nabi Mohammad saw diboeat sebagai perkakas mendjilat', *Fadjar Asia*, 7 September 1928
'Perbandingan', *Fadjar Asia*, 7 July 1929
'Perbedaan', *Fadjar Asia*, 30 June 1928
'Perbedaan dan perselisihan', *Fadjar Asia*, 11 August 1928
'Perdjalanan ketanah soetji', *Fadjar Asia*, 20 July 1928
'Pergerakan dan korban', *Fadjar Asia*, 18 September 1928
'Pergerakan pemoeda dan politiek', *Fadjar Asia*, 19 April 1929
'Perkara jang benar susah pakainya', *Fadjar Asia*, 17 August 1928
'Perkara tanah: Bangsa mendjadi oekoeran hak', *Fadjar Asia*, 16 August 1929
'Permoeliaan manoesia', *Fadjar Asia*, 31 August 1928
'Peroebahan zaman', *Fadjar Asia*, 24 September 1928
'Pertjaja kepada diri sendiri dan ...', *Fadjar Asia*, 31 October 1928
'Pertjakapan di dalam kereta api', *Fadjar Asia*, 15 May 1928
'Poetoesan dan keterangan', *Fadjar Asia*, 2 February 1929
'Polisi dan ra'iat', *Fadjar Asia*, 3 October 1928
'Politie yang ganas', *Fadjar Asia*, 26 April 1929
'Politiek djadjahan dan igama', *Fadjar Asia*, 2 June 1928
'Politiek djadjahan dan igama II', *Fadjar Asia*, 4 June 1928
'Politiek djadjahan dan igama III', *Fadjar Asia*, 13 June 1928
'Politiek djadjahan dan igama IV', *Fadjar Asia*, 14 June 1928

'Politiek djadjahan dan igama V', *Fadjar Asia*, 16 June 1928
'Ra'iat dan nasibnja', *Fadjar Asia*, 12 February 1929
'Randjau pergerakan', *Fadjar Asia*, 13 August 1929
'Ratap tangis dan keloeh kesah si "Lemah"', *Fadjar Asia*, 13 October 1928
'Rintangan dan larangan', *Fadjar Asia*, 14 May 1929
'Rintangan di Soengai-Batang (Menindjau)', *Fadjar Asia*, 1 August 1929
'Riwajat AlMahroem Raden Adjeng Kartini', *Fadjar Asia*, 23 April 1929
'Roedjak Sentoel', *Fadjar Asia*, 17 July 1929
'Roesland dan Tiongkok', *Fadjar Asia*, 12 September 1929
'Sambil laloe: Lagi tentang persatoean', *Fadjar Asia*, 12 March 1929
'Sambil laloe: Lagi tentang persatoean II', *Fadjar Asia*, 15 March 1929
'Sambil laloe: Pikiran sehat', *Fadjar Asia*, 7 September 1929
'Sambil laloe: Soeara baroe! Model lama', *Fadjar Asia*, 4 May 1929
'Samboetan', *Fadjar Asia*, 14 November 1929
'Satoe boekti gampangnja hak ra'iat djadjahan dilanggar ataoe terlanggar', *Fadjar Asia*, 23 February 1929
'Sedikit tentang oeloel amri', *Fadjar Asia*, 23 May 1930
'Selamat djalan', *Fadjar Asia*, 2 May 1929
'Serangan dan balasan', *Fadjar Asia*, 20 July 1929
'Seroean oemoem komite zakat fitrah', *Fadjar Asia*, 1 March 1929
'Siapa jang tidak setoedjoe dengan kita, ialah moesoeh kita', *Fadjar Asia*, 9 July 1929
'Sifat binatang', *Fadjar Asia*, 10 July 1929
'Sikap jang berbahaja neutraal', *Fadjar Asia*, 17 October 1929
'Soe'al kaoem boeroeh dan madjikan', *Fadjar Asia*, 3 June 1929
'Soe'al persatoean', *Fadjar Asia*, 10 September 1929
'Soeap!', *Fadjar Asia*, 22 September 1928
'Soenan dan kebangsaan', *Fadjar Asia*, 16 January 1929
'Tentang sembahjang djoem'ah dan pendirian masdjid', *Fadjar Asia*, 11 April 1930
'Tetap dalam pendirian kita', *Fadjar Asia*, 24 July 1929
'Troenodjojo', *Fadjar Asia*, 12 November 1928
'Vergadering ISDP', *Fadjar Asia*, 2 April 1928
'Warta bagi pers', *Fadjar Asia*, 13 September 1929
'Zaman terbalik', *Fadjar Asia*, 25 April 1929

Pamphlets (in chronological order)

Sikap hidjrah PSII, 10 September 1936
Daftar oesaha hidjrah PSII, March 1940

Haloean politik Islam, 16 August 1946
Perang sabil, 27 Ramadhan 1366/15 August 1947
ad-Daulatul Islamiyah, March 1949

NII documents (in chronological order)

Qanun asasy Negara Islam Indonesia, 22 Syawal 1367/27 August 1948
Proklamasi Negara Islam Indonesia, 12 Syawal 1368/18 August 1949
Manifesto politik 1/7, 1 Dzulqa'idah 1368/26 August 1949
Hukum pidana, 1949

Glossary

adat	custom’ary law or traditions
amir	leader, commander
amir ul-mu’minin	commander of the faithful
bait al mal	Islamic communal treasury
bughat	rebel
bupati	regent
dar al-Islam or dar-ul-Islam	house of Islam, Islamic territory
ad-daulatul Islamiyah	Islamic state
desa	village
dewan fatwa	advisory council
dewan imamah	Ministerial Cabinet
dewan partij	Party’s Central Board
fard al-‘ayn	individual duty
fard al-kifaya	collective duty
fatwa	legal opinion
fiqh	jurisprudence
haram	forbidden
hijrah	migration; in politics: non-cooperation
hukum	law
hukum pidana	criminal code
‘ibada	worship
imam	leader
iman	faith
Jawi	Southeast Asians
jihad	struggle
jihad al-akbar	greater struggle
jihad al-asghar	lesser struggle
kafir	infidel
kaum	group, people
keris	a dagger with an undulate blade, deemed to possess spiritual essence
ketuhanan	belief in God

kiyai	Islamic scholar
konsepsi	vision
laskar	militia
majelis syuro	consultative assembly, parliament
majelis Islam	Islamic council
menak	Sundanese aristocracy
negara	state
perang sabil or suci	holy war
pergerakan, gerakan	movement
pesantren	traditional Islamic (boarding) school
priyayi	Javanese courtly elite, transformed into bureaucratic elite by the colonial administration
sikap	policy, effort
Soeffah	educational institution in Medina at the time of the Prophet; Kartosuwiryo's pesantren
tauhid	monotheism, unity of God
ulama	religious scholar
ummah, ummat	community
wahyu (Ar.) – pulung (Jv.)	divine revelation
wajib	obligatory

Bibliography

Archives

Arsip Angkatan Bersenjata Republik Indonesia, Jakarta
- D.I.-T.I.I. Ja.Bar.

Arsip Nasional Republik Indonesia, Jakarta
- Kabinet Perdana Menteri Republik Indonesia, Yogyakarta. 1949-1950
- Jogjakarta Documenten, 1945-1949
- Kementrian Pertahanan Republik Indonesia
- Kepolisian Negara Republik Indonesia, 1947-1949
- Pemerintah Darurat RI, 1948-1949
- Kabinet Presiden, 1950-1959
- Kabinet Presiden Republik Indonesia Serikat, 1949-1950

Nationaal Archief, The Hague
- Archief van de Procureur-Generaal
- Archief van het Ministerie van Koloniën, 1900-1963
- Archief van de Algemene Secretarie, 1944-1950
- Archief van het Ministerie van Koloniën, Rapportage Indonesië, 1945-1950
- Archief van het Ministerie van Koloniën, Supplement (1664), 1826-1952
- Archief van de Marine en Leger Inlichtingendienst, Netherlands Forces Intelligence Service en Centrale Militaire Inlichtingendienst in Nederlands-Indië

National Archives of the United Kingdom, Kew
- Foreign Office Archives
- War Office Archives

Periodicals and newspapers

A.P.B.
al-Djihad

Algemeen overzicht van de Inlandsche (Maleisisch-Chineesche en Arabische) Pers
Antara News
Asia Raya
Berita
Berita Indonesia
Berita Masjumi
Berita Priangan
Darmokondo
Fadjar Asia
Harian Berita
Harian Ra'jat
Indonesia Merdeka
Indonesisch pers en radio overzicht, Java
Java Post
Keng Po
Kedaulatan Rakyat
Logbericht
Majalah Tempo
Merdeka
Nieuwe Courant
Overzicht van der Inlandsche en Maleisisch-Chineesche Pers
Pandji Islam
Pandji Poestaka
Panji Masyarakat
Pewarta Surabaja
Politiek-politioneele overzichten van Nederlandsch-Indië
Sabili
Sin Po
Soeara MIAI
Soeara PSII
TIME Magazine
Trompet Masjarakat
Vrjie Pers
Warta Indonesia

Publications

35 Tahun Siliwangi
1981 *35 tahun Siliwangi, 20 Mei 1946-20 Mei 1981.* Bandung: Dinas Penerangan dan Hubungan Masyarakat Kodam 6/Siliwangi.

Abdurrahman
1999 'Jong Islamieten Bond, 1925-1942 (sejarah, pemikiran, dan gerakan)'. Thesis, IAIN Sunan Kalijaga, Yogyakarta.

Abeyasekere, Susan
1976 *One hand clapping: Indonesian nationalists and the Dutch, 1939-1942.* Clayton: Centre of Southeast Asian Studies, Monash University. [Monash Papers on Southeast Asia 5.]
1973 'The Soetardjo petition', *Indonesia* 15:80-108.
1972 'Partai Indonesia Raja, 1936-42: A study in cooperative nationalism', *Journal of Southeast Asian Studies* 3-2:262-76.

Abuza, Zachary
2003 *Militant Islam in Southeast Asia: Crucible of terror.* Boulder: Lynne Rienner.

Adams, Cindy
1965 *Soekarno: An autobiography.* Indianapolis: Bobbs-Merrill.

Ahmad, Zainal Abidin
1964 *Negara utama (madinatu'l fadilah).* Jakarta: Djambatan.
1956 *Membentuk negara Islam.* Jakarta: Widjaya.
1952 *Dasar-dasar ekonomi Islam.* Jakarta: Pustaka Antara/Aida. [First edition Jakarta: Sinar Ilmu, 1950.]
1952 *Konsepsi negara Islam.* Bandung: Al Ma'arif.
1949 *Konsepsi tata negara Islam.* Jakarta: Sinar Ilmu.
1946 *Konstitoesi negara, pendjelasan landjoet tentang oendang-oendang dasar negara Republik Indonesia.* Bukit Tinggi: Poestaka Islam.

Aiko, Kurasawa
1986 'Japanese occupation and leadership changes in Javanese villages', in: Jurrien van Goor (ed.), *The Indonesian Revolution: Papers of the conference held in Utrecht, 17-20 June 1986,* pp. 57-78. Utrecht: Instituut voor Geschiedenis. [Utrechtse Historische Cahiers, jaargang 7, 2/3.]

Amelz
1952 *H.O.S. Tjokroaminoto: Hidup dan perdjuangannja.* Jakarta: Bulan Bintang. Two vols.

Amiq
1998 'Two fatwas on jihad against the Dutch colonisation in Indonesia: A prosopographical approach to the study of fatwa', *Studia Islamika* 5-3:81-124.

Anderson, Benedict R.O'G.
1972 *Java in a time of revolution: Occupation and resistance, 1944-1946.* Ithaca, NY/London: Cornell University Press.

Anshari, Endang Saifuddin
1997 *Piagam Jakarta 22 Juni 1945: Sebuah konsensus nasional tentang dasar negara Republik Indonesia, 1945-1959.* Edisi 3. Jakarta: Gema Insani Press. [First edition 1981.]

Anshari, Fauzan al-
2005 *KUHP Syariah dan penjelasannya.* Jakarta: Departemen Data dan Informasi MMI. 'Proposal for a Criminal Code for the Republic of Indonesia adjusted to accord with the syari'ah of Islam', issued by Central Headquarters of the Majelis Mujahidin Jl.Veteran no. 17, Jogjakarta, Indonesia.

Anshary, Isa
1951 *Falsafah perdjuangan Islam.* Medan: Saiful. [First edition 1949.]

Ansyori, Muhammad Isa
2007 'Respons Masyumi terhadap gerakan Darul Islam di Jawa Barat (1949-1960)'. Thesis, Universitas Pajadjaran, Jatinangor.

Aspinall, Edward
2009 *Islam and nation: Separatist rebellion in Aceh, Indonesia.* Singapore: NUS Press.

Awwas, Irfan
2008 *Trilogi kepemimpinan Negara Islam Indonesia.* Yogyakarta: Uswah.
2007 *Jejak jihad S.M. Kartosuwiryo.* Cetakan ke-3. Yogyakarta: Uswah. [First edition 1999.]
1999 *Menelusuri perjalanan jihad S.M. Kartosuwiryo: Proklamator Negara Islam Indonesia.* Yogyakarta: Wihdah Press.

Aziz, M.A.
1955 *Japan's colonialism and Indonesia.* The Hague: Nijhoff.

Azra, Azyumardi
2004 *The origins of Islamic reformism in Southeast Asia: Networks of Malay-Indonesian and Middle Eastern 'ulamā' in the seventeenth and eighteenth century.* Honolulu: University of Hawai'i Press.

Balfas, M.
1952 *Dr Tjipto Mangoekoesoemo, demokrat sedjati.* Jakarta: Penerbit Djambatan. [Seri Tjermin Kehidupan.]

Barton, Greg and Greg Fealy (eds)
1996 *Nahdlatul Ulama, traditional Islam and modernity in Indonesia.* Clayton: Monash Asia Institute, Monash University. [Monash Papers on Southeast Asia 39.]

Beinin, Joel and Joe Stork (eds)
1997 *Political Islam: Essays from Middle East report.* Berkeley, CA: University of California Press. [Published in cooperation with Middle East Research and Information Project.]

Benda, Harry J.
1958 *The crescent and the rising sun: Indonesian Islam under the Japanese occupation, 1942-1945.* The Hague: Van Hoeve, New York: Institute of Pacific Relations.
1960 'Non-Western intelligentsias as political elites', *Australian Journal of Politics and History* 6:205-18.
1962 'The structure of Southeast Asian history: Some preliminary observations', *Journal of Southeast Asian History* 3:106-38.

Boland, B.J.
1982 *The struggle of Islam in modern Indonesia.* The Hague: Nijhoff. [KITLV, Verhandelingen 59.]

Bruinessen, Martin van
2002 'Genealogies of radical Islam in post-Suharto Indonesia', Utrecht University Website, http://www.let.uu.nl/~Martin.vanBruinessen/personal/publications/genealogies_islamic_radicalism.htm.
1995 'Muslims of the Dutch East Indies and the Caliphate question', *Studia Islamika* 2-3:115-40.

Bush, Robin
2012 'Islam and constitutionalism in Indonesia', in: David Linnan (ed.), *Legitimacy, legal development and change: Law and modernization reconsidered.* Surrey: Ashgate.
2008 'Regional sharia regulations in Indonesia: Anomaly or symptom?', in: Greg Fealy and Sally White (eds), *Expressing Islam: Religious life and politics in Indonesia,* pp. 174-91. Singapore: Institute of Southeast Asian Studies. [Indonesia Update Series.]

Chaidar, Al
2000 *Sepak terjang KW9 Abu Toto (Syekh A.S. Panji Gumilang) menyelewengkan NKA-NII pasca S.M. Kartosoewirjo.* Cetakan ke-2. Jakarta: Madani Press. [Serial musuh-musuh Darul Islam 1.]
1999 *Pemikiran politik proklamator negara Islam Indonesia S.M. Kartosoewirjo: Fakta dan data sejarah Darul Islam.* Jakarta: Darul Falah.
1999 *S.M. Kartosoewirjo: Pemberontak atau mujahid.* Jakarta: Suara Hidayatullah.

1998 *Wacana ideologi negara Islam.* Jakarta: Darul Falah.

1996 'Ideologi Negara Islam di Asia Tenggara: Telaah perbandingan atas terbentuknya diskursus politik Islam dalam gerakan-gerakan pembentukan negara di Indonesia dan Filipina pasca kolonialisme'. Thesis, Universitas Indonesia, Jakarta.

Cribb, Robert

1991 *Gangsters and revolutionaries: The Jakarta people's militia and the Indonesian revolution, 1945-49.* Sydney: Allen & Unwin. [Asian Studies Association of Australia, Southeast Asia Publications Series 20.]

1986 'Administrative competition in the Indonesian revolution: The dual government of Jakarta, 1945-1947', in: Jurrien van Goor (ed.), *The Indonesian Revolution: Papers of the conference held in Utrecht, 17-20 June 1986*, pp. 129-46. Utrecht: Instituut voor Geschiedenis. [Utrechtse Historische Cahiers, jaargang 7, 2/3.]

Dahm, Bernhard

1969 *Sukarno and the struggle for Indonesian independence.* Translated from the German by Mary F. Somers Heidhues. Ithaca, NY/London: Cornell University Press. [Originally published as *Sukarnos Kampf um Indonesiens Unabhängigkeit: Werdegang und politische Ideen bis zu seiner Wahl zum ersten Präsidenten der Republik Indonesien im August 1945.* Kiel: n.n., 1964.]

Dhofier, Zamakhsyari

1992 'The intellectualisation of Islamic Studies in Indonesia', *Indonesia Circle* 58:19-31.

Dick, Howard

2002 *Surabaya, city of work: A socioeconomic history, 1900-2000.* Athens, OH: Ohio University Press. [Research in International Studies.]

Dinas Sedjarah Kodam VI Siliwangi

1968 *Siliwangi dari masa ke masa.* Jakarta: Fakta Mahjuma.

Dinas Sejarah TNI, Jakarta

1978 *Album peristiwa pemberontakan DI-TII di Indonesia.* Jakarta: Dinas Sejarah Tentara Nasional Indonesia Angkatan Darat.

Dinas Sejarah TNI, Bandung

1982 *Penumpasan pemberontakan DI/TII, S.M. Kartosuwiryo di Jawa Barat.* Bandung: Dinas Sejarah Tentara Nasional Indonesia Angkatan Darat. [First edition 1974.]

Dijk, Cornelis van
1981 *Rebellion under the banner of Islam: The Darul Islam in Indonesia.* The Hague: Nijhoff. [KITLV, Verhandelingen 94.]
Dudung
1987 Peristiwa Cipari. Thesis, Universitas Padjadjaran, Bandung.
Ekadjati, Edi S.
1979 *Sejarah kebangkitan nasional daerah Jawa Barat.* Jakarta: Proyek Penelitian dan Pencatatan Kebudayaan Daerah Jawa Barat, Pusat Penelitian Sejarah & Budaya, Departemen Pendidikan dan Kebudayaan.
Elson, Robert E.
2008 *The idea of Indonesia: A history.* Cambridge: Cambridge University Press.
Elson, B. and C. Formichi
2011 'Why did Kartosuwiryo start shooting?', *Journal of Southeast Asian Studies* 42-3:458-86.
Ensering, Else
1984 'Afdeeling B of Sarekat Islam. A rebellious Islamic movement', in: Dick Kooiman, Otto van den Muijzenberg, and Peter van der Veer (eds), *Conversion, competition, and conflict: Essays on the role of religion in Asia.* Amsterdam: VU Uitgeverij. [Anthropological Studies Free University 6.]
Esposito, John L.
2002 *Un-holy war: Terror in the name of Islam.* Oxford: Oxford University Press.
Fakkih, Markhaban
1970 'Golongan santri dan peristiwa 426 di Klaten'. Thesis, Universitas Gadjah Mada, Yogyakarta.
Fasseur, Cornelis
1992 *The politics of colonial exploitation: Java, the Dutch, and the cultivation system.* Translated from the Dutch by R.E. Elson and Ary Kraal. Ithaca, NY: Southeast Asia Program, Cornell University. [Studies on Southeast Asia 8.] [Originally published as *Kultuurstelsel en koloniale baten: De Nederlandse exploitatie van Java 1840-1860.* Leiden: Universitaire Pers, 1975.]
Fealy, Greg
1996 'Wahab Chasbullah, traditionalism and the political development of Nahdlatul Ulama', in: Greg Barton and Greg Fealy (eds), *Nahdlatul Ulama, traditional Islam and modernity in Indonesia*, pp. 1-41. Clayton: Monash Asia Institute, Monash University. [Monash Papers on Southeast Asia 39.]

Fealy, Greg and Virginia Hooker (eds)
2006 *Voices of Islam in Southeast Asia: A contemporary sourcebook.* Singapore: Institute of Southeast Asian Studies.
Fealy, Greg and Sally White (eds)
2008 *Expressing Islam: Religious life and politics in Indonesia.* Singapore: Institute of Southeast Asian Studies. [Indonesia Update Series.]
Federspiel, Howard M.
2001 *Islam and ideology in the emerging Indonesian state: The Persatuan Islam (Persis), 1923 to 1957.* Revised second edition. Leiden: Brill. [Social, Economic and Political Studies of the Middle East and Asia 78.] [First edition 1970.]
Feener, R. Michael
2010 'New networks and new knowledge: Migrations, communications, and the refiguration of the Muslim community in the nineteenth and early twentieth centuries', in: Robert Hefner (ed.), *The new Cambridge history of Islam.* Vol. 6, pp. 39-68. New York: Cambridge University Press.
2007 *Muslim legal thought in modern Indonesia.* Cambridge: Cambridge University Press.
Feillard, Andrée and Rémy Madinier
2011 *The end of innocence? Indonesian Islam and the temptation of radicalism.* Translated by Wong Wee. Singapore: NUS Press. [Originally published as *La fin de l'innocence? L'islam indonésien face à la tentation radicale de 1967 à nos jours.* Paris: Indes Savantes, 2006.]
Feith, Herbert
1957 *The Indonesian elections of 1955.* Ithaca, NY: Modern Indonesia Project, Cornell University.
1962 *The decline of constitutional democracy in Indonesia.* Ithaca, NY: Cornell University Press.
Feith, Herbert and Lance Castles (eds)
1970 *Indonesian political thinking, 1945-1965.* Ithaca, NY: Cornell University Press. [Asian Literature Program of the Asia Society, New York.]
Feith, H. and D.S. Lev
1963 'The end of the Indonesian rebellion', *Pacific Affairs* 36-1: 32-46.
Florida, Nancy K.
1995 *Writing the past, inscribing the future: History as prophecy in colonial Java.* Durham, NC: Duke University Press.

Formichi, Chiara
2012a 'Mustafa Kemal's abrogation of the Ottoman Caliphate and its impact on the Indonesian nationalist Movement', in: Madawi al-Rasheed, Carool Kersten and Marat Shterin (eds), *Demystifying the caliphate: Historical memory and contemporary contexts,* pp. 95-115. London: Hurst, New York: Columbia University Press.
2012b 'Review article: Is an Islamic democracy possible? Perspectives from contemporary Southeast Asia', *Journal of Southeast Asian Research* 20:100-6.
2010 'Pan-Islam and religious nationalism: The case of S.M. Kartosuwiryo and Negara Islam Indonesia', *Indonesia* 90:125-46.

Foulcher, Keith
2002 '*Sumpah Pemuda*: The making and meaning of a symbol on Indonesian nationhood', *Asian Studies Review* 24-3:377-410.

Geertz, Clifford
1960 *The religion of Java.* Chicago/London: University of Chicago Press.

Gerakan separatisme
2003 *Gerakan separatisme Indonesia tahun 1945-1965.* Jakarta: Arsip Nasional Republik Indonesia.

Goor, Jurrien van (ed.)
1986 *The Indonesian Revolution: Papers of the conference held in Utrecht, 17-20 June 1986,* pp. 57-78. Utrecht: Instituut voor Geschiedenis. [Utrechtse Historische Cahiers, jaargang 7, 2/3.].

Gunaratna, Rohan
2003 *Terrorism in the Asia-Pacific: Threat and response.* Singapore: Eastern Universities Press.
2002 *Inside al-Qaeda: Global network of terror.* New York: Columbia University Press.

Hakim, L.E.
1955 *Konstitusi negara-negara Islam.* Jakarta: Bulan Bintang.
1951 *Konstitusi negara2 Islam.* Bandung: Al Ma'arif.

Hanneman, Samuel and Henk Schulte Nordholt (eds)
2004 *Indonesia in transition: Rethinking 'civil society', 'region' and 'crisis'.* Yogyakarta: Pustaka Pelajar.

Hardacre, Helen
1989 *Shintō and the state, 1868-1988.* Princeton, NJ: Princeton University Press.

Harvey, Barbara Sillars
1974 *Tradition, Islam and rebellion: South Sulawesi, 1905-1965.* PhD thesis, Cornell University, Ithaca, NY.
1977 *Permesta: Half a rebellion.* Ithaca, NY: Cornell University Press. [Cornell Modern Indonesia Project, Monograph Series 57.]

Hasan, Noorhaidi
2006 *Laskar Jihad: Islam, militancy, and the quest for identity in post-New Order Indonesia.* Ithaca, NY: Southeast Asia Program, Cornell University. [Studies on Southeast Asia 40.]

Hefner, Robert W.
2010 (ed.) *The new Cambridge history of Islam. Vol. 6: Muslims and mondernity; Culture and society since 1800.* New York: Cambridge University Press.
2000 *Civil Islam: Muslims and democratization in Indonesia.* Princeton, NJ: Princeton University Press. [Princeton Studies in Muslim Politics.]

Heinrichs, W., Peri Bearman, and B. Weiss (eds)
2008 *The law applied: Contextualizing the Islamic sharia.* London: I.B. Tauris.

Hering, Bob
2002 *Soekarno: Founding father of Indonesia.* Leiden: KITLV Press. [Verhandelingen 192.]

Hilmy, Masdar
2010 *Islamism and democracy in Indonesia: Piety and pragmatism.* Singapore: Institute of Southeast Asian Studies. [ISEAS Series on Islam.]

Horikoshi, Hiroko
1975 'The Dar-ul-Islam movement in West Java (1942-62): An experience in the historical process', *Indonesia* 20:59-86.

Hosen, Nadirsyah
2007 *Shari'a and constitutional reform in Indonesia.* Singapore: Institute of Southeast Asian Studies. [ISEAS Series on Islam.]

Ibrahim, Ahmad, Sharon Siddique and Yasmin Hussain (eds)
1985 *Readings on Islam in Southeast Asia.* Singapore: Institute of Southeast Asian Studies. [Social Issues in Southeast Asia.]

Ingleson, John
1988 'Urban Java during the depression', *Journal of Southeast Asian Studies* 19-2:292-309.

Iskandar, Mohammad
2001 *Para pengemban amanah: Pergulatan pemikiran kiai dan ulama di Jawa Barat, 1900-1950.* Yogyakarta: MataBangsa.

Ismail
1998 'Perjuangan K.H. Mustofa Kamil pada masa penjajahan dan kemerdekaan di Garut antara tahun 1914-1945'. Thesis, IAIN Sunan Gunung Jati, Bandung.

Jackson, Karl D.
1980 *Traditional authority and national integration: A study of Indonesian political behavior.* Berkeley, CA/London: University of California Press.

Jauhari, Usman
1987 'Peranan Hizboellah-Sabilillah dalam perlawanan bersenjata terhadap Belanda di Jawa Barat pada masa revolusi fisik (1945-1959)'. Thesis, Universitas Padjajaran, Bandung.

Johns, Anthony H.
1985 'Islam in Southeast Asia: Problems of perspective', in Ahmad Ibrahim, Sharon Siddique and Yasmin Hussain (eds), *Readings on Islam in Southeast Asia,* pp. 20-4. Singapore: Institute of Southeast Asian Studies. [Social Issues in Southeast Asia.] [First printed in 1976.]

Jones, Sidney
2005 'Recycling militants in Indonesia: Darul Islam and the Australian embassy bombing', *Asia Report.* Singapore/Brussels: International Crisis Group.

Jong, J.J.P. de
1986 'Winds of change: Van Mook, Dutch policy and the realities of November 1945'. In Jurrien van Goor (ed), *The Indonesian Revolution,* Utrecht: Rijksuniversiteit Instituut voor Geschiedenis, pp. 163-82.

Kahin, George Mc Turnan
2003 *Nationalism and revolution in Indonesia.* Ithaca, NY: Cornell Southeast Asia Program Publications. [First edition 1952.]

Kamus Besar
2001 *Kamus Besar Bahasa Indonesia.* Jakarta: Balai Pustaka.

Keddie, Nikki R.
1969 'Pan-Islam as proto-nationalism,' *The Journal of Modern History* 41-1:17-28.

Kementerian Penerangan
1953 *Republik Indonesia: Propinsi Djawa Barat.* Jakarta: Kementerian Penerangan.
Kooiman, D., O. van den Muijzenberg, and P. van der Veer (eds)
1984 *Conversion, competition, and conflict: Essays on the role of religion in Asia.* Amsterdam: VU Uitgeverij.
Laffan, Michael F.
2004 'An Indonesian community in Cairo: Continuity and change in a cosmopolitan Islamic milieu', *Indonesia* 77 (April): 1-26.
2003 *Islamic nationhood and colonial Indonesia: The* umma *below the winds.* London: Routledge.
Landau, Jacob M.
1994 *The politics of pan-Islam: Ideology and organisation.* Oxford: Oxford University Press.
Latief, Hasyim
1995 *Laskar Hisbullah.* Surabaya: Lajnah Ta'lif wan Nasyr PBNU.
Latif, Yudi
2008 *Indonesian Muslim intelligentsia and power.* Singapore: Institute of Southeast Asian Studies.
Legge, John David
1981 '*Daulat Ra'jat* and the ideas of the Pendidikan Nasional Indonesia', *Indonesia* 32 (October): 151-68.
Liddle, R. William
1978 'Indonesia 1977: The New Order's second parliamentary election', *Asian Survey* 18-2 (February): 175-85.
Lindsey, T. and J. Kingsley
2008 'Talking in code: Legal Islamisation in Indonesia and the MMI shari'a criminal code', in Heinrichs, W., Peri Bearman, and B. Weiss (eds), *The law applied,* pp. 295-320. London: I.B. Tauris.
Linnan, David (ed)
2012 *Legitimacy, legal development and change: Law and modernization reconsidered.* Surrey, UK: Ashgate.
Lubis, Nina Herlina
2003 'Religious thoughts and practices of the *kaum menak*: Strengthening traditional power', *Studia Islamika* 10-2: 5-7.

Madewa, Lukman

1977 *Esa hilang dua terbilang; Album kenangan KODAM 6/Siliwangi, 1946-1977.* Bandung: Komando Daerah Militer (KODAM) 6/Siliwangi.

McGregor, Katharine E.

2007 *History in uniform: Military ideology and the construction of Indonesia's past.* Singapore: NUS Press.

McMillan, Richard

2009 'British military intelligence in Java and Sumatra, 1945-46', *Indonesia and the Malay World* 37-107:65-81.

2005 *The British occupation of Indonesia, 1945-1946.* London: RoutledgeCurzon.

McVey, Ruth Thomas

2006 *The rise of Indonesian communism.* 1st Equinox ed. Singapore: Equinox Publishing. [First edition 1961.]

1981 'Reviewed work: Traditional authority, Islam, and rebellion: A study of Indonesian political behavior by Karl D. Jackson', *Pacific Affairs* 54-2:260-87.

Melik, Sajuti

1953 *Negara nasional ataukah Negara Islam.* Yogyakarta: Kedaulatan Rakjat.

Millard, Mike

2004 *Jihad in paradise: Islam and politics in Southeast Asia.* Armonk, NY: M.E. Sharpe.

Mobini-Kesheh, Natalie

1999 *The Hadhrami awakening: Community and identity in the Netherlands East Indies, 1900-1942.* Ithaca, NY: Cornell University Southeast Asia Program.

Museum Waspada Purbawisesa

1997 *Museum Waspada Purbawisesa: Buku panduan.* 3rd ed. Jakarta: Markas Besar Angkatan Bersenjata RI, Pusat Sejarah dan Tradisi ABRI. [First edition 1995.]

Nasution, Abdul Haris

1978 *Sekitar perang kemerdekaan Indonesia.* Bandung: Angkasa.

1968 *Tentara Nasional Indonesia.* Jakarta: Seruling Masa.

Nasution, Harun

1965 The Islamic state in Indonesia: The rise of the ideology, the movement for its creation and the theory of the MASJUMI. MA thesis, McGill, Montreal.

Natsir, Muhammad

2008 *Capita selecta*. 3 vols. Jakarta: Abadi-Yayasan Capita Selecta.

1957 *Islam sebagai dasar negara*. Jakarta: Pimpinan Fraksi Masjumi dalam Konstituante.

Niel, R. van

1960 *The emergence of the modern Indonesian elite*. The Hague: Van Hoeve.

Niemeijer, A.C.

1972 *The Khilafat movement in India, 1919-1924*. The Hague: Martinus Nijhoff.

Nieuwenhuijze, C.A.O. van

1958 *Aspects of Islam in post-colonial Indonesia: Five essays*. The Hague/Bandung: Van Hoeve.

1950 'The Darul Islam movement in Western Java ' *Pacific Affairs* 23-2:169-83.

Noer, Deliar

1973 *The modernist Muslim movement in Indonesia, 1900-1942*. Singapore: Oxford University Press.

1960 *Masjumi: Its organization, ideology and political role in Indonesia*. Master's thesis, Cornell University, Ithaca.

Noer, D. and Akbarsyah

2005 *K.N.I.P.: Komite Nasional Indonesia Pusat. Parlemen Indonesia 1945-1959*. Jakarta: Yayasan Risalah.

Nur Ichwan, Moch

2001 'Differing responses to an Ahmadi translation and exegesis: The Holy Qur'ān in Egypt and Indonesia', *Archipel* 62:143-61.

Oates, William A.

1968 'The Afdeeling B: An Indonesian case study', *Journal of Southeast Asian History* 9-1 (March): 107-16.

Oliver-Dee, Sean

2009 *The Caliphate question: The British government and Islamic governance*. Lanham, MD: Lexington Books.

Panitya Buku Peringatan Muhammad Natsir

1978 *Muhammad Natsir 70 tahun kenang-kenangan kehidupan dan perdjuangan*. Jakarta: Pustaka Antara.

Pinardi

1964 *Sekarmadji Maridjan Kartosuwirjo*. Jakarta: Aryaguna.

Platzdasch, Bernhard

2009 *Islamism in Indonesia: Politics in the emerging democracy*. Singapore: Institute of Southeast Asian Studies.

Poeze, Harry
2007 *Verguisd en vergeten: Tan Malaka, de linkse beweging en de Indonesische revolutie, 1945-1949.* 3 vols. Leiden: KITLV Uitgeverij. [KITLV Verhandelingen 250.]

Rambe, Safrizal
2008 *Sarekat Islam: Pelopor nasionalisme Indonesia, 1905-1942.* Jakarta: Yayasan Kebangkitan Insan Cendekia.

Rasheed, Madawi al-, Carool Kersten and Marat Shterin (eds)
2012 *Demystifying the caliphate: Historical memory and contemporary contexts.* London: Hurst Publishers; New York: Columbia University Press.

Ricklefs, Merle Calvin
2007 *Polarizing Javanese society: Islamic and other visions (c.1830-1930).* Singapore: NUS Press.
2001 *A history of modern Indonesia since c.1200.* 3rd ed. Basingstoke: Palgrave.
1985 'Islamization in Java: Fourteenth to eighteenth centuries', in Ahmad Ibrahim, Sharon Siddique, and Yasmin Hussain (eds), *Readings on Islam in Southeast Asia,* pp. 36-43. Singapore: Institute of Southeast Asian Studies. [First published in 1979.]

Rizki Ridyasmara
2004 'Yang pertama kali mendukung kemerdekaan Republik Indonesia 1945', *Majalah Saksi* 4-21 (18 August 2004), http://hensyam.wordpress.com/2006/08/18/yang-pertama-kali-mendukung-kemerdekaan-republik-indonesia-1945 (accessed 5 May 2009).

Roff, William R.
1970 'Indonesian and Malay students in Cairo in the 1920s', *Indonesia* 9 (April): 73-87.

Santosa, Kholid
2006 *Jejak-jejak sang pejuang pemberontak: Pemikiran, gerakan & ekspresi politik S.M. Kartosuwirjo dan Daud Beureueh.* 2nd ed. Bandung: Sega Arsy.

Sato, Shigeru
1994 *War, nationalism, and peasants: Java under the Japanese occupation, 1942-1945.* Asian Studies Association of Australia. St. Leonard's, NSW: Allen & Unwin.

Schiller, A. Arthur
1955 *The formation of federal Indonesia, 1945-1949.* The Hague: Van Hoeve.

Schwarz, Adam
1999 *A nation in waiting: Indonesia's search for stability.* St Leonard's, NSW: Allen & Unwin.

Shiraishi, Takashi
1990 *An age in motion: Popular radicalism in Java, 1912-1926.* Ithaca/London: Cornell University Press.

Singh, Bilveer
2004 *Jemaah Islamiyah in Southeast Asia.* Singapore: Institute of Southeast Asian Studies.

Sjariffudin, Amak
1963 *Kisah Kartosuwirjo dan menjerahnja.* 3 ed. Surabaya: Grip.

Slamet
1946 *The holy war 'made in Japan'. Vol. 2: Japanese machinations.* Batavia: n.n.

Smail, John R.W.
1964 *Bandung in the early revolution, 1945-1946: A study in the social history of the Indonesian revolution.* Ithaca, NY: Department of Asian Studies Cornell University.

Soekarno
1960 *Dibawah bendera revolusi.* Jakarta: Panitia Penerbit Dibawah Bendera Revolusi.

Sudrajat, Suryana
2006 *Kearifan guru bangsa: Pilar kemerdekaan.* Jakarta: Erlangga.

Suherly, Tanu
1981 'Kekuatan gerilya di daerah Priangan pada waktu divisi Siliwangi hijrah tahun 1948'. Paper, Seminar Sejarah Nasional ke-3, Jakarta, 10-14 November.

Suswadi, M.A. and E. Pristiwaningsih (eds)
2003 *Sumpah Pemuda: Latar sejarah dan pengaruhnya bagi pergerakan nasional.* Jakarta: Kementerian Kebudayaan dan Pariwisata Indonesia.

Swift, Ann
1989 *The road to Madiun.* Ithaca, NY: Cornell Modern Indonesia Project.

Temby, Quinton
2010 'Imagining an Islamic state in Indonesia', *Indonesia* 89 (April): 1-36.

Tempo
2011 *Kartosoewirjo.* Seri buku Tempo: Tokoh Islam di awal kemerdekaan. Jakarta: Gramedia.

Tickell, Paul
1987 'Taman Pewarta: Malay medium-Indonesian message', in Paul Tickell (ed.), *The Indonesian press: Its past, its people, its problems*, pp. 7-14. Annual Indonesian Lecture Series. Melbourne: Monash University.

Tohari, Ahmad
1999 *Lingkar tanah, lingkar air.* Yogyakarta: LKiS.

Velthoen, Esther
2004 '*Hutan* and *kota*: Contested visions of the nation-state in southern Sulawesi in the 1950s', in Samuel Hanneman and Henk Schulte Nordholt (eds), *Indonesia in transition: Rethinking 'civil society', 'region' and 'crisis'*, pp. 147-74. Yogyakarta: Pustaka Pelajar.

Wahdani, Dani
2003 Politik militer Angkatan Perang Negara Islam Indonesia (A.P.N.I.I.) di Jawa Barat pimpinan Imam S.M. Kartosoewirjo. Thesis, Universitas Padjadjaran, Jatinangor.

Wahyudi
2006 Aktivitas K.H. Yusuf Tauzirie dalam mengembangkan syiar Islam di desa Cipari kecamatan Wanaraja kabupaten Garut (1926-1981). Thesis, UIN Sunan Gunung Jati, Bandung.

Wilson, Greta O. (ed.)
1978 *Regents, reformers, and revolutionaries: Indonesian voices of colonial days.* Honolulu: University Press of Hawaii.

Zubaida, Sami
1997 'Is Iran an Islamic state?', in Joel Beinin and Joe Stork (eds), *Political Islam: Essays from* Middle East Report. Berkeley: University of California Press.

Index

9 789067 183864